THE
GATHERING
OF ZION

The Story of the Mormon Trail

by Wallace Stegner

University of Nebraska Press
Lincoln and London

Copyright © 1964 and 1981 by Wallace Stegner
All rights reserved
Manufactured in the United States of America

First Bison Book printing: 1992

Library of Congress Cataloging-in-Publication Data
Stegner, Wallace Earle, 1909–
The gathering of Zion: the story of the Mormon Trail / by Wallace Stegner.
p.   cm.
"Bison book."
Originally published: New York: McGraw-Hill, 1964, in series: The
American trails series.
Includes bibliographical references and index.
ISBN 0-8032-9213-9 (pa)
1. Mormon Trail. 2. Mormons—West (U.S.)—History. 3. West (U.S.)—
Description and travel—To 1848. 4. West (U.S.)—Description and
travel—1848–1860. 5. West (U.S.)—Description and travel—1860–
1880. I. Title.
F593.S85   1992
978—dc20   91-41841
CIP

Reprinted by arrangement with Wallace Stegner, represented by Brandt
and Brandt, Literary Agents, Inc.

Illustrations from Frederick Hawkins Piercy's *Route From Liverpool to Great
Salt Lake Valley* are used with the generous assistance and permission of
the University of Utah Marriot Library, Special Collections Division.

♾

Contents

ⲦⲦⲦⲦⲦⲦⲦⲦⲦⲦⲦⲦⲦⲦ

Acknowledgments

In making this book I have benefited from the helpfulness of many individuals and several institutions. For suggestions, corrections, clarifications, and the generous loan of their time and their personal collections of documents, I am especially grateful to Juanita Brooks and Dale L. Morgan—and while I am at it I should thank them as well for the example of their personal integrity and erudition. I owe Dr. Merrill Mattes of the National Park Service for many suggestions and for aid in the collection of trail accounts, and like many another who writes books about the West, I have leaned heavily on the friendship and learning of George R. Stewart. My thanks go also to Louise Stegner of Omaha, Nebraska, a late-discovered relative with a fortunate addiction to Western history; to Deon Lee of Castro Valley, California, and Newell Hart of Walnut Creek, California, for providing me with copies of important journals; to Robert Lee Hough of the University of Nebraska for running down some leads at the east end of the Mormon Trail; to Fawn Brodie and David Lavender for the instruction their books and their conversation have provided; to William Smart of the *Deseret News* for enlightenment on the trail through the Wasatch. Finally, I thank dozens of Utah friends, many of them descendants of people I have written about here, who have taught me to respect their heritage and their singular virtues even when I disagreed with the faith that set their world in motion.

Several libraries have helped to compensate for the fact that the most logical source of information, the library of the Church of Jesus Christ of Latter-day Saints, is opened to scholars only reluctantly and with limitations. From the Stanford University Library, and especially from Acting Director Elmer Grieder and Ralph Hansen of the Manuscript Division, I have had the fullest and most enthusiastic aid, as I have had also from Chad Flake of the Special Collections division of the Brigham Young University Library, from Everett Cooley, John James and others of the Utah Historical Society, and from the staffs of the Bancroft Library of the University of California at Berkeley, the library of the University of Vermont in Burlington, and the Baker Memorial Library of Dartmouth College.

Thanks for permission to quote from manuscript and typescript journals go to the Brigham Young University Library and to the Utah Historical Society. A version of the chapter entitled "Ordeal by Handcart" appeared in *Collier's*, the chapter entitled "The Man That Ate the Pack Saddle" in *Esquire*.

Checkpoints on the Road
to New Jerusalem

1805

DECEMBER 23   Joseph Smith born in Sharon, Vermont.

1823-1827

Each September 21 for four years, Joseph visited by angel who reveals the burial place of the golden plates; on September 21, 1827, Joseph is permitted to take the plates home for translation by means of the miraculous Urim and Thummim.

1830

MARCH 26   *The Book of Mormon* published in Palmyra, N.Y.

APRIL 6   The Church of Christ (which later became the Church of Jesus Christ of Latter-day Saints) established with six members.

1831

JANUARY   Joseph Smith arrives in Kirtland, Ohio, to establish the Church in the West.

AUTUMN   A Mormon colony settles near Independence, Jackson County, Missouri.

1832

MARCH 24   Joseph Smith and his counselor Sidney Rigdon are tarred and feathered in Hiram, Ohio, the first of a succession of violences against the self-styled Prophet and his Church.

NOVEMBER   Brigham Young arrives as a convert in Kirtland.

1833

SPRING   The first Mormon Temple is begun in Kirtland.

JULY   The Mormon colony near Independence is driven out by Missouri mobs.

OCTOBER 31   The Mormon colony west of the Big Blue River is attacked and burned.

NOVEMBER 4   A pitched battle between Missourians and
             Mormons leaves two Gentiles and one Mor-
             mon dead, and results in the expulsion of the
             whole Mormon population of Jackson County.
             Most of them move north into Clay, Daviess,
             and Caldwell Counties, Missouri.

1834

APRIL 24–30 Missourians, aroused by word of a Mormon
             "army" being organized, burn 150 Mormon
             houses in Jackson County.
MAY 5   Joseph leads "Zion's Camp" of 200 armed men
             from Kirtland toward Independence, with the
             aim of regaining seized Mormon property.
JUNE 17   A Missouri raid against Zion's Camp swamps
             in the Missouri River; several Missourians
             drowned.
JUNE 19   "The Battle of Fishing River" is broken up by
             a great storm; cholera breaks out in Zion's
             Camp.
JULY 9   Joseph leaves part of his "army" in Clay
             County and returns to Kirtland.

1835

AUGUST   The Church issues the first of several official
             denials that it is practising polygamy, though it
             has in fact been practised, first by Joseph Smith
             and later by his most trusted counselors, from
             as early as the year 1831.

1836

MARCH 26   The Kirtland Temple is dedicated; elabora-
             tion of the mystic rites of washing, anointing,
             and sealing.
JUNE 29   Renewed trouble in Missouri; Clay County
             Mormons invited to leave.

1837

JANUARY 1   Joseph Smith organizes the Kirtland Safety
             Society Bank Company and prepares to issue
             paper money.

JANUARY 2   When the Ohio Legislature refuses to incorporate the bank, Joseph reorganizes it as the Kirtland Safety Society Anti-Banking Company.

JANUARY 27   The Anti-Bank stops payment on its paper.

FEBRUARY 8   A warrant is sworn out against Joseph by Samuel Rounds—the first of more than a dozen legal actions that will harass him during the next year.

JUNE 29   Sidney Rigdon is brought to court on the charge of making spurious money, and the Anti-Bank finally stops issuing notes.

JUNE   Out of the turmoil of collapsing Kirtland, Joseph sends Heber Kimball, Orson Hyde, and Willard Richards to establish what will become the fabulously successful English Mission.

1 8 3 8

JANUARY 12   Joseph flees Kirtland in the midst of apostasy, panic, and lawsuits and makes his way to Far West, the Mormon center in Clay County, Missouri.

JUNE   To resist and counterattack the Missourians, the Mormons organize the "Sons of Dan," who will become known in the penny dreadfuls as "Destroying Angels." Raids and night-riding increase.

JULY 4   Sidney Rigdon makes an inflammatory speech in Far West that alarms all anti-Mormon Missouri and increases tension.

JULY 6   The remnant of the Kirtland faithful, between 500 and 600 people with all their personal goods, start by wagon from Kirtland to Far West.

AUGUST 6   Election day riot between Mormons and Missourians in Gallatin, Missouri.

OCTOBER 1   Missourians besiege the river town of DeWitt when the Mormons refuse to leave.

OCTOBER 4   The Kirtland Saints arrive in Far West to find it an armed camp in the midst of crisis.

OCTOBER 15   Apostle David Patten and a band of Danites raid Gallatin and plunder it.

OCTOBER 24	In the "Battle of Crooked River" Apostle Patten and several other Mormons are killed, but the Missourians are driven back.
OCTOBER 27	Governor Boggs issues to the Missouri militia the order that the Mormons must be "exterminated or driven from the state."
OCTOBER 30	A mob massacres 17 Mormons and wounds 15 others at Haun's Mill.
OCTOBER 31	Joseph and other Mormon leaders surrender; Mormons give up arms and agree to leave Missouri.
NOVEMBER 30	Joseph and other Mormon leaders put in Liberty jail, awaiting trial.

1 8 3 9

FEBRUARY	Last of the Mormon refugees begin making their way back to the Mississippi and across into Illinois.
APRIL	Joseph and his fellow prisoners bribe their way out of the hands of guards taking them to trial, and escape into Illinois. The city of Nauvoo is established near the site of the village called Commerce.

1 8 4 0

DECEMBER 16	The Illinois Legislature grants Nauvoo a charter of an extraordinary liberality.

1 8 4 1

MAY	Joseph is kidnapped by Missouri sheriffs; is released on a writ of habeas corpus and the Missouri warrant is quashed by Judge Stephen A. Douglas—a testimonial to Joseph's political importance.

1 8 4 2

MARCH 15	A Masonic lodge is installed in Nauvoo, and out of its rituals Joseph elaborates the temple ordinances, destined to become the "endowments" so important in the Mormon Church.

MAY   Ex-Governor Lillburn Boggs is seriously wounded by an assassin; Joseph's bodyguard O. P. Rockwell accused.

JUNE 23   John C. Bennett, Joseph's counselor, is excommunicated and expelled from Nauvoo on morals charges; his case begins the polygamy scandals that will eventually destroy both Nauvoo and Joseph Smith.

1843

JANUARY 5   Joseph is cleared in probate court of Sangamon County of complicity in the attempt on Boggs' life.

AUGUST 12   Joseph's revelation on polygamy is read to the High Council, and the doctrine thus becomes official, though still a secret to all but the leaders of the Church.

DECEMBER 12   Porter Rockwell returns from months in jail in Missouri, freed for lack of evidence.

1844

MARCH 11   Joseph selects the secret Council of Fifty, which ordains and crowns him King of the Kingdom of God.

MAY 17   Joseph announces himself a candidate for the Presidency of the United States, and is nominated in convention.

JUNE 7   The reform newspaper *The Nauvoo Expositor* issues its first and only number; the shop is wrecked and the type pied by the Nauvoo Legion, on Joseph's order.

JUNE 24   Joseph and Hyrum Smith, who have fled across the river to Iowa to escape arrest, return and give themselves up to authorities in Carthage.

JUNE 27   Joseph and Hyrum are murdered by militiamen in Carthage jail.

AUGUST 8   Brigham Young, as President of the Quorum of the Twelve Apostles, assumes leadership of the Mormon Church.

1845

JANUARY   Nauvoo's charter revoked by the Illinois Legislature.

SEPTEMBER 24   Brigham and the Twelve, to allay night-riding and violence, agree to leave Illinois "as soon as grass grows and water runs."

1846

FEBRUARY 4   Charles Shumway takes the first refugees out of Nauvoo and across to Sugar Creek Camp on the Iowa side of the Mississippi.

JULY 20   Mormon Battalion, organized among the Mormons on the Missouri, starts its march toward Fort Leavenworth, and thence to Santa Fe and the Pacific Coast.

AUGUST   Winter Quarters established on the Missouri, at the site of modern Florence, Nebraska.

SEPTEMBER 17   The last of the Mormons driven from Nauvoo by mobs after a three-day battle.

1847

APRIL 17   The Pioneer Company starts westward from its rendezvous on the Elkhorn.

JULY 21   Orson Pratt and Erastus Snow, scouts for the Pioneer Company, enter Salt Lake Valley.

JULY 24   Brigham Young, ill with mountain fever, is brought into the Valley in Wilford Woodruff's carriage, and the selection of Salt Lake Valley as the site of the City of Zion is assured.

1850

Territory of Utah established.

1857-1858

Autumn and winter—the Utah War.

1869

MAY 10   Golden Spike joins the Union Pacific and Central Pacific at Promontory, Utah.

1877

AUGUST 29   Death of Brigham Young.

1882-1890

Polygamy prosecutions under the Edmunds-
Tucker Act of 1882.

1890

SEPTEMBER 25   Wilford Woodruff, as President of the Mormon Church, issues the "Manifesto" abandon-
ing the practise, though not the doctrine, of
polygamy.

1896

Utah admitted to the Union as the forty-sixth
state.

Introduction: *The Way to the Kingdom*

Close to the heart of Mormondom, as close as the beehive symbol of labor and cohesiveness that decorates the great seal of Utah, is the stylized memory of the trail. For every early Saint, crossing the plains to Zion in the Valleys of the Mountains was not merely a journey but a rite of passage, the final, devoted, enduring act that brought one into the Kingdom. Until the railroad made the journey too easy, and until new generations born in the valley began to outnumber the immigrant Saints, the shared experience of the trail was a bond that reinforced the bonds of the faith; and to successive generations who did not personally experience it, it has continued to have sanctity as legend and myth.

It is fully, even monotonously, documented. Attics and archives are crammed with its records, for in addition to the official journals authorized by a history-conscious church, it seems that every second Mormon emigrant kept a diary, and every Mormon family that has such a diary cherishes it as part of the lares and penates. Great-granddaughters edit the jottings of their pioneer ancestors as piously as they go to the temple to be baptized for the dead, and if great-grandfather was too occupied to keep notes, his recollective yarns will be gathered up and published as reminiscences, with a genealogical chart to show all the branches and twigs that have sprung from the pioneer root. Any people in a new land may be pardoned for being solicitous about their history: they create it, in a sense, by remembering it. But the tradition of the pioneer that is strong all through the West is a cult in Utah.

Symbols of the trail rise as naturally out of the Mormon mind as the phrase about making the desert blossom as the rose—and that springs to Mormon lips with the innocent ease of birdsong. Those symbols—white bows of covered wagons, horned cattle low-necked in the yoke, laboring files of handcarts, booted and bearded pioneers, sunbonneted Mothers of Zion—are recurrent, if not compulsive, in Mormon art, which runs strongly to monumental sculpture and is overwhelmingly historical in emphasis. One might expect to find artistic treatment of Joseph's revelations from God or His angels, the early persecutions and martyrdoms, the massacre at Haun's Mill, the assassination of Joseph and Hyrum Smith in Carthage Jail. But these things, though remembered, have not emerged as abiding symbols. Instead, one finds the trail.

No responsible historian can afford to underestimate the literalness of Mormon belief. These emigrants were convinced that they went not merely to a new country and a new life, but to a new Dispensation, to the literal Kingdom of God on earth. In the years between Joseph's vision and its fulfillment, persecution and hardship discouraged many, and others fell away into apostasy, but what might be called the hard core of Mormonism took persecution and suffering in stride, as God's way of trying their faith. Signs and wonders accompanied them, their way was cleared by divine interventions. Rivers opportunely froze over to permit passage of their wagons, quail fell among their exhausted and starving camps as miraculously as manna ever fell upon the camps of the Israelites fleeing Pharaoh, the sick (even sick horses) upon whom the elders laid their hands rose up rejoicing in health, the wolves that dug up Oregonian and Californian graves and scattered Gentile bones across the prairies did not touch the graves of the Lord's people. If they were blessed with an easy passage, they praised God for His favor; if their way was a via dolorosa milestoned with the cairns of their dead, they told themselves they were being tested, and hearkened to counsel, and endured.

Patience Loader, a girl who could not have been more aptly named, said it for all of them in the journal she kept across the plains in 1856: "It seemed the Lord fitted the back for the burden. Every day we realized that the hand of God was over us and that he made good his promises unto us day by day.... We know that his promises never fail and this we prooved day by day. We knew that we had not strength of our own to perform such hardships if our heavenly Father had not help us ..."

The Lord fitted the back for the burden. And however heavy or light the burden, it was on the trail that the back was generally shaped. Especially for those who had not come through the early drivings and burnings (and this means nearly every Mormon emigrant after the evacuation of Kanesville in 1852) the crossing of the plains provided a testing that most proselytes welcomed. The Kingdom of God should not be too easily come at. Those who felt such things must have understood that the hard trail was both religiously and artistically right: a labor to be performed, difficulties to be overcome, dangers to be faced, faithfulness to be proved, a great safety to be won. Welsh converts aware of their own folklore might have remembered the heroes who after great trouble arrived at the Isle of Glass and succeeded in making their way across to it on a sword-edge bridge.

Having endured, and crossed to safety, they began at once to transform their experience into myth. In this they were aided by the patriarchal character of Mormon society. The head of the family then was, and in theory still is, a sun around which revolved planetary wives and offspring. The adjuration to be fruitful and multiply—good practical doctrine in a desert wilderness and at a time when numbers meant strength—was reinforced by the spiritual doctrine that the more numerous a man's offspring were, the greater would be his glory in heaven. When the patriarch was also a pioneer, one of those who had most suffered for the faith, filial pride as well as filial duty tended to magnify him.

So long as any were still alive, pioneers were a revered club in Utah, and the club included not only the exclusive members of the original 1847 party and the 1856 handcart companies, but anyone who had crossed into Utah before the coming of the railroad. The one universally celebrated Mormon holiday is Pioneer Day, July 24, the day on which Brigham Young entered Salt Lake Valley. The honorific societies based on inheritance are not called Sons and Daughters of Nauvoo, or Sons and Daughters of the Three Witnesses, but Sons and Daughters of the Utah Pioneers. Their principal activity is an assiduous collecting and memorializing of the history of the migration and settlement. In their loving memorials, the men and women who came out the hard way look like photographs taken by infra-red light, imposing but transparent and unreal. They loom taller as time passes; their harsh and violent qualities soften; their beards achieve a Mosaic dignity; they walk through Mormon history with the tread of Jacob or Abraham.

Mormonism was in several ways—and its persecutors rightly felt it so—antipathetic to the unlicked democracy out of which it grew. Far from separating church and state, it made them synonymous. ("Theoretically," said Apostle Franklin D. Richards in 1880, "Church and State are one. If there were no Gentiles and no other Government there would be no Civil Law.") Instead of celebrating the free individual, it celebrated the obedient group. For the will of the people it substituted the will of God as announced by the priesthood. Its internal elections showed only one slate, its votes were not choices between competing candidates but "sustaining votes" for candidates proposed by the hierarchy—and it took a bold man to vote Nay. Its shibboleths were not the catchwords of republicanism, but were lifted from the patriarchal vocabulary of the Old Testament, especially Isaiah. What they went to build in the Great Basin was not a state, not a republic, but a Kingdom. Hierarchic, theocratic, patriarchal, this strange descendant of New England puritanism was in some ways wildly un-puritan—or seemed so. For ever since some time in the 1830's the doctrine of plural marriage had been secretly making its way among them. Not an indulgence but a divine command, it had been revealed privately by Joseph to his most confidential counselors, had been put into writing in 1843 for the eyes of the High Council and of Joseph's difficult wife Emma, and had finally been publicly admitted in 1852. As if all this were not enough, the Mormons tended to vote solid in state and national elections, and as a "closed" society surrounded by an open one, they had a tendency to attract outlaws looking for asylum, to breed fearful rumors, and to infuriate the Gentiles with their smug assumption that they alone held the keys of truth, they alone were the chosen of the Lord.

And yet in at least one way Mormonism was profoundly of its time and place: its movement was inevitably westward beyond the frontiers. The pioneering itch troubled Mormon flesh and spirit quite as much as did the contemporary religious stirrings, the talking and interpreting in tongues, the magical healings, the millennial hopes, the revelations, the direct interventions of God in man's affairs. If the martyrdom of Joseph and Hyrum Smith assured the persistence of this sect, which doctrinally was a pastiche of the revivals that had swept New York State's "burned-over ground" in the 1820's, the combination of millennialism and the westward movement assured its growth. All but one of the splinter sects that refused to follow when the mass of Mormondom went west were shortly extinct; that one, though it was headed by Joseph's wife Emma and her sons, remained essentially dormant. The main body of Mormonism chose to fulfill its millennial destiny by moving with the current that carried the nation west, and in good part because of that choice, it throve. Millennium and Manifest Destiny turned out to be hardly more than variant spellings for the same thing.

Nothing so emphasizes Mormonism's simultaneous identity with and separation from the tide of western expansion as its presence on wheels in the Platte valley during all the years from 1847 to the completion of the transcontinental railroad. It was part of the tide—but across the Platte from most of it; it was going the same direction—but stopping short. Looking for an escape from the Missouri "pukes" and the Illinois mobbers and the other agents of Manifest Destiny, the Mormons were in fact inextricably entangled with them. They built up their own solidarity and morale by listening disapprovingly to the language of Missouri wagontrains. When the gold that their own young men helped to discover pulled fortune-hunters toward California in thousands, the Mormons were not only caught in the rush, but profited by it, sold it cattle and fresh teams, vegetables and flour, melons and the home-made whiskey called Valley Tan. They solidified themselves in their chosen valley on the profitable trade of their enemies. Fleeing America, they fled it by that most American of acts, migration into the West.

So there are more than theological reasons for remembering the Mormon pioneers. They were the most systematic, organized, disciplined, and successful pioneers in our history; and their advantage over the random individualists who preceded them and paralleled them and followed them up the valley of the Platte came directly from their "un-American" social and religious organization. Where Oregon emigrants and argonauts bound for the gold fields lost practically all their social cohesion en route, the Mormons moved like the Host of Israel they thought themselves. Far from loosening their social organization, the trail perfected it. As communities on the march they proved extraordinarily adaptable. When driven out of Nauvoo, they converted their fixed property, insofar as they could, into the instruments of mobility, especially livestock, and became for the time herders and shepherds, teamsters and frontiersmen, instead of artisans and townsmen and farmers. When their villages on wheels reached the valley of their destination, the Saints were able to revert at once, because they were town-and-temple builders and because they had their families with them, to the stable agrarian life in which most of them had grown up.

They built a commonwealth, or as they would have put it, a Kingdom. But the story of their migration is more than the story of the founding of Utah. In their hegira they opened up southern Iowa from Locust Creek to the Missouri, made the first roads, built the first bridges, established the first communities. They transformed the Missouri at Council Bluffs from a trading post and an Indian agency into an outpost of civilization, founded settlements on both sides of the river and made Winter Quarters (now Florence, a suburb of Omaha) and later Kanesville (now Council Bluffs) into outfitting points that rivaled Independence, Westport, and St. Joseph. They defined the road up the north side of the Platte that is now the route of both U.S. 30 and the Union Pacific Railroad. Their guide books and trail markers, their bridges and ferries, though made for the Saints scheduled to come later, served also for the Gentiles: according to Irene Paden in *The Wake of the Prairie Schooner*, a third of the California and Oregon travel from 1849 on followed the Mormon Trail.

That is to say, the Mormons were one of the principal forces in the settlement of the West. Their main body opened southern Iowa, the Missouri frontier, Nebraska, Wyoming, Utah. Samuel Brannan's group of eastern Saints who sailed around the Horn in the ship *Brooklyn*, and the Mormon Battalion that marched 2,000 miles overland from Fort Leavenworth to San Diego, were secondary prongs of the Mormon movement; between them, they contributed to the opening of the Southwest and of California. Battalion members were at Coloma when gold gleamed up from the bedrock of Sutter's millrace. Battalion members crossed the Sierra in the spring of 1847 when the dismembered bodies of the Donner Party victims were still scattered through their ghastly camps. Battalion members opened for wagons the Hensley route around the north end of Great Salt Lake that California trains increasingly took after 1850. And Brigham Young's colonizing Mormons, taking to wheels again after the briefest stay, radiated outward from the Salt Lake, Utah, and Weber Valleys and planted settlements that reached from Northern Arizona to the Lemhi River in Idaho, and from Fort Bridger in Wyoming to Genoa in Carson Valley under the loom of the Sierra, and in the Southwest down through St. George and Las Vegas to San Bernardino.

With much of this activity, central though it is to the story of western settlement, this book has nothing to do. Neither does it concern itself, except for the indispensable summary of event and belief, with the history of Mormonism before the expulsion from Nauvoo. Because that early history is hardly credible, and because the Mormon faith has seemed to historians in need of explanation, apologetics, or ridicule, books dealing with any aspect of Mormon history have had a tendency to go over the whole ground from the Hill Cumorah to the Edmunds-Tucker Act. A history of the Mormon Trail is subject to the same temptations. In electing otherwise, I have had to make some arbitrary limitations, choices, and definitions.

The Mormon Trail ends in Salt Lake City, but where does it begin, and how many branches does it have, and how shall we compute its duration? From the time of Joseph Smith's first visions, he and the church he founded were in motion; and the church stayed in motion, with short breathing spaces in Ohio, Missouri, and Illinois, until it found its sanctuary in the mountains. Does a proper discussion of the Mormon Trail begin at the Hill Cumorah, near Palmyra, New York, where the angel showed young Joseph the golden plates and chose him, out of all men in these latter days, to receive the true priesthood? Or at Manchester, New York, where Joseph organized six members into what he then called the Church of Christ, on April 6, 1830? Or at Kirtland, Ohio (now a suburb of Cleveland), the site of the first divinely ordered Gathering and of the first temple, from which Joseph and his diminished faithful fled in a fog of apostasy, bankruptcy, and criminal charges resulting from the prophet's ill-advised experiments in the banking business? Or at Independence, Missouri, where a colony of Mormons made a short-lived attempt to build the Kingdom, only to be driven out by settlers suspicious of their groupiness and their potentially Abolitionist vote? Or at Far West, Missouri, and the near-by town they called Adam-ondi-Ahman, from which they were driven bloodily in the fall and winter of 1838–39? Or at Nauvoo the Beautiful, on the Mississippi, where for a few years they flourished, where they built their second temple and a city over which Joseph ruled like an oriental potentate, and from which they were again driven, almost before their crowding feet had settled the temple's truss floor? Or at Winter Quarters on the Missouri, where they built a transient town of huts and dugouts from which, next year, they started on the 1,032-mile traverse of the wilderness that brought them finally to safety?

This is a strange, often incredible, sometimes terrible story, and it has been told so generally by partisans full of piety, hatred, or paranoia that it would be worth trying to tell it again. But not here, and not so long as Dale L. Morgan has it in his mind to tell it. For purposes of simplification, this narrative begins at Nauvoo in the last months of 1845; its primary subjects are the Mormon migration from the bank of the Mississippi to the bank of City Creek in Salt Lake Valley, and the Gathering of Zion that took place over essentially the same route during the next twenty-two years.

There is one extension of the trail that cannot be ignored. The peculiar Mormon commandment known as the Gathering of Zion had effective implementation and devoted agents. In the very agony of their exodus from Nauvoo, elders obediently left wives and families to make their way as they could, and turned back eastward to do missionary work in the "black counties" and the textile cities of England; and once Zion was established and the Gathering reinstituted, the trickle of European converts that had formerly run by gravity toward Nauvoo was put under pressure, with pumping stations at New Orleans (later New York or Boston or Philadelphia) and at some frontier staging point, generally Council Bluffs or Florence. Between 1847 and 1868, the last year of overland emigration by trail, nearly 50,000 British, Scandinavian, and German converts were pumped along that pipeline into Salt Lake City.* During the

* Figures for Mormon immigration, like many of the data of Mormon history, are profuse but contradictory. Mr. Earl Olsen of the Church Historian's Office supplies a figure of 68,028 for the emigration of European Saints between 1847 and 1868, but this is almost surely the total influx into the Salt Lake Valley, and therefore must include many from the Missouri frontier and from the United States. Kate B. Carter's compilation in *Heart Throbs of the West* adds up to 46,972, but Mrs. Carter is not always reliable in such details. Unfortunately the most reliable tabulation, that by James Linforth in the notes to Piercy's *Route from Liverpool to Great*

peak year of 1855 it was said that a third of all the emigrants from the British Isles to the United States were Mormons. Because for a very large proportion of Utah's early settlers the Mormon Trail began at the Liverpool docks, I have given some space to the structure of conversion and emigration that the Mormons developed before 1840 and matured in the 1850's, and I have followed at least one party of European Saints from Liverpool all the way to the valley.

From the Missouri west, despite the assertion of many journals and many histories that the Mormons were breaking a new road, the trail was known and traveled before they came. Both sides of the Platte valley, that almost inescapable level highway into the West, had been an Indian travel route for generations. Traders between Fort Laramie and the Missouri River posts had sometimes traveled the north bank. The missionaries who in 1844 built a mission to the Pawnee on Loup Fork had used it. The Stevens Party of 1844 had gone that way. According to George R. Stewart, there had been wagons up the north bank as early as 1835.

From Fort Laramie to just beyond South Pass the Mormon Trail, Oregon Trail, and California Trail were synonymous. From South Pass to Fort Bridger the Mormon Trail followed the older fork of the Oregon-California Trail. West from Fort Bridger on through Echo, Weber, and East Canyons and over the Wasatch to Salt Lake Valley, the Mormon pioneers were following the dim and barely passable route that Lansford Hastings had so lamentably sold to the Donner-Reed party of 1846. There was nothing at all new about the Mormon Trail except the two hundred miles across western Iowa and the little loop at the very western end known as Golden Pass, which circumnavigated the difficulties of Big and Little Mountains and came into Salt Lake Valley through Parley's Canyon instead of through Emigration. It was opened in 1850 as a toll road,

---

Salt Lake Valley (1855) ends with the year 1854. A combination of Linforth's figures and later figures from Gustive Larson's *Prelude to the Kingdom* gives a total of 47,099, which is close enough to Mrs. Carter's total to substantiate the general order of magnitude her summary suggests.

but maintenance problems in the canyon caused it to be abandoned after only a brief period of use.

What was new about the Mormon migration was that it was the permanent hegira of a whole people—grandparents, parents, children, flocks and herds, household goods and gods. In the composition of its wagontrains, the motives that drove them, the organization and discipline of the companies, it differed profoundly from the Oregon and California migrations. These were not groups of young and reckless adventurers, nor were they isolated families or groups of families. They were literally villages on the march, villages of a sobriety, solidarity, and discipline unheard of anywhere else on the western trails, and not too frequent in the settled United States.

Moreover, the Mormon Trail was a two-way road to an extent that neither the California nor the Oregon Trail was. It saw a steady eastward traffic in elders headed for the mission fields, a constant flow of wagons and strong teams going back to pick up supplies and new converts at the Missouri, or to meet faltering companies, generally at some point between the last crossing of the North Platte and Fort Bridger, and help them on in to Salt Lake. After 1861 the immigration was handled largely by Church trains that came east from Salt Lake, picked up passengers and freight at the Missouri, and returned the same season. Few California or Oregon emigrants gave a thought to people coming after them, unless they feared a company behind them might pass them and use up the grass. There are recorded instances of their destroying rafts and ferries to prevent their use by other groups. Not so the Mormons. The first thought of the pioneer company was to note good campgrounds, wood, water, grass, to measure distances and set up mileposts. They and succeeding companies bent their backs to build bridges and dig down the steep approaches of fords. They made rafts and ferry boats and left them for the use of later companies—and twice left men with them to make an honest dollar ferrying the Gentiles. They threw rocks off the road on the rough stretch between Fort Laramie and the Mormon Ferry at modern Casper, Wyoming; they cut and grubbed the abominable willows in the East Canyon bottoms. By the improvements they made in it, they earned the right to put their name on the trail they used.

Thus it is not primarily the route, but the people who traveled it, and how, and why, that is my subject. My betters have been before me at least part of the way. It is a brave man who attempts to tell the story of the Mormon expulsion from Nauvoo after Bernard DeVoto's brilliant account in *The Year of Decision, 1846*. Yet I must attempt it, for Nauvoo is where the trail began. Fortunately for me, DeVoto's account follows the Mormons west of Winter Quarters only in brief summary. There are objective and dependable histories of the pioneer and later companies west of the Missouri, but most are either narrowly focused, as are Dale Morgan's meticulous studies of the ferries on the North Platte, or are inclined to treat the migration incidentally, as part of the larger history of Mormonism or as part of the western movement. The most detailed histories of the trail itself have been written in the spirit of celebration and faith-promotion, and though most of them make extensive use of journals, they end by dehumanizing the emigrants almost as much as do the debunkers who see the migration as a movement of dupes led by blackguards. For the celebrators characteristically enlarge and mythify, and hence falsify, people who in their lives were painfully and complicatedly human. They leave out matters that they or the Church authorities feel to be embarrassing, they wash out of the mouths of Brigham Young, Heber Kimball, and others the strong language that stress and humor sometimes put there, they minimize frictions and gloss over personal animosities.

I should prefer to deal with the Mormon pioneers, if I can, as human beings of their time and place, the earlier ones westward-moving Americans, the later ones European converts gripped by the double promise of economic betterment and eternal life. Suffering, endurance, discipline, faith, brotherly and sisterly charity, the qualities so thoroughly celebrated by Mormon writers, were surely well distributed among them, but theirs also was a normal amount of human cussedness, vengefulness, masochism, backbiting, violence, ignorance, selfishness, and gullibility. So far as it is possible, I shall take them from their own journals and reminiscences and letters, and I shall try to follow George Bancroft's rule for historians: I shall try to present them in their terms and judge them in mine. That I do not accept the faith that possessed them does not mean I doubt their frequent devotion and heroism in its service. Especially their women. Their women were incredible.

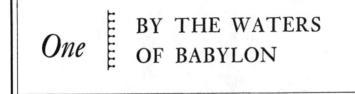

One BY THE WATERS
OF BABYLON

Joseph Smith

1

ттттттттттттт

"Is There No Help for the Widow's Son?"

JOSEPH SMITH, THE PROPHET, Seer, Revelator, and President of
the Church of Jesus Christ of Latter-day Saints, and his brother
Hyrum, its Patriarch, were shot to death by a black-face mob in
the upper room of the jail at Carthage, Illinois, on June 27, 1844.
That act of ruffianism, which culminated (though it did not end)
the hostility of the middle border toward Joseph's peculiar people,
was expected to scotch the Mormons for good. Instead, it did two
things: it tempered their already well-tempered steel in the blood
of martyrs, and made zealots out of men and women who might
otherwise have been only die-hards; and it assured the carrying-out
of migration plans that had been fitfully contemplated long before
Joseph's death.

Both Joseph and his earliest followers were Americans of their
time—New Englanders and upstate New Yorkers mainly, with a
sprinkling from Ontario and from Kentucky, Tennessee, Pennsylvania, and the Virginias. In their education, background, and experience, and in the intensity of their religious seeking, they did not
much differ from contemporary members of other sects, and many
had in fact been Methodists, Baptists, Shakers, Millerites, Campbell-
ites, and Cumberland Presbyterians, or all of these in succession,
before hearing the true gospel from Mormon missionaries. Several

17

of the leaders, notably Sidney Rigdon, Parley P. Pratt, and Newel K. Whitney, had been prominent in the Campbellite sect. They and others embraced Mormonism presumably because it had everything the other religions had, and more: not only total immersion, seizures, the gift of tongues and other aspects of the Holy Ghost, baptism for remission of sins, and the promise or threat of the imminent Second Coming, but also the true apostolic succession and the renewal of the ancient personal communication with God. Those who bought that package revealed a susceptibility that was characteristically nineteenth-century American. And they bought it the more eagerly because the package also contained the promise of the Kingdom of God on earth, the New Jerusalem.

New Jerusalem would have been unthinkable in the settled East. It was a dream that could flourish only in the new soil of the West, for it was the spiritual counterpart, the purified image, of the dream of new opportunity that drew the whole nation toward the frontiers. The Gathering preached by Joseph and his missionaries was the more plausible because impulse already yearned that way; it was possible for a New Hampshire convert to sell his farm and move to Kirtland, Ohio, because plenty of his neighbors were already on the move to the Western Reserve for quite unspiritual reasons. Or it was possible, if the prophet so counseled, to keep on going, clear to the outpost of Zion in Jackson County, Missouri, near Independence. Kirtland became the Mormon headquarters after January, 1831; the Independence colony was established six months later. Years before the panic of 1837 and the collapse of Joseph's "anti-bank" broke up the Kirtland community, Joseph had prophesied the ultimate removal of all the Saints to the frontiers: "And from this place ye shall go forth into the regions westward; and inasmuch as ye shall find them that will receive you, ye shall build up my Church in every region, until the time shall come when it shall be revealed unto you from on high, where the city of the New Jerusalem shall be prepared, that ye may be gathered in one..."

Joseph may already have been anticipating defeat by the non-Mormons and apostates around Kirtland, or he may simply have been dreaming of more stately mansions in a new country where his imagination and his ambition could run unchecked. Certainly when trouble did come upon the Mormons, their natural move was west, though there was considerable wavering on the question of precise locality. Independence, the site of the Garden of Eden, where revelation had said would one day be built "the chief city of the Western Hemisphere" (it turned out to be Kansas City) turned hostile almost at once. The Saints were driven from it into more northerly and less-settled counties in 1833, and Joseph's attempt to restore them to their homes in the next year with a two-hundred-man "army" ended in one of those ludicrous but somehow constructive failures with which his whole career was marked. Zion's Camp, as it was called, marched nearly 1,000 miles from Kirtland to the Missouri, bickering all the way. On Fishing River it was spared an attack when a providential storm wrecked the scow of the rampant Missourians and drowned a couple of them. But cholera did what the Missourians were temporarily prevented from doing. Joseph said the plague was visited on them for their lack of faith. Fourteen of them died, and finally, tamely, the rest disintegrated and dribbled off into Clay County or back to Kirtland. A fiasco. Yet on that long and foolish march was created a major unit of Church authority, the Quorum of the Twelve Apostles, which would hold the Saints together after Joseph's murder ten years later; and among the members of Zion's Camp were Brigham Young, Joseph Young, Charles Coulson Rich, Heber C. Kimball, Orson and Parley Pratt, Orson Hyde—men whom neither hardship nor failure nor absurdity could discourage, and who would utilize Joseph's organizational units of tens, fifties, and hundreds when they had to lead, later on, more successful marches than this.

Thrown out of Jackson County, the Saints settled in Caldwell and Daviess Counties, in the towns of Far West (now Kerr, Missouri) and Adam-ondi-Ahman. The first, said Joseph when he arrived there from the debacle of Kirtland in the spring of 1838, was the exact spot where Cain had killed Abel; the second was the place where Adam and Eve had lived after their expulsion from the Garden near Independence. Holy ground, and rich, and free from Gentile interference—for a time.

At Far West began the first attempt at the City of Enoch, the New Jerusalem, and to Far West the faithful began to gather. From apostasy-riddled Kirtland, on July 6, 1838, started a caravan composed of fifty-eight wagons and 515 people and hundreds of cattle, sheep, swine—the first of the villages on wheels that would rock through Mormon history. Like most of those later caravans it was fleeing trouble and hunting sanctuary. Unfortunately, on July 4, two days before it set out, Joseph's counselor Sidney Rigdon had made a fire-eating speech at Far West, daring the Gentiles to come on and threatening what would happen to them if they did. The Lord three days later sent a sign, ambiguous and troubling, by blasting the flagpole in the square of Far West with a thunderbolt. Rumors of Rigdon's words and rumors of the Mormon secret avengers who called themselves the Sons of Dan spread through Gentile Missouri growing more fearsome with each repeating, and all Missouri that was not already in arms to harass the Mormons flew to arms to repel them. When the Kirtland company dragged wearily in on October 4 they found not sanctuary but bloody crisis. Missourians and Danites were raiding each other and burning farms and looting. On October 26 they clashed at the Battle of Crooked River, with casualties on both sides. Three days later two hundred men, either militiamen or mobbers (the Mormons saw no reason to make a distinction), burst upon a little group of Mormon families gathered for safety at Haun's Mill. They killed several at the first fire. The women and children ran screaming for the woods, men and boys dove for shelter into the blacksmith shop. The mobbers put their guns to the cracks and shot them as they huddled together or tried to hide behind the forge. When the women crept back later they found seventeen dead and fifteen others shot to bits but still living. Stiff with horror, terrified for their own lives if the mob should return, they dragged the bodies of their husbands and sons across the yard and dumped them into the well, and with their wounded escaped to Far West.

On October 31 Gen. Samuel Lucas with nearly 3,000 militiamen was drawn up before Far West, preparing to put into effect
Governor Lillburn Boggs' frantic order to drive the Mormons from
the state or exterminate them. But George M. Hinkle, an elder
who figures as Judas in the Mormon hagiography, arranged a surrender that disarmed the outnumbered Mormons and turned their
leaders, including Joseph and Hyrum Smith, over to the troops.
So furious was the feeling against them that they would have been
summarily shot if Col. Alexander Doniphan had not refused to
obey his superior's order. Joseph and the other leaders who had
surrendered went to jail; the Crooked River combatants, much
wanted by the militia, slipped away by night; and all through the
last month of 1838 and the first months of 1839 destitute families
made their way as they could up the "Mormon Road" to the rapids
of the Des Moines and thence across the Mississippi into Illinois.

They were hungry, freezing, dispossessed, sullen with hatred
and the sense of wrong, and the name of Boggs was a curse in their
mouths. Eliza Snow, seamstress and poetess whose brother would
become the fifth president of the Mormon Church and whose husbands would be, successively, Joseph Smith and Brigham Young,
labored up that road with her parents under conditions so bleak
that sometimes their only food was frozen bread broken into milk
warm from the cow. One day they met a man who watched them
struggle through the freezing mud. "If I were in your places," he
said finally, "I should want the Governor of the state hitched at the
head of my team." Eliza remarked tartly to her father that she had
not heard so sensible a speech from a stranger since entering Missouri.

It is the accepted Mormon version of this story that Brigham
Young, for the first time given a job commensurate with his talents,
superintended the evacuation of the Saints from Missouri. Contemporary records examined by Stanley Ivins and other reputable
scholars do not bear out this early importance of Brother Brigham.
He came into the area on March 14, 1838, but took up a farm some
distance from Far West, and was not involved in most of the trouble,

though he was in town when Joseph surrendered. On December 10 he was present, inconspicuously, at a meeting, and on December 19 he presided at another—meetings which drew up and then re-affirmed resolutions bearing on the best plan of action. But on February 14, 1839, he himself fled from Missouri into Illinois, near Quincy, leaving John Taylor and others to manage the evacuation.

"Inasmuch as ye shall find them that will receive you," Joseph had said back in Kirtland, "ye shall build up my Church in every region." But in Missouri there had been few who would receive them, for they were a different tribe from their neighbors on that border. Col. Thomas Kane, who is all but deified in Mormon history for his friendliness to the Church in its times of trouble, first met the Mormons in Council Bluffs in 1846, and found them then many cuts above their enemies.

> Wherever I was compelled to tarry, I was certain to find shelter and hospitality, scant, indeed, but never stinted, and always honest and kind. After a recent unavoidable association with the border inhabitants of Western Missouri and Iowa, the vile scum which our own society, to apply the words of an admirable gentleman and eminent divine (Dr. Morton of Philadelphia) "like the great ocean washes upon its frontier shores," I can scarcely describe the gratification I felt in associating again with persons who were almost all of eastern American origin—persons of refined and cleanly habits and decent language.

Colonel Kane was a partial witness, so partial that many suspect him of having been baptized during his sojourn among the Saints on the Missouri. He overlooked a roughneck element among the Mormons, and he erred in implying that all who resisted the Saints were scum. But he was an intelligent and educated man, and his general opinion of the border scum would have been seconded by plenty of people. That scum, in fact, was already a literary type, even a stereotype. Hector St. John Crèvecoeur had found the re-lapsed frontier American barely human, lost to all the nobilities and graces of civilization. Cooper had drawn him with fascinated dis-taste as Ishmael Bush in *The Prairie*. In the years immediately after

the Mormons' expulsion from Missouri, J. J. Hooper would carica-
ture him as the shifty scoundrel Simon Suggs. As the Pike, he
would shortly be a stock character in California. And Mark Twain,
a Missourian whose family settled in Hannibal the year after the
Mormons were driven from Daviess and Caldwell Counties, would
do him for keeps in Pap Finn. To imagine the worst sorts of prejudice and hoodlumism that the Mormons encountered in Missouri
and Illinois, we should imagine the mobs as made up of Pap Finns
led by Simon Suggses.

So Mormonism reeled back from Missouri to lick its wounds for
one winter on the east bank of the Mississippi, and then, in a dazzling
display of recuperative power, gathered again around its escaped
Prophet to build the city of Nauvoo, a city whose name Joseph said
meant "beautiful plantation" in Hebrew. They did not stop to check
the Hebrew dictionary; they simply came and dug in. In five years
they transformed a stretch of high prairie and wooded bluffs, a
malarial riverbottom swamp, and a fever-and-ague hamlet called
Commerce into the city of Zion, the largest town in all of Illinois
and the show-place of the upper Mississippi, with a population of
20,000 and a partly completed temple that was surely the most
grandiose building in the Middle West, and would shortly be the
most imposing ruin.

Five years, it took them. Five years to demonstrate that the possibility which had so scared the Missourians was an inevitability if this
society was allowed to go its way without interference. Five years
to show what a people organized like an anthill or a beehive, and
guided by what they believed to be the direct word of God, could
do in a new country. Five years to develop, with the aid of the
liberal charter that a sympathetic legislature granted them, a city-
state owing scarcely any duty to the state of Illinois. By a mere
ordinance it could countermand court orders, by a writ of habeas
corpus set at liberty Mormons wanted by outside law. Among those
wanted was Joseph Smith, especially after someone over in Missouri
filled ex-Governor Boggs with buckshot. The Gentiles swore that
Joseph's bodyguard Porter Rockwell had done it, and the accused

many years later modestly admitted the soft imputation. But no matter how much vengeful Missouri sheriffs might want Joseph or Rockwell, they found them untouchable. For Joseph ruled this city. He was unquestioned—or nearly unquestioned—head of both church and state; he was Lieutenant General of the Nauvoo Legion, a private army of 4,000 men, well-drilled and armed as a wing of the Illinois militia, whose parades were so gorgeous with blue coats, white trousers, jackboots, feathers, and the music of Captain Pitt's Brass Band, that passing steamboats tied up at the landing to watch, and at least once Stephen A. Douglas adjourned his court in Carthage to come up and see the show.

Five years to grow great, to put the Mormons solidly into Illinois politics, to consolidate a missionary system that was having astonishing success in England and Wales, to raise Joseph Smith into such prominence and confidence that in 1844 he announced himself as a candidate for the Presidency of the United States and set his domestic missionaries to electioneering. Five years to lead the prophet into the indulgences that he called the will of God and the Gentiles called abominations, five years to start the whispers and the scandals and breed up the internal and external enemies. Five years to bring Illinois, once markedly friendly, to a hostility as savage as that of Missouri ever was, and to start the whole state, from high-placed politicians to the lowest border ruffian, crying that the Mormons must go.

As Fawn Brodie remarks in her distinguished biography of the prophet, *No Man Knows My History*, the troubles of the Mormons had different causes in Ohio, in Missouri, and in Illinois. For our purposes the differences hardly matter. One way and another, the Mormons managed to get on ill terms with anyone, given time. A chosen people is probably inspiring for the chosen to live *among;* it is not so comfortable for outsiders to live *with.*

Nauvoo was in deep trouble from the time when Joseph broke with his First and Second Counselors, the scalawag John C. Bennett and the upright William Law, and turned them into enemies. It was in deeper trouble when at Joseph's orders the Nauvoo Legion wrecked the press and pied the type of the *Nauvoo Expositor*, Law's rash opposition newspaper. It was doomed from the time when Joseph plunged bleeding, crying "Oh Lord, my God!" from the upstairs window of Carthage jail.

Though it was his enemies who killed him, Joseph had put himself in their hands by alienating some of the men who might have been his buckler and his shield. John C. Bennett, opportunist, abortionist, and enthusiastic believer in Joseph's principle of plurality of wives, was thrown out of Nauvoo on June 23, 1842; between July and September he published in the *Sangamo Journal* of Springfield a lurid "expose" composed of truths, half-truths, and sensational lies which was carried by the press over the country. Much of it could be discounted because of its outrageous exaggeration, and even the truths could be parried because of Bennett's own character, which gave him no moral right to cast the first stone. But William Law, whose alienation began in 1843 and was irrevocable by mid-1844, was another matter.

He was one of the most prosperous, as well as one of the most honorable and devoted, of all Nauvoo's leading men, and his distaste for some of Joseph's practises was tempered by his belief that, though a somewhat corrupted prophet, Joseph was still a prophet. Nevertheless he found himself in stiff opposition to Joseph's business methods. During the long and delayed construction of the Nauvoo House, which Joseph had projected as a combination home and official house of entertainment, and which was being built by tithes and contributions, Law came to believe that Joseph was using these Church monies to finance his personal land speculations. Moreover, Joseph attempted to monopolize in the Church's name all the extensive construction of public and private buildings in Nauvoo. Eventually Law and his associate Robert D. Foster rebelled, bought Wisconsin lumber that was being rafted down to Nauvoo, and set up as private contractors. They paid wages where the Church paid only in scrip and supplies, and their introduction of private enterprise into the anthill diverted some of the Nauvoo work force from Nauvoo House and the temple. Joseph denounced their operations

without being able to stop them. Then, driven by some unde-
terminable combination of eroticism, Caesarism, faith in his divine
mission, and perhaps the desire to retaliate upon his rebellious counselor, he made a proposal of spiritual marriage to Law's "amiable
and handsome" wife Jane.

It was the sort of proposal that he had made to other married
women, and that some of them had accepted. Even some of the
husbands had accepted, standing up to witness the ceremony that
sealed their wives to the prophet for eternity. The Apostle Parley
P. Pratt was one who thus bent his neck; Henry Jacobs, the husband of Zina Huntington, was another. Likewise several prominent
Mormons, including Heber C. Kimball and Newel K. Whitney,
willingly gave their young daughters to Joseph in plural marriage,
and the daughters willingly (but still discreetly, because of the
rampageous first wife Emma) entered the prophet's bed. But Jane
Law did not respond to Joseph's proposal, and William Law responded with grief and anger. He had long known about the revelation on spiritual marriage and about the secret plural wives, and had
kept silence, hoping that Joseph would come to his senses. Instead,
he had come to Jane.

Law had a bitter confrontation with the prophet and demanded
that he confess and repudiate his concupiscence before the High
Council; if he did not, Law threatened to tell all he knew, and add
his facts to the charges of John C. Bennett. Joseph gave him no
satisfaction, made him no promises, and offered no confession; and
in his agonized dilemma, which put him into commercial and moral
conflict with the man he sincerely believed to be the prophet of
God, Law was forced further onto the side of the apostates and
dissidents. In the spring of 1844 conversation among the discontented
ones uncovered the fact that not only Jane Law but Austin Cowles'
wife and Hiram Kimball's wife and Robert D. Foster's wife had
been offered spiritual marriage by Joseph. What had been private
discontent was whipped into group fury. Spies carried to Joseph
reports of what was being said among the disaffected, and he sum-
moned Foster for trial before the High Council on April 20. That

trial was never held, because Joseph discovered that Foster was prepared to bring along forty-one witnesses, all ready to swear to some polygamous relationship or polygamous offer. Meeting secretly in advance, the High Council summarily cut off William and Wilson Law, Jane Law, and Robert Foster from the Church.

Though these difficulties affected only a few, and did not immediately show their full effects, the excommunication of the Laws and Foster was the beginning of the end of Nauvoo, for as Fawn Brodie points out, Law was no ordinary trouble-maker or apostate. Even excommunicated he was still a believer. His purpose was not to denounce Joseph and the Church, but to bring them back to health, and so did not pull out of Nauvoo, but stayed on, in constant fear of his life from the Sons of Dan, to see what he could accomplish in the way of reform. Clearly there was no road to reform that did not involve direct attack on Joseph. Accordingly Law and his associates prosecuted the attack with energy. One of the somewhat disreputable Higbee brothers who had been smeared in the Bennett scandals of 1842 sued Joseph for slander; Foster and Joseph H. Jackson had little trouble persuading the Mormon-hating grand jury of Carthage to indict the prophet for false swearing; and William Law himself got him indicted for adultery and polygamy. While they were waiting for the law of Illinois to take its course, the rebels ordered a printing press, intent upon airing within the holy city itself the smell of Joseph's sins.

Joseph responded not by denying the charges but by assuming their absurdity, and by a vicious vilification of his enemies—murderers, thieves, fornicators and bearers of false witness. In the midst of that the press arrived and was set up, and the first issue of the *Nauvoo Expositor* appeared on the streets on June 7, 1844. It did not vilify or fulminate. It kept its temper and a reasonable tone. But it rocked Nauvoo to the deep foundations of the temple, for it denied Joseph's right to the autocratic power he wielded, accused him of abusing the city charter, doubted his political revelations, charged him with using Church money for land gambles. Worse, it published a little parable about an innocent English girl who came to

Nauvoo for her faith's sake and was instructed in the mysteries of spiritual marriage; and along with that story it printed affadavits by William Law, Jane Law, and Austin Cowles that they had personally seen a copy of Joseph's revelation allowing the faithful Saint ten virgins.

The *Expositor's* first issue was its last, for Law and Cowles were too well known to be dismissed, like Bennett, as fornicators whose own foul breath was blowing back in their faces. Within hours Joseph had declared the paper a libelous nuisance, and the Nauvoo Legion had wrecked the shop and thrown the type into the street. The Laws and others escaped to Carthage, taking with them what they knew and the word of Joseph's response to their attack. Before a week was up, the *Warsaw Signal* was screaming for war against the Mormons, and the mob violence that had driven the Saints from Missouri was running like a grass fire through western Illinois. But here, as Mrs. Brodie suggests, it was sure to be more dangerous. Here it was not primarily the response of border scum to a potentially abolitionist immigration. Here the anti-Mormon could call himself anti-theocracy, anti-tyranny. He could point to Nauvoo's fusion of church and state, to its flouting of due process, to its bald outrage against the freedom of the press. He did not even need the charges of polygamy and the rumors of holy murders by the Sons of Dan, but those two things were like gasoline on a fire that was already burning hotly without them. Illinois exploded.

The militia was already assembling—without orders—when Governor Ford reached Carthage. Desperate to avert a civil war, Ford wrote Joseph ordering him to appear and answer the charges against him before the militia got out of hand. Joseph had said he would come if he could bring a military escort of the Nauvoo Legion to protect him from mob violence. Ford told him to leave the Legion at home if he wanted violence prevented. In no doubt about the mood of his enemies, Joseph held a conference with his brother Hyrum, and decided that if he appeared in Carthage he was a dead man. By midnight he and Hyrum were in flight across the Mississippi into Iowa.

But that flight was a brief flurry of panic. Porter Rockwell and other messengers, carrying word back and forth, brought Joseph the realization that with its leader gone Nauvoo was a coop of scared chickens. Governor Ford sent reassurances guaranteeing his safety if he gave himself up—reassurances that Hyrum was inclined to credit but that Joseph saw coldly. "If you go back," he told Hyrum, "I will go with you, but we shall be butchered." Nevertheless he had to go back. He was caught in the consequences of his own personal leadership. Prophet, revelator, Mayor of Nauvoo, General of the Legion, and even (by the secret election of the Council of Fifty), King, he could not run away and leave his people to be scattered by their enemies. Whatever else Joseph Smith was, he was at the end neither a scoundrel nor a coward. On June 24, 1844, he rode to Carthage and delivered himself up, and there is no doubt at all that he knew he rode to his death.

Death was only three days coming. Though his talks with Governor Ford had convinced Joseph that there would be no such "extermination order" as Governor Boggs had issued in Missouri, he had endeavored to extract a promise from Ford that he would not go to Nauvoo without taking Joseph along. He did not trust the militia even for an hour if Ford should leave town. But on June 27 he got word that Ford had gone to Nauvoo after all, intent upon talking the Mormons out of their will to resist by force the processes of law. Ford had taken the precaution to send home the most rabid of the militiamen, those from Warsaw; but he had left the jail to be guarded by the Carthage Greys, who were almost as hot for Joseph's blood. The moment that word came, Joseph smuggled out a note by Willard Richards, the only Mormon still able to go in and out of the jail, asking Jonathan Dunham to bring the Legion.

If Dunham had acted on the prophet's order, and brought the Legion galloping the fifteen miles to Carthage, history would have had to record a battle, and perhaps the beginning of a civil war. But Dunham for some reason never brought the Legion, and instead of a battle there was a martyrdom. The noises that Willard Richards, John Taylor, and the two Smiths heard at the door—the shouts and shots and calls to surrender—were not the Legion thundering to the rescue, but the Warsaw militia, returning as soon as the Governor was well out of sight, to join the Carthage guards in a lynching.

The four Mormons had, for defense, two canes, a six-shooter, and a single-barreled pistol that friends had smuggled in. As the steps pounded up the stairs they threw themselves against the door, but bullets tore through it and they fell back. The door burst in, slugs from a half dozen guns caught Hyrum in the body and face. Over his body Joseph emptied the six shooter through the doorway, while Willard Richards stood beside the door knocking down gun barrels with his cane. John Taylor fell with five bullets in him, Joseph flung the empty revolver aside and leaped to the window. Below were the bayoneted guns and the painted faces of a hundred militiamen.

It was a moment certain to be amplified and intensified into myth. Perhaps, as he poised there, arrested in mid-leap, Joseph comprehended in an instant of nervous lightning his whole career, his martyrdom, the rightness of this violence to which revelation and the hand of God had led him. Perhaps he gave, as Zina Huntington later said, the Masonic sign of distress. Perhaps he cried out, as one witness said, "Is there no help for the widow's son?" And perhaps, after a bullet from the doorway struck him in the back and he hung in agony from the sill, he cried out again, "Oh Lord, my God!" before he fell to the ground. It is certain that they dragged him to the well-curb in the yard and that four men fired bullets into him there, and that then, either because their job was done or because they were panicked by a beam of accusing sun that broke through the clouds and touched Joseph's body, they scattered. A long time later, Willard Richards, miraculously unwounded, crept from the roaring silence of the jail to the reverberating quiet of the yard to drag the prophet's body inside.

For more than a year and a half after Joseph's death, his people hung on, preparing for inevitable eviction from their city. One of the curious aspects of the journals which record those months is the matter-of-factness with which these much-driven people accepted the fact that they must lose all once more for their faith's sake. They had been taught to expect persecution; their solidarity was moulded by hostility from without; their faith was the more secure, the more it showed that it could bear. There was a streak of puritan masochism in many early Mormons—one feels that without tribulation they would hardly have felt confident of their identity as Saints. Perhaps as important, eviction from Nauvoo meant a heading west, and west was where the Kingdom of God, purged of Gentile persecution, could finally be built. It is likely that few of them had ever thought of their brilliant city as the final City of Zion. It was another way station, vital because of the temple and the "endowments" that could be obtained only there, but a way station nevertheless, a gathering place until the Lord should speak His final mind. Joseph himself was half in flight from Nauvoo for more than a year before they killed him.

Even earlier, if one reads the signs right. Once in Kirtland, ministering to Brigham Young's brother Lorenzo, he had promised that Lorenzo would recover fully and live to a ripe age among the Saints in the Rocky Mountains. That early, before Nauvoo could have been imagined, Joseph's eyes had gone all the way west. As a man of his time, and one who had lived in Independence when it was the head of the Santa Fe and Oregon Trails, he would have had to catch that vision. If he had not, someone would have suggested it to him.

James Arlington Bennett, the New York lawyer who for a while was Joseph's choice as a running mate in the Presidential race of 1844, had watched conflict intensify in Nauvoo and had recommended in an open letter to the New York *Herald* that Joseph take his people and establish an independent empire in Oregon. In the summer of 1843 Joseph and his advisors, soberly pondering migration, sent an agent to hunt out the best route to the Missouri. In the spring of 1844 the prophet directed James Emmet and John L. Butler to take a few families and put in crops somewhere up the Missouri, so that the Saints would have a supply point and resting

place when they left. (The Emmet party did go out, but not until
after Joseph was dead and not along the route that the Saints
ultimately traveled.) At about the same time as the Emmet instructions, Joseph told the apostles that they should send a party to look
into the possibilities of California and Oregon (which then meant
anything beyond the crest of the Rockies), "where we can remove
after the temple is completed, and where we can build a city in a
day, and have a government of our own, get up into the mountains,
where the devil cannot dig us out." Henry Clay and Stephen A.
Douglas were both recommending Oregon; Bishop George Miller
and Apostle Lyman Wight were hot for Texas. (Both would
later apostatize over essentially that issue, and lead a splinter-group
southwest.) The secret Council of Fifty, which was made up of the
most trusted leaders, went so far in 1844 as to send Lucian Wood-
worth to negotiate for a grant from the Republic of Texas; if the
request had not been so extravagant, and if Brigham Young had
not been shrewd, the Mormons might have found themselves
squarely in the midst of the Mexican War. And in March, 1844,
three months before his death, Joseph proposed to Congress what
Mrs. Brodie calls "the most grandiloquent scheme of his whole
life." He requested appointment as an officer, with power to raise
100,000 volunteers "to open the vast regions of the unpeopled west
and south." It could hardly have astonished him that his request was
denied. But the fact that he made it at all is one more evidence of
his restless casting about for a western solution to his problems.

He did not live to fix his vague impulse upon any definite locality,
and it is possible that he would not have even if his life had been
spared, for in spite of its internal and external turmoil, Nauvoo must
have been sweet to him—a city that he had raised up by his own
imaginative energy, a city that offered him not only the somewhat
puerile pleasures of uniforms and a white horse, but the real pleasures of power and the still discreetly veiled pleasures of the multiple marriage bed. On July 12, 1843, apparently as a way of quiet-
ing opposition, including that of his first wife Emma, Joseph dictated to William Clayton the revelation on celestial marriage, but

he had been taking plural wives well before, as had others of the hierarchy. In the last three or four years of his life, if Mrs. Brodie's count is accurate, Joseph had taken forty-eight wives besides Emma. And though the doctrine of celestial marriage stressed responsibility and duty and greater glory in Heaven and even a sort of eugenics as its justifications, and though many of the priesthood, including Brigham Young, entered into it in anguish of spirit and only because it was God's commandment, there is little evidence that to the full-blooded prophet polygamy was especially puritan.

Nauvoo had everything to make his life good to him—everything but tranquility—and it is possible that it would have taken violence to start him out of even an untranquil Nauvoo. In the event, it was not Joseph who led the Mormons west, but Brigham Young, and Brigham was another sort of genius, a man as practical as Joseph was visionary, as efficient in administration as Joseph was fertile in invention. He put to practical use the doctrines and the organization that Joseph had created; he found means to bind the Mormon people to him as firmly almost as they had been bound to Joseph; and he exercised, when he felt forced to it, a ruthlessness that Joseph could never have stomached. Golden-haired, blue-eyed, stocky, approachable, liable to pungent speech and direct action, inclined to thunderous wrath when crossed, he was as low-born as Joseph himself, like Joseph a farm boy from Vermont with a mainly home-made education. At the time of Joseph's death he was forty-three, with a kind of experience peculiarly Mormon: wide travel as a missionary "without purse and scrip" throughout the East and Middle West, wide experience of handling crowds, much practise in public speaking, some weeks of soldiering with Zion's Camp, some months of difficult logistics in the flight from Missouri, many months of missionarying in England. Farm boy or not, half-educated or not, by 1845 he was a man of the world, and so were the rest of the Twelve Apostles.

It was Brigham who, returning with the other apostles from the Eastern States Mission after Joseph's death, stood off the claims to the succession made by Sidney Rigdon, James Jesse Strang, and others. In a miraculous manifestation that hundreds attested, his pudgy body on the platform had assumed the length and beauty of the dead prophet's; his mouth had opened to send abroad not his own voice but the incontrovertible voice of Joseph. After that speech there was no question who would lead the Church, but it was as President of the Quorum of the Twelve Apostles, and not as prophet and revelator, that Brigham assumed command. He made his position sound humble, but neither then nor later did his actions indicate that Brother Brigham possessed humility in any excessive quantity. Nor, faced with what he was faced with, would humility have served.

2

TTTTTTTTTTTTTT

As Soon as Grass Grows and Water Runs

THROUGH THE EARLY MONTHS of 1845 there were few acts of hostility between Mormon and Gentile. Not even the trial and acquittal of Joseph's murderers (it took three days, John Hay said, to find twelve men ignorant enough to form a jury) caused any breaches of the peace. In its embattled way, Nauvoo prospered. Irene Hascall Pomeroy, who arrived with her husband in late May expecting that Nauvoo "would look like poordunk or something," found it "the prettiest place I ever saw for a large place." She wrote her mother back in New Salem, Massachusetts, urging her to come on, and reassuring her that the Saints were not worried about the mobbers, "for they fear us more than we do them."

At that point, she was probably not far wrong; and the stalemate into which the young bride moved might have continued a good while, perhaps even until the Mormons got all their preparations made, if it had not been for the ant-like swarms of laborers working on the temple. In June, more than three hundred men were at work on it. They had built fully half the great building since Joseph's death, and had laid the top tier of stone, with hosannas, the day before Irene arrived. From her cottage she could hear them sing and shout as they raised the timbers of the steeple.

The Gentiles who passed by could hear them, too. They asked

themselves why, if the Mormons intended to move out, they poured
every tithing dollar and every available man-hour of labor into
this building. And why, though the Nauvoo charter had been revoked by the legislature in January, the Legion had not only not
disbanded, but refused to hand over its ordnance to the militia. (The
Mormons would have replied that they remembered Far West, and
Boggs, and the traitorous Hinkle.) Gentiles looked at the thriving
crops and the humming town, and counted the people who still
kept disembarking from the river boats, and heard that 25,000 had
attended the spring conference in April. It looked more like growth
than decline, more like staying than moving out.

What the Gentiles did not know was the importance of the
temple to this sect which could get only from the hands of its own
ordained priesthood the rites and endowments that meant salvation. Hence the mystical power of the Gathering upon such people
as Irene Pomeroy. Her letters to her mother are full of the urgency
of apocalypse: "Mother if it is a possible thing you must come. It
will be perfectly right if you come and leave everything that you
cannot get to come with you and every body." Irene had had her
patriarchal blessing, a sort of official horoscope, which had told her
that if faithful she would be the means of saving all her living and
dead friends in the first resurrection, "so if you have to leave Father
and Grandmother there is a way they can be saved in the first
resurrection. Everyone has to be tried and make a sacrifice like faithful Abraham when he offered his son Isaac." If it sounds a little
cold-blooded, her willingness to sacrifice skeptical members of the
family, it is quintessentially Mormon. This new and pregnant bride,
thrilling to the work of finishing the temple "with a tool in one hand
and a sword in the other," would not have felt herself worthy if her
faith had not been tested by the sacrifice of at least a father or
brother, all her worldly goods, the fruit of her womb, or some other
worthy offering. Eventually, eleven years hence, she would lose an
arm in another Saintly flight, and die of it in full beatitude.

More than Irene Pomeroy were aflame with salvation and sacrifice. By October, the Church was ready to issue an official letter

urging all Saints in the United States to sell their property, gather to Nauvoo to receive their endowments in the temple, and then join the migration westward. Without the completion of the endowments, the Mormons' departure from Nauvoo would have been only flight. But with the endowments completed, they could go a saved and covenanted people. "The main purpose in gathering the people of God," Joseph had told them, was "to build unto the Lord a house wherein He could reveal to them the ordinances and glories of His Kingdom." There was only one true priesthood, passed on by Joseph, upon whom it had been conferred by the angel of God. "Can you get an endowment in Boston?" Brigham Young had asked a gathering in Boylston Hall in 1843. "No, only in that place which God has appointed.... If you do not help to build the Temple ... if you do not help to build up Zion and the cause of God, you will not inherit the land of Zion. Be faithful or you will not be chosen; for the day of choosing is at the door."

There had been no temple ceremonies since Kirtland, seven years earlier. Now thousands yearning for the initiation that would complete their covenant with God watched the steeple rise, and the roof go on, and were assured that they would have their endowments by the time snow flew. The Gentiles watched too, steadily more exasperated and alarmed. By September there were renewed outbreaks of violence, burnings, raids, and though Irene wrote proudly that the words *Nauvoo Legion* struck terror to the mobbers' hearts, the mobbers grew daily more dangerous and the reprisals more violent. In September the Legion had to rescue two hundred people from the village of Lima and bring them for safety to Nauvoo. On the road between Nauvoo and Carthage a gang chased Sheriff Backenstos, who had shown signs of taking the Mormon side, and had enlisted Mormons as a posse to keep the peace, until the sheriff encountered a pair of Mormons one of whom was Porter Rockwell. Rockwell had been promised by Joseph that no bullet would ever touch him. He wore his hair long in remembrance of that prophecy, and in a long life that his enemies said included upwards of a hundred holy murders (his most scrupulous biographer guesses twenty) the promise held good. He was illiterate, nerveless, tireless, dedicated, an utterly dependable zealot. Now at the sheriff's frantic command he lifted his rifle and shot off his horse one of the pursuers, a Mormon-eater named Worrell, and the Mormon-Gentile hostility was once again renewed in blood. On September 24, 1845, under heavy pressure, the Twelve issued a proclamation aimed at bringing about a truce: they said that the Saints would move out of Nauvoo "as soon as the grass grows and water runs." From that time on the Mormon hive had two crash programs—the temple and the preparations for migration. Men cut and kiln-dried oak for wagons, pickled in brine the hickory for axles, fired up the forges to beat out tires and chains, twisted hemp in the long rope-walks along the river. The sisters, as fall came on, multiplied their housewifely accumulations of dried squash, dried fruits, pickles, vinegar. While they visited together, and were in turn visited by the Holy Ghost, and spoke and interpreted in tongues, and related dreams, and told how one or another had risen up cured when the elders had anointed him with oil and laid on hands and rebuked the illness, their hands were busy sewing tents, wagon covers, and sacks for flour and crackers.

At the end of September, at the instance of the Twelve, Apostle Parley P. Pratt estimated the required outfit for a family of five: one wagon, three yoke of oxen, two cows, two beef cattle, three sheep, 1,000 pounds of flour, twenty pounds of sugar, one rifle and ammunition, one tent and poles—a total weight of 2,700 pounds. Later he enlarged the estimate to include two pounds of tea, five of coffee, and a keg of alcohol for each two families, plus other items. All of these estimates, in the event, would prove to be pipe-dreams. For as soon as it was announced that all of the Twelve, with their families, would go west with the first company, every Saint wanted to go too. Wherever the priesthood was, there was the heart of the Church. Outfit and provisions were secondary.

Work on the temple went on, and the pressures from the Gentiles increased. General Hardin of the militia swore he would come to Nauvoo and arrest Port Rockwell if he had to unroof every house in the place to find him. But he didn't; he wouldn't have dared. When marshals or officers came to Nauvoo these days they found themselves always under the eyes of lolling loungers, young men with hard faces who watched them silently, and took out their bowies to whittle, and followed the marshals, whittling, wherever they went. Those "whittling deacons," they knew, were members of the Nauvoo Legion, part of the police force of Col. Hosea Stout. It would have taken more nerve than Hardin or any other Gentile official had to challenge them inside Nauvoo. Angry letters went back and forth between the Mormons and the Governor, under whose guarantees of safety Joseph Smith had been killed and who now vacillated between helplessness ("The whole state is a mob," he told Bishop George Miller) and somewhat cynical scorn. Both parties, he said, were "so enraged that they were, as they said, anxious to be permitted to fight, though . . . their ardor sensibly abated when the obstacle to a fight should be removed." Quite correctly, the Saints expected no help from him. He was a little man, and they expressed their contempt in a song:

> Governor Ford, he is so small
> He has no room for a soul at all.

But fighting was only one of the possibilities the Mormons faced. Another was the constant threat of legal action, on one charge or another, against their leaders. The making of "bogus" was one of the methods of livelihood adopted along the river, and Nauvoo, hitherto nearly immune to raids by law officers, looked to the Gentiles like the place where it centered. Perhaps they were right, for Hosea Stout, in his capacity as police chief of Zion, later discovered bonafide counterfeiters among the Saints in Winter Quarters. Brigham Young and others of the Twelve, as the most obvious targets of Gentile law, began to move circumspectly and to keep to their houses or to the temple where they could not be seized.

Yet they went steadily about their preparations, gathering everything needed for the migration of the whole people. Even history: though they did not quite go so far as to carry with them an Ark

of the Covenant, they chose to carry along the history of how their
Church had been created and its priesthood ordained and its com-
municants persecuted. Apostle Willard Richards, as Church Historian, sent out a call for any documents relevant to the Church's
story, and with William Clayton and other clerks set about to put
them in order. Letters from the prophet, deeds to old Missouri
property, written accounts of remarkable providences, journals
and lists and organizational charts, took their place in the preparations beside wagon hubs and tent poles. In rare breathing spaces,
Brigham had Richards or Parley Pratt or one of the other more
literary apostles read aloud from Frémont and Hastings and other
authorities on the West.

An inventory on November 23 showed 3,285 families organized,
on the model of Zion's Camp, into tens, fifties, and hundreds. There
were then 1,508 wagons ready and 1,892 begun, all of the new
ones built to specifications laid out by Brother Brigham and announced in the Gathering letter of October. In that same letter, in
the midst of advice about building wagons to a track of five feet
and using well-selected, well-seasoned lumber, the Twelve had, as
if casually, mentioned that there were many good locations on the
Pacific, especially at Vancouver's Island. That was a public nudge,
a power play calculated to gain concessions from the United States,
for Vancouver Island was part of disputed Oregon, over which
the United States and Great Britain were close to war. Fifteen or
twenty thousand disciplined settlers who hated the United States
and threw their weight on the side of Great Britain could tip the
balance on that sparse frontier and make impossible a settlement
favorable to America. There is little evidence that Brigham ever
seriously intended taking his people to Vancouver Island or anywhere near it; but he was the last man to overlook the advantage of
seeming to lean that way. So now on December 11 Apostle Orson
Pratt, Parley's brother and Mormondom's chief scholar, returned
from the Eastern States Mission (he said in leaving that he hoped
not a Saint would be left in the United States by spring) bringing
$400 worth of Allen's pepperbox revolvers and the word from Sam-

uel Brannan, entirely false, that the United States was planning to use force, if necessary, to prevent the Mormons from going west. Brigham would surely have been able to appraise that rumor at its true value, knowing Sam Brannan and knowing something about rumor-mongering himself. Governor Ford was widely suspected later of having helped circulate the rumor of federal force in order to hurry the Mormons on their way. But for the rank and file the threat served admirably as a spur. More persecution. They took a deep refreshed breath and pushed ahead, protected on their fringes by Charles Coulson Rich's undiminished Legion and within Nauvoo by Hosea Stout's hard-handed police.

By December 10, 1845, the temple's upper rooms were sufficiently finished so that the endowments could begin. Night and day the faithful crowded in to have their turn at baptisms and sealings and washings and anointings, to witness the symbolic Adam and Eve drama acted out by the Twelve and others of the priesthood, and to be initiated as full members of the New Dispensation. The ceremonies, freely adapted by Joseph from Masonic rituals, have been described more than once, though they were then and are now held secret by the Church. To the good Saint they have always been incomparably holy; in the temple and the temple ceremonies reside the keys to the Kingdom. Now men and women so crowded the unfinished rooms that they wore out the priesthood, and finally made Brigham wish a little irritably that they could postpone the whole business of the endowments to insure their safe departure. He could not, of course, frustrate so much pious desire, but his journal and the day-by-day Church history indicate how much of a burden the endowments added to a burden already enormous.

For they were dickering about the sale of their property, including the temple, to the Catholic Church. They were dickering with the President of the United States trying to get a contract to build and temporarily man posts along the Oregon Trail. They were debating the problem of their destination, and planning advance parties to go ahead and prepare the way "in some good valley in the neighborhood of the Rocky Mountains. . . . Here we will make a resting place, until we can determine a place for permanent location." They were ducking marshals and sheriffs armed with warrants, they were gathering tithing corn, urging along the wagon-building, preparing boats and lighters for the crossing of the river. They were sifting rumors, writing letters, officiating at the endowment ceremonies, inspecting the progress of work—which still stubbornly continued—on the temple. In the middle of it, Brigham's team fell through a bridge, and with a concern and a practicality that were entirely characteristic, he personally spent several hours and used up half a gallon of whiskey rubbing them down to prevent their catching cold and going stiff.

By the end of January there were rumors that the Twelve were about to be arrested. Gentiles were supposed to have danced in warpaint over in Keokuk, threatening to take the Twelve as soon as they crossed the river. But the Mormon population in Lee County, Iowa, immediately across from Nauvoo, was heavy, and that region was at least as safe as the Illinois side. Moreover, Illinois warrants were no good there. It was more and more probable that the Gentiles were not going to wait until grass grew again. For the safety of the Twelve and the placation of mob ugliness, at least a token move had to be made. The weather was not severe—it hung in that mildness of January thaw that tobacco growers call "case weather." Abruptly, not because he or his people were ready but because his estimate of the situation told him he must, Brigham decided to move.

3

TTTTTTTTTTTT

Sugar Creek

THUS THEIR GOING was something between orderly withdrawal and flight—neither the well-equipped exodus that Church leaders had tried for nor the panicked and empty-handed rout that would be the fate of those who because of health or economics dared the wrath of the Gentiles through the following summer. Despite the months of organization and planning, few of the hundreds of families who crowded to the riverbank in February were provided with all the things that Parley Pratt had thought essential; and despite their organization into tens and hundreds they did not finally go as Irene Pomeroy had pictured them going, orderly as ducks in a shooting gallery, "every company a half mile apart, every waggon ten rods apart." They went as they could, and with the outfits they had been able to get together, and many, out of fear of the Gentiles or exhilaration at receiving their endowments or a simple desire to be with the Twelve, reported themselves readier than in fact they were.

Charles Shumway, one of the discreet and powerful Council of Fifty, crossed the Mississippi on February 4 and located a campground in the timber on Sugar Creek, about seven miles from Nauvoo. (That same day, the ship *Brooklyn* sailed from New York, bound for San Francisco Bay with 238 Saints under the leadership of Sam Brannan.) And now that whole people heaved into motion, plan became fact, the City of Zion began to be transformed into the Camp of Israel.

They cherished historical parallels: a chosen people would not be a chosen people without an acute sense of role. The Yankees among them, who were many, remembered the Pilgrim Fathers, similarly driven for their faith's sake; and out in the flooded creek-bottoms of Iowa some Saints would soon be reading, with the satisfaction of shared martyrdom, a book about Siberian exiles. But the surest image they had of themselves was that of an Old Testament tribe. They were the tribe of Joseph, of the seed of Jacob, this was their flight out of Egypt, Brother Brigham was their Moses, the Mississippi was their Red Sea, Governor Ford was a reasonable facsimile of Pharaoh. Shortly the river would get into the spirit of its role by providentially freezing over to let some of their wagons cross on the ice, and Mormon writers ever after would note the miracle, though it was a miracle that nearly froze a couple of thousand Saints.

But mainly they had a cold, wet, muscle-wrenching, wagon-straining job of loading all they owned onto flatboats and lighters and skiffs and getting it across from the uneasy truce of Nauvoo to the uncertain neutrality of Iowa. The wilderness before them was broad and their destination dubious; they were leaving behind them the only prosperity and security many of them had ever known, and abandoning their holy place to the infidel. Nevertheless, the Lord had promised a Canaan. Their mood was characteristically neither fear nor sorrow, but resolution. "To your tents, O Israel!" someone is supposed to have cried, and if anyone did indeed say those improbable words, we may be sure no one smiled, for the command expressed their united impulse in their natural phraseology.

One could have stood on the river bank in the raw wind and seen a cross-section of Zion wallow down to the ferry landing to wait a turn. A random sampling will introduce us to both leaders and followers whom we shall meet again.

On February 6, Bishop George Miller with six wagons. Miller will always be out ahead; he is impatient and headstrong, one who does not readily accept counsel, especially the counsel of Brother Brigham. He will lead the first party of Saints out into the plains beyond the Missouri, and will winter among the Poncas at the mouth of the Niobrara, west of modern Yankton, South Dakota. But when the pioneer Mormon party starts west in the spring of 1847 he will not be with them; he will be off to Texas with Apostle Lyman Wight, both of them disfellowshipped.

On February 8, among many others, John Smith, uncle of the Prophet, President of the Nauvoo Stake of Zion, who will be the first president of the still-to-be-founded stake in Great Salt Lake Valley—a nominal leader only, a pious figurehead; and Albert Carrington, graduate of Dartmouth College, now a sort of clerk or secretary, destined one day to become one of the Quorum of the Twelve Apostles; and Brigham Young's slow, massive, stubborn brother Lorenzo, with two wives and five children, some of them by a previous marriage of his first wife's.

On February 9, William Huntington, who long ago sold his New York State farm to gather to Kirtland, and fled out of Kirtland to gather to Far West, and fled out of Far West before the mobs and the militia, losing his wife to the hardships of that winter. He has just consecrated, i.e., deeded over, his Nauvoo property to the Church, and now heads west with a skimpy outfit behind a team borrowed from the Church authorities. He is important to us for several reasons, none of them related to the fact that his grandfather was a signer of the Declaration of Independence. Two of his daughters have been plural wives of Joseph Smith while both were still ostensibly married to rank and file Saints. The younger and more beautiful one, Zina, was recently taken over by Brigham as Joseph's proxy, being sealed to him for time and to Joseph for eternity in the Nauvoo temple, with her still-undivorced husband Henry Jacobs standing witness. The older, Prescindia, who has borne a son almost surely of Joseph's fathering, will in a few months be sealed for time to Brigham's counselor, Heber C. Kimball. Two of Huntington's sons have been Danites; one, Dimick, will march with the Mormon Battalion. Many years from now a son of Dimick's, Lot Huntington, a boy gone a little wild on the frontier, will be blown to hell by old Porter Rockwell, a family friend since before Lot's birth. In its New England origin and its history of sacrifice, devotion, and fanaticism the Huntington family is a compendium of early Mormonism. William Huntington himself will not survive the trail.

There are omens of trouble and hardship. On the ninth, while Huntington and Thomas Grover and the family of Apostle George A. Smith are preparing to cross, someone looks back up the hill and cries out that the temple is afire. Prompt work by bucket brigades puts the fire out in a half hour, with minor damage to the roof, but there were some, surely, whose hearts dropped like stones to see that smoke, and others who would fiercely have welcomed so final a sign of their sacrifice as the destruction of the whole building. They have no time for examining their feelings, for the river is fast, icy, and a mile wide. A skiff gets in trouble and has to be rescued by a scow, which in turn gets in trouble so that several people, among them members of the family of Hosea Stout, are marooned cold and wet on an island. And Thomas Grover's loaded flatboat too: someone (some accounts say a mischievous boy, the official *Church History* says a "filthy wicked man") spits tobacco juice in the eye of one of Grover's oxen, which in his lumbering dismay plunges overboard, knocking the sideboards out of the scow and dragging another ox with him. The flatboat sinks, the two oxen drown, the load of clothing and food is spoiled or lost. An incident, merely—an instance of the hazards they will face at every major river along their route. An object lesson also on the evils of tobacco, whose use is frowned on in Joseph's dietary revelations called the Word of Wisdom. But also some valuable experience to Grover, who a little over a year hence will be left behind with a crew to superintend the Mormon Ferry at the last crossing of the North Platte, a thousand miles west.

They come in an irregular procession, horses humped back in

the breeching down the slope, oxen heaving to drag loaded wagons through the mud, men with whips and goads, boys driving loose stock, women tight-mouthed on the wagon seats, children peering out from the bows or darting between the wheels. There are more women than men; and some of the women, risking themselves against all caution and all necessity, are far gone in pregnancy. No one actually is pressing them this hard: they could stay a week or a month and have their babies under a roof. But it is as if they covet the opportunity to drop their young like animals in any crude shelter available to God's driven people.

During these early days of February the mild weather chills, the rutted mud freezes, there is a skim of snow, ice reaches out from the shore of protected coves. Working in shifts day and night, the ferrymen have a bleak job. Superintending them, in the time allowed by his duties as head of the Nauvoo police, is Hosea Stout, a colonel in the Legion, a veteran of the Missouri troubles and one of the warriors of Crooked River. Like William Huntington, he has lost a wife to the hardships of the Missouri exodus, though when he sees her grave at Sugar Creek on February 13 he will be able to console himself: "Instead of being deprived of my lost bosom friend, I now have three equally dear and confiding to me."

On February 12, Hosea sends across the first installment of the family of his brother-in-law, Charles Coulson Rich. Rich is another of Brigham's dependables, a six-foot-four Tennesseean, Major General of the Legion, a fighter and doer. In marriage, as in other things, he has shown himself more dutiful than emotional. At the suggestion of the elders, he proposed to his first wife by mail, and married her sight-unseen. Not to be outdone in faithfulness, she has selected four of her friends to be his plural wives (one of them is a daughter of Thomas Grover) and stood up in the temple with them when they were sealed to him. On the trail she will give him another, and they will live together in harmony all their lives as if determined to prove the rightness of Joseph's revelation on marriage. Rich is destined to become a member of the Quorum of the Twelve; like many of these Nauvoo refugees, he will be important

in the history of the West, and less than a decade later he and Amasa
Lyman will found a city called San Bernardino in California. Now
he starts his multiple family across the Mississippi a wife at a time,
but he is wiser than some husbands: he holds back number two, Eliza,
so that she can have her baby in a warm house instead of in a tent.

Also on February 12 comes that other Eliza, Eliza Snow the
prophetess, traveling in the buggy of Stephen Markham with her
feet on a charcoal footstove. Eliza is forty-two, and widowed by
the guns that slew Joseph Smith. Though she now has another husband, having been sealed to Brigham for time and to Joseph for
eternity during the passion of temple work that preceded the departure, Brigham will not extend his personal protection to her until 1848, well after she reaches Salt Lake City. For one thing, he
has taken on a good many women lately, including several other
former wives of Joseph, thus setting an example to the priesthood
to support the unsupported. For another, he has plenty to do just
getting the Saints on the road. For still another, polygamy is even
yet, and even among the Saints, not generally admitted. So Eliza
will depend upon Brother Markham, one of the stalwarts, a member of the Council of Fifty, and will concentrate her energies upon
memorializing the exodus in verse. She is exceedingly pious, enjoys
the gifts of the Holy Ghost, loves a good session of tongues. In her
poems she can be, according to the occasion, hortatory, martial, or
mortuary, and she will be all three; but during the nearly two years
during which she will be on the road to Zion she will be called
upon more often to record Israel's losses than to urge on its lagging
feet. A dreadful number of her poems of the next months will begin,
"Mourn not for him, he's gone to rest," or "Mourn not for them
—their bodies rest/ So sweetly in the ground," or "Mary's gone—
she's gone; but whither?/ To the paradise of love," or "Round the
grave there are no shadows—/ 'Tis no more a dread to die."

On February 13, Brother Serrine comes in from Michigan, re-
porting seventy families of Saints on their way from there, well
fitted out for the West. That same day, Brigham sends his baggage

wagons over, and Appleton Harmon, one of Hosea Stout's policemen whom we shall meet again, makes it across to the Iowa side.
Next day, Apostle Parley Pratt ferries the river with his teams—
one of the eloquent mouths of Mormonism, once a Campbellite
preacher; a man whose enthusiasm sometimes outruns his discre-
tion but who can be oddly humble when rebuked. He will live to
be one of the explorers of Utah and to see his name on a canyon in
the Wasatch above Salt Lake City, and in 1857 he will be shot down
in Arkansas by the furious ex-husband of one of his converts, and
so become, next to Joseph and Hyrum, the most famous of Mormon
martyrs.

Finally, on February 15, in company with Eliza Snow's brother
Lorenzo and the Apostles Willard Richards and George A. Smith,
Brigham ferries the river and flounders out the frozen-mudhole road
to Sugar Creek, where for ten days the growing camp of Saints has
been uncomfortably waiting, with its morale shredding apart in the
icy wind and its brotherly love beginning to freeze solid.

He is an extraordinary leader. His presence has the instant clari-
fying and precipitating effect of glycerin in a cloudy liquid. On
February 17, he hauls a wagon into the center of the camp and
climbs on it and makes them one again in a half hour. He tells them
why they are held up there in the cold: they are waiting for Heber
C. Kimball, William Clayton, and Bishop Newel K. Whitney to
secure and forward Church property and put the Church's affairs
in order for the trustees who will be left behind. He braces up those
who are sagging from cold or illness or want, orders the owners
of horses with distemper to get them out of camp at once, promises that dogs which are not kept leashed will be shot, organizes a
Lost and Found, appoints a commissary for animal fodder, rebukes
those who have been careless with firearms or wasteful of food.
He is a terrible and rewarding man to be scolded by. There has never
been a people that so dearly loved a scolding, and Brigham under-
stands them down to the ground. "We will have no rules we cannot keep," he tells them, "but we will have order in camp." The

next day he has them organized into companies with captains and sub-captains and specifically assigned duties, and dismisses them saying, "Brethren, you are the best set of fellows there is in the world but there is great chance for improvement."

Sugar Creek is notorious in the histories as a place of intense hardship, as if it had held a huddle of refugees without rags to cover them or a bone to gnaw. Some of that over-dramatization stems from the error of confusing Sugar Creek with the Poor Camp of September; some stems from Eliza Snow's report that nine babies were born in the ice-bound tent town the night before she arrived. As we have seen, most of the women wouldn't have had to bear their children in the snow if they had not chosen to; and Sugar Creek was not a rabble of starving and freezing victims but a well-ordered camp of people who had been preparing for this move for months. Most of them had well-made wagons, good tents, and a certain amount of provisions. There was plenty of timber for fires. The principal trial at Sugar Creek was the cold, which went close to or below zero every night now. On February 19, a blizzardy storm blew down some tents and dropped six or seven inches of snow on the camp, and the next day the temperature fell until the ice reaching out from both banks of the Mississippi began to meet and fuse. No one who has camped out in a tent in below-zero weather would pretend it was cozy; nevertheless this was not a place of the bitterest hardship: that would come later. Once Brother Brigham arrived and played the father to them all, there was little wrong with them except a shortage of fodder and an impatience to be gone. They would have "felt to agree," as the Mormon idiom went, with Eliza Snow, who on the snowy nineteenth wrote a marching song:

> Altho' in woods and tents we dwell
> Shout, shout O Camp of Israel!
> No Christian mobs on earth can bind
> Our thoughts, or steal our peace of mind.

On the eighteenth, Brigham and Heber Kimball had gone back to Nauvoo to hurry Clayton and Whitney along. On the twenty-second, when the Saints gathered for meeting in the temple, their weight on the unstabilized truss floor settled the timbers with an alarming crack, causing a near panic. Several people jumped out the windows, one mashing his face and another breaking an arm—both, reports Willard Richards comfortably, Strangites, and therefore near apostasy. That night Brigham and Heber crossed the Mississippi in a skiff among the running ice cakes, in company with Apostle John Taylor, who had been shot along with Joseph and Hyrum but had survived his wounds. Brigham found the camp so restless in the cold—Orson Pratt's thermometer showed twelve below zero on February 24—that on the twenty-fifth he let the hasty George Miller take sixteen wagons and thirty or forty pioneers to lay out a road along the divide between the Des Moines and the Missouri. The rest waited. Finally, on the twenty-seventh, Clayton and Bishop Whitney arrived, having driven across the Mississippi on the ice.

These are both men of interest to us. Whitney, one of the most devout of the Kirtland converts, had personally given his seventeen-year-old daughter to Joseph as a polygamous wife; and to Clayton, as confidential secretary, Joseph had dictated his revelation on celestial marriage. He has been appointed clerk of the Camp of Israel. His more-or-less-official journal, this year and next, we shall find indispensable.

Now the reasons for the delay are past. On February 28, Stephen Markham, having traded his buggy for a wagon, leads out a party of additional pioneers, and on March 1, nearly a month after the first crossings of the Mississippi, the main camp begins to roll. Company after company, the spaced wagons heave up out of the stained creekbottom and onto high ground. Hosea Stout's company of guards post themselves as outriders, the artillery company and Captain Pitt's Brass Band, converted en masse in England and a thing of absolutely incalculable value to the Saints ever since, fall in line among the companies led by Brigham, Heber Kimball, Amasa Lyman, George A. Smith, John Smith, Orson Pratt, and Willard Richards. Fanning across the snowy prairie, or tied to the endgates, move their hundreds of cows and sheep and spare oxen and horses and mules. All across Iowa, in good weather or in foul, unimaginative men seeing that people in movement, hundreds of wagons, thousands of animals, two or three thousand men, women and children, will catch their breath with the momentary feeling that they have looked back through more than two thousand years at the veritable Children of Israel.

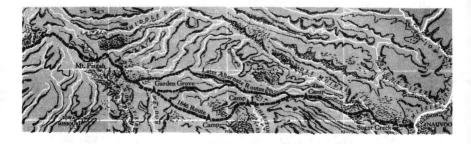

4

~~~~~~~~~~~~~~~~~

Go Down, Moses

THE ROUTE THAT THEY FOLLOWED, and in its western parts established, became in the 1850's a major road between the Mississippi and the Missouri. Though it no longer exists as a road, it can be traced with considerable accuracy. Starting from Sugar Creek, it angled northwest along the Des Moines, passing through the settlement of Farmington and crossing the Des Moines at Bonaparte, then called Bonaparte Mills. From there it took a course essentially west; as far as a little beyond modern Centerville it is paralleled by, and for some stretches is synonymous with, Iowa 2. On a branch of Chequest Creek the Camp of Israel halted to repair wagons, hire out gangs of rail splitters and corn huskers, and play concerts for some of the nearby communities; and that camp at Richardson's Point became the first of the way stations on the road. A little above present Bloomfield, in Appanoose County, the trail crossed Fox River and struck a track of the Mormons' own making—the trail between Muscatine and Caldwell County, Missouri, along which many Saints had entered Missouri and back which many had fled. Hosea Stout and Lorenzo Young had some reminiscent conversation about that road, for they had been among the Crooked River combatants who labored along it for their lives in the late fall of 1838. Now, when the Camp of Israel came along, there were settlements and farms that grew thinner and rattier the farther west one went, until in Wayne County began the sea of grass, all but empty to the Missouri.

On the Chariton, just above Centerville, the Camp of Israel established a second station. Rain and floods that turned the prairie to quagmire forced them to stay with the old Mormon Road, bad as it was; it took them southwest to Shoal or Locust Creek, almost at the Missouri border, where they made their third permanent camp. But it would have taken more than a road to lure them into Missouri. From Shoal Creek they turned northwest across the roadless prairie into Decatur County, Iowa, recently surveyed but not yet settled. On April 24, they were bogged down over a good many miles in the center of that vacant county, the advance companies gathering themselves to erect a permanent town and farm for the benefit of those too used up to go farther and of the companies which would come after.

Characteristically, they started at the sound of a trumpet, just as they characteristically were led on each day's journey by the sound of the temple bell carried in one of the lead wagons. A trumpeter from the band blew, and a hundred men raised their axes against the bottomland trees, forty-eight fell upon the downed timber to cut it into logs for cabins, a gang went to work building a bridge across a branch of Grand River, another gang started digging a well, another making wooden plows, still another taking off into Missouri to trade dishes, furniture, and other dispensables for provisions. Like Caesar's armies fortifying themselves in enemy country, they could build towns overnight. On May 11, when they pulled out again, they left a cluster of log cabins, plowed and planted and fenced fields, a bridged creek, wells, a plain road, a Branch of Zion: a town, Garden Grove. It is there yet.

On May 18, forty-five miles northwest on the middle fork of Grand River, near the present village of Talmadge, they started another town, Mt. Pisgah. By the end of the month most of the Twelve and large companies of the Saints had moved on into Adair

County, and thence westward in two southward-drooping loops, past the Pottawattamie village on the Nishnabotna and on to where Indian Creek flows into the Missouri. The temporary settlement they formed there was at first called Miller's Hollow, later Kanesville. It is in the heart of modern Council Bluffs.

That was essentially the route that was followed up to 1852 by all the Mormon refugees from Nauvoo and southeastern Iowa, by several thousand European Saints brought up the Mississippi as far as Keokuk in the 1850's, and by a growing number of California- and Oregon-bound emigrants from 1848 on. The most northerly road then linking the Mississippi and the Missouri, it funneled travelers into the Council Bluffs staging area, which was two hundred miles closer to the west coast than were Independence, Westport, or St. Joseph; and this northerly emigration naturally passed on out the north side of the Platte on the Mormon route across the plains. A major route into the West, the Mormon Trail beginning on the Iowa shore across from Nauvoo was more than a trace marked by ruts and mudholes. However far it was from being a modern highway, it was a road: its creeks were generally bridged, its fords were dug down and made passable, it developed and maintained a string of roadside stations through thinly inhabited country.

Later travel made a few variations on the route laid out by the Camp of Israel. Learning to love high ground, later refugees from Nauvoo straightened the route by bearing northward from the crossing of Fox River, at modern Bloomfield, and staying north of the Chariton to near the present town of that name, where they established a station. From this they went west on the route of contemporary US 34 until they met the Camp of Israel road a few miles south of Osceola. The new route was both shorter and easier, for it avoided some bad river crossings and much muddy lowland. But it had the disadvantage that it passed well north of the way station at Garden Grove, which lay at about mid-point between Mississippi and Missouri and which provided not only refreshment and supplies but blacksmithing and other services. So a third com-

promise route came to be used. It branched off at Bloomfield, but
instead of going far enough north to head the Chariton, it crossed
the river above the present village of Griffinsville and went almost
due west to Garden Grove and a junction with the original road.

The difficulties of this road did not include very much of the
hostility that the Saints had had reason to fear. They were the usual
difficulties of a frontier trace—mudholes, steep and boggy stream
crossings, stiff hills, slithering descents into the bottoms. The hills,
even with double- and triple-teaming, wore out their animals, and
even a new and solid wagon was not proof against the strains put on
it. The heavy gumbo stuck in bucket-sized clumps to the feet, or
jammed like tar between wheel and wagonbox. They had agreed
with their enemies that they would move as soon as the grass grew
again, but they had left sooner than they intended, and now in
March and early April they were between hay and grass. Their
corn and fodder had been so depleted at Sugar Creek that most companies were hard up for feed before they ever started. Many a night
they fed their animals on the twigs and bark of felled cottonwoods
and elms.

Where they had opportunity, they cleared land or split rails
or shucked corn for settlers along the way, and took their pay in
corn or fodder. When it was invited—and it was invited with enthusiasm at Farmington and Keosaqua and other places—the band
played concerts in towns whose only music up to that hour had been
the hymns of infrequent camp meetings or the singing of a girl
gathering eggs with her mind on more romantic things. Sometimes
the band was paid by a cash collection, sometimes in corn, once
with a pail of honey that a band member later stole for his own
family's use. As they toiled west, those opportunities dwindled and
finally ceased. The organization of companies was weakened by
breakdowns, overloading, illness, sick or lost or dying stock, until
they were stretched out across many miles, coagulating briefly for
rest and reorganization at the principal way stations and then
stretching out again. Let us follow a few individuals along that
road.

Lorenzo Young, though a man of great strength, great devotion, and a stubborn honesty, was not particularly bright. He never was given a place in the hierarchy commensurate with his position as Brigham's brother, but he remained entirely faithful. On the journey out of Sugar Creek his hardships and difficulties were if anything worse than the average, but his diary, set down at first in his own hand and in his own incomparable spelling, and later kept by his wife Harriet with a considerable improvement in both, is as matter of fact as the rain. It is our privilege to visualize him up to his boot tops in heavy, slippery mud, wielding goad or whip or voice on oxen that slither and slip and flinch and stall, while boys and wives heave at the spokes to keep the wheels turning, and the rain comes down with the gray of sleet in it, dimming their sight of the wagons ahead, closing off the road behind . . . On that unseasonable journey such a day was more normal than not. But that is not the way Lorenzo reports it. His diary is as dry as the squash cakes that thrifty Mormon wives put away, and sometimes served up along the trail in squash pies without sugar or spice:

> I started with my company of ten; traveled 5 milds; broke a nexeltree to one of my wagons. We went on one mild, then went back and got the lode and wagon and campt for the night. Put in a new exeltree. The nex day started on our gerny. Neer night Wm. Worken broke a wagon whel.
> The next day we traveled through Garmenton [Germantown]. Campel 4 milds above the town. The next day we went through Bonipart. Crosed the Dismoin. Camped on Bank of the river. The next day traveled 4 milds; campt on the edg of the perara. The next morning I lost my red cow, but fortunately found her again. Traveled to Deer Creek that day; broke the tung out of my big wagon but put in a nother in about one our.

Four miles, five miles, was as much as human and animal flesh could manage after the thaws softened the prairie and the rains began. They were a month making a hundred miles; and though it would have disheartened them to know it in advance—the more naive of them set out with high hopes of driving straight through

to the mountains—they would be a good four months on the road
before the first wagons of them would cross the Missouri. From
their journals, it appears that it rained just about half the time
during those four months; on several occasions, as in mid-March
and at the end of April, it rained steadily and hard for days on end.
The Mormon Trail across Iowa was made through almost interminable mud, and when in mid-April they had a brief spell of fine weather
and the ground dried out a little and the grass began to come on
green, the rattlesnakes came out with the grass in such numbers
as to dismay them, bit the noses of oxen and horses, killed some and
sickened many more. During that sunny spell someone, Indian or
white, fired the old grass so that some companies of the Saints had
to backfire in self defense, and they slept those few dry nights on
charred ground under the falling ash and soot of prairie fires, until
the rains came again and returned them to the mud.

Chilblained feet went morning after morning into sodden, mis-
shapen shoes that had been soaked for weeks. Children sniffled and
sickened and had to be whipped from their beds in the mornings
to milk the cow or hunt up the teams. The beds themselves, wet
when tents blew down or all-night rains dripped through the wagon
covers, or muddied from being spread on wet ground, might stay
wet and muddy for days before a combination of weather and wood
let them be dried out. Several times whole companies, caught by
storms out of reach of timber, spent the night on the open prairie
without fire, and with no food except flour gruel or parched corn,
and none too much of that. Even the phlegmatic Lorenzo was moved
nearly to lamentation by the night of March 23, when they had just
made the exhausting crossing of the Chariton.

> We camped on the hill. It began to rain about noon and
> raind the rest of the day. About nine oclock P.M. it began to
> roar in the west, and the wind began to bloe. I steped to the
> doare of my tent and took hold to hold it, but in A moment
> there came A gust of wind and blue the tent flat to the ground.
> My nex care was to hold my carage, which was under the tent,
> from blowing a way. The rain came down in torants so fast
> that it put out the fire. In a few minuits it was all darkness, and

> it was so cold that it seemed as though I must perish. I stood and
> held the . . . end of the carage about one our. The rain wet me
> through and through, and I never felt in my life as though I
> must perish with the col more than I did then.

Thus Lorenzo, a man more inured to hardship than most. It is painful to imagine how that night may have been for Zina Huntington
Jacobs (Young), who the night before had given birth to a son,
named Chariton after the creek they were camped on, with no at-
tendant except Mother Lyman, the aunt of Apostle George A.
Smith. Or for the nameless woman that Eliza Snow heard about,
who gave birth "in the rude shelter of a hut—the sides formed of
blankets fastened to poles stuck in the ground—a bark roof, through
which the rain was dripping: Kind sisters held dishes and caught
the water—thus protecting the mother and her little darling from
a shower-bath on its entrance to the stage of human existence."

Eliza herself was uncomfortable enough, for before leaving Sugar
Creek Brother Markham had traded his buggy for a wagon, and
loaded it so heavily with Church baggage that there was hardly
room for Eliza and Sister Markham to sit. But her discomfort was
so far only discomfort. On some, the trip wore more heavily.

Hosea Stout, for instance, a hard man and one who took seriously
his job of keeping the peace, and who was widely hated in consequence, started from Sugar Creek with several wagons and drivers,
three wives, one of them pregnant, and three children. His duties
as captain of the guard left him little time to provide for his family, and they suffered early from lack of food. Through what was
potentially hostile country Hosea wore two six-shooters and a
bowie, and he imposed his will harshly on malefactors and shirk-
ers. But his family life could not be managed by a show of will or
force. As they wallowed from the Fox River down toward Locust
Creek his pregnant wife Louisa, down with pleurisy and nearing
her time, was jolted and thrown around the wagon on the worst
road Hosea had ever seen. "It was up and down sloughs on spouty
ridges and deep marshes, and raining all the while. The horses would
sometimes sink to their bellies."

On April 21, Louisa gave birth to a girl child in the wagon. They rested three days at Hog Creek and then drove on eight miles. That night the two older children came down with whooping cough. With Louisa gritting her teeth in agony at every jar and jolt of the springless wagon, the children languid with malnutrition, burning with fever, and racked with hollow coughs, they made it into the way station that the Camp of Israel was constructing at Garden Grove. From there Hosea had to send two of his drivers and wagons back to pick up the goods of his sister Anna, stranded back on the trail because her husband had gone to hunt work in the settlements. With his family all sick and his helpers gone, he herded his stock himself, and came in before night "almost fainting with a headache, which later confined me to my bed." (All through Stout's journal these migraines regularly recur.) On May 6, he had to swallow his pride and beg food from the Twelve, for he was entirely out. Three days later his son Hyrum, who had been growing daily weaker with his combination of whooping cough and "black canker," or scurvy, died in Hosea's arms. "I shall not attempt to express my feelings at this time because my family is still afflicted. My wife, Louisa, is yet unable to get about. Little Hosea, my only son, is now wearing down with the same complaint. I have fearful forebodings of coming evils. We are truly desolate and afflicted, and entirely destitute of anything to eat, much less to nourish the sick."

The day before they left Garden Grove, on May 27, word came of the war between the United States and Mexico. Said Hosea, speaking for the whole Mormon people, "I confess that I was glad to learn of war against the United States. I hoped the war might never end until the States were entirely destroyed, for they had driven us into the wilderness, and now were laughing at our calamities." An eye for an eye—this was an Old Testament people in its hatred of its enemies as well as in its covenant with the Lord. They had conned the Biblical record of the flight out of Egypt and the Babylonian captivity, and they felt to agree with the psalmist: *Remember, O lord, the children of Edom in the day of Jerusalem; who said, Rase it, rase it, even to the foundation thereof. O daughter of*

*Babylon, who art to be destroyed; happy shall he be, that rewardeth
thee as thou hast served us. Happy shall he be, that taketh and dasheth
thy little ones against the stones.* In the minds of such men as Hosea
Stout and John D. Lee the road through the wilderness, added to
the persecutions of Missouri and Illinois, was preparing the spirit
of tribal vengeance that in eleven years would bring about, far to
the west in the place called Mountain Meadows, the most horrible
atrocity in western history.

Hosea, by pooling teams with another, made it to the new settlement of Mt. Pisgah, and there in June took a week or two of rest
from travel. We may leave him there and follow William Huntington and his three wives, who started out with Apostle Amasa Lyman's company a day behind the main camp and stayed behind it
all the way to Locust Creek. For the first month they had a reasonably prosperous journey. Huntington celebrated his sixty-third
birthday on Fox River on March 28, and the day after that his wives
got into a giddy spirit of imminent spring by braiding some palm
leaf hats. On Locust Creek Huntington found his daughter Zina
nursing the healthy child she had borne in the rain on the Chariton.
His tone at that time is cheerful.

Brigham had reorganized the Camp of Israel on Locust Creek,
hoping to keep it from straggling and to increase the mutual helpfulness of its parts. But the road out of the bottoms was very bad,
and some teams immediately pulled ahead and left others to flounder.
At noon it began to rain,

> with some 200 teams then scattered over the wet flat Pararies
> for three milds the rain increased the roads soon became im-
> passable teams ware stauled in every direction men Doubling
> and thribling teams but to no effect with many wagons left
> stalled in the mud in every direction many families remained
> on the pararie over the night with out fire with their clothing
> wet and cold . . . Spent one of the most uncomfortable nights
> that so many of the church ever suffered in one night rained
> steady all night verry cold and a high wind the ground filled
> with water the mud ne deep around our tents and Little or no
> feed one cow through fatigue Laid down by the waggon on

the paraie chilled and died A general sene of suffering for man
and beast.

Others agreed. "We all sufered verry mutch," said Lorenzo
Young. "The most severe time we have had," wrote William Clayton. And as the strains became worse, the human kindness of some
gave way to selfishness. Though many drivers helped one another
through the mud, William Huntington got no help, and suffered
accordingly. Out of feed, they cut elm branches at Elm Creek to
feed their animals, and after four days of pleasant weather were
able to get to Louse Creek, short of Garden Grove, "as butiful a
site as ever was seen in this region of cuntry a city of tents and
waggons inhabited by the saints of the last days."

"Butiful" or not, it brought little relief to Huntington. On April
18, Brigham called for all Church teams to be given up so that they
could be used to haul public property and carry the advance party
that he still planned to send to the mountains that year. Families such
as Huntington's which had been using Church teams would
be left at Garden Grove until they could assemble stock and supplies. "Here," said Huntington, "I have one of the most trying sens
I ever have had as I have no team nor waggon here of my own I
expect on Monday morning to onload the waggon I have ben useing
put my goods on the ground and be helped up to the stopping place
having agreable to councel previous to leaving nauvoo given a deed
of my lot to the trustees in order to fulfill my covenant made at
October conference ... therefore I am now according to the President's order to be left on the camp ground and my effects to be
carried up to grand river settlement and fit out myself."

Next day, Brigham relented and told Huntington he could use
the team to go on west if he could provision himself. Huntington
accepted, but finding provisions was easier to imagine than to do.
Within ten days he was confessing to his journal that he was now
"out of provision or I have none of conciquence have no meat no
flower no meal save a few quarts of pearched corn meal no milk
have a few crackers how I shall be provided for the Lord knows
I do not."

In Garden Grove, in late April and early May, Huntington's condition was more the rule than the exception. Scores were sick, some dying; all were pinched for food. Brigham's problem as Moses of this people was to get them safely across a country that by now provided grass for the stock but no food for human beings except the occasional turkeys and prairie chickens that hunters brought in. At various times he sent off John D. Lee, Howard Egan, and Jackson Redding with wagon loads of furniture, dishes, and clothing to trade for food in Missouri; he sent back, or settled at Garden Grove, people too feeble, ill-equipped, or faint-hearted to go on; he exhorted those who still had provisions to share them; he dispensed, frugally, emergency rations from the Church stores. And somehow he brought them on across that wild prairie and left a track and way stations for those who, according to word brought by Shadrach Roundy, were now fleeing Nauvoo in greater numbers before the threats of the mobs.

Not remarkably, rifts and lesions had begun to show among them. Faith and mutual helpfulness sometimes broke down along with strength and cheerfulness. The sermon that Brigham preached on Sunday, April 12, had some pointed comments on thievery; he felt to deplore it even when it was practised against the Gentiles. A little later, James Hemmic challenged Wilbur Earl to a duel, and had to be thrown out of camp as a trouble-maker. There were warnings against bogus makers hiding among the Saints, there were troubles with men wanting to turn back to get their families in Nauvoo. Minds and tempers began to crack. On May 4, William Huntington noted that William Edwards had gone out of his head and was thought dangerous. On May 7, the daughter of Peter Haws threw a cup of scalding coffee into the face of one of her father's young teamsters, all but blinding him. "The Lord reward her," said Lorenzo Young.

On the last day of April Huntington wrote in his journal while waiting in a thin rain, a day's journey short of Garden Grove, for the return of the Missouri trading expedition. His health was not good, he had a cold that he could not get rid of. His family, he re-

flected sadly, were scattered over half the nation: his sons Oliver
and Chauncey on missions in New York State, his sons Dimick and
William still in Nauvoo preparing to start west, his daughter Prescindia in Lima, separated from her husband and in danger from
the mobs, his son John off trading in Missouri, and only his daughter Zina with him, accompanied by her husband Henry Jacobs. He
might have been expected to murmur, this man who except for the
word brought by Mormon missionaries might now be living on a
prosperous New York State farm surrounded by his children and
grandchildren. He did not murmur; in his journal, though there
may be dismay at the sacrifices demanded of him, there is no word
of regret or doubt.

William Clayton was not quite so long-suffering. As secretary
to the Twelve, Clayton had access to the deliberations and decisions hidden from the rank and file, and he must be reckoned among
the second echelon of leaders, for he was in charge of the band
and the band's wagons, was either a member or the clerk of the
Council of Fifty, and had taken plural wives, one of whom, Diantha,
had remained behind in Nauvoo to bear her child. But Clayton
frequently felt himself abused and overworked; he was troubled
by a stream of minor irritations and by ominous dreams which he
interpreted with the passion of an analyst. He suffered from rheumatism, and made himself worse by exercising and by helping to
get others' wagons out of the mud. His wives Lydia and Margaret
were out all the time, continually getting soaked and chilled, so that
he worried about them as much as about Diantha back in Nauvoo.
He is a constant reminder that in reconstructing this exodus we
must remember to bring into it not only the always threatening
Trail, with its epidemics of malaria, typhoid, and cholera, but the
arthritis, sinus infections, migraines, colds, croup, dysentery, and
plain anxieties that trouble any modern; the difference is that a Mormon on this road could give in to none of them, but had to go on
exposing himself to precisely the conditions most calculated to make
him worse.

On April 15, Ellen Kimball, one of Heber's wives, came to tell

Clayton that Diantha had had a fine fat son, but was herself suffering from ague and mumps. Clayton felt to rejoice at the news, but was sorry to hear of Diantha's other sicknesses. That night he held a christening party in his tent, a party that included some fellow members of the band and also, rather oddly considering Clayton's civilized English background and clerkly temperament, two men he might have been expected to shun. One was Howard Egan, a tough Irishman who was already, with Port Rockwell, John D. Lee, Hosea Stout, and some others, among the trusted frontiersmen, dispatch bearers, and general strong-arm men of Brother Brigham; the other was Return Jackson Redden, or Redding, who had a reputation as a Mississippi River outlaw but who then and ever afterward was a good Saint. They had a pleasant evening singing and drinking the health of young William Adriel Benoni Clayton, and the proud father composed what was shortly to become the great camp song of Zion:

> Come, come ye saints,
> No toil nor labor fear,
> But with joy wend your way;
> Though hard to you
> This journey may appear,
> Grace shall be as your day.
>
> 'Tis better far for us to strive
> Our useless cares from us to drive;
> Do this, and joy your hearts will swell.
> All is well! All is well!

William Clayton was a man of real abilities, and he performed his many duties with thoroughness and devotion. But he sometimes found it hard to follow the advice of his own song, and however he strove to drive away his useless cares and with joy to wend his way, he felt his injustices, and like all the rest of them he felt them more as the journey lengthened and the hardships increased. What begins in his journal as no more than a self-righteous censoriousness, a waspish way of taking satisfaction out of the discomfiture of those he disapproved of, becomes sharper as the days wear on. He grumbles that he can't move out with the rest of his company because he has to make inventories of the Church property and records in his charge. Just at the moment when Brigham sends out his call for all Church teams, Clayton loses a horse to a rattlesnake bite —or to the snake's master root ("rattlesnake weed") boiled in milk that they gave him as an antidote—and is left hard up for teams. Stalled at Garden Grove, he begins to hear murmuring from the families of band members.

> I have been informed that Esther Kay has been offering bitter complaints because they do not fare as well as some others. The hint was thrown at Margaret and she understood that it was for me. I have today let Miss Kay [have] a pair of shoes and took down a large bag of biscuits and divided it amongst those who are needy. I have all the time let them have flour, sugar, bacon, and other things as I had them and to hear of dissatisfaction because I will not let them have the last I have grieves me.

Grief curdled into grievance. The journal begins to be cluttered with complaints against teamsters who, although they are hauling Church goods, still expect to live on Clayton's private stores; teamsters who have quit working for him but still come around to be fed; Saints remaining behind at Garden Grove who expect him to grubstake them until their crops come on. Stalled without sufficient teams, Clayton could get no satisfaction from anyone, including Brigham Young, who promised teams but did not produce them. Then past Clayton's grumbling camp on Sunday, May 17, came Bishop George Miller's company, pushing on ahead as usual; "but he did not leave me any cattle although he has plenty and many cows. This agrees with his course, for from about two months before we left Nauvoo to the present, he has done nothing but for himself."

All the time, his sense of doing more than others and getting less reward than they rubbed blisters on Clayton's self-love. He grew impatient and angry even at the Twelve. When they left Garden

Grove the High Council voted to leave Samuel Bent, with two
counselors, in charge. A letter of authority was to be written by
Apostle Willard Richards, the historian,

> but he made me copy it, and afterwards when the President
> spoke to him to write to O. P. Rockwell he favored me to do
> that although I left three men waiting to weigh my loading and
> my wagon. The fact is, I can scarcely ever go to council but
> Dr. Richards wants me to do his writing, although I have
> more writing to do as clerk of the camp than I can possibly
> do. Moreover I have to unpack the chest and wait on all of
> them with the public goods in my charge which keeps me busy
> all the time. President Young, Heber, Dr. Richards and Bishop
> Whitney have all made out to get lumber sawed to make their
> wagons comfortable but I can't get enough to make a hind
> board for one of my wagons which has none. They are tolera-
> bly well prepared with wagons and teams but I am here with
> about five tons of stuff and only six wagons and five yoke of
> oxen to take it. I have dealt out nearly all my provisions and
> have to get more before I can go on. It looks as if I had to be
> a slave and take slave's fare all the journey.

Thus William Clayton, Clerk of the Camp of Israel, sitting in
the endless rain while Brigham's improvised logistics struggled to
take care of the hundred other problems as pressing as William
Clayton's. Eventually Brother Brigham found six teams and sent
them back to him, and on May 26 Clayton got his wagons in to Mt.
Pisgah. A few days later, with most of the Twelve and with large
companies of the better equipped and healthier Saints, he went on
toward the Missouri.

Like Garden Grove, Mt. Pisgah was conceived as a rest camp for
those unable to continue, and a refreshment and supply station for
later companies. Many, like Hosea Stout, fell into it grim and suffering. Some, like Sister Markham and Eliza Snow, fatigued and
unwell, camped there in crude cabins while their men went back
to the States to get new teams or pick up other members of the family. And some, like William Huntington, had destitution compounded by duty. On May 21 he had been appointed President

of the Mt. Pisgah Council, with Charles Rich and Ezra Taft Benson for his counselors, and that, as he confided ruefully to his journal, effectively tied his hands. He had neither teams nor supplies to go on west, and as President of the Council he had no time to acquire them. He stayed there through the summer, while company after company, several members of his family among them, came in from the east, rested briefly, and crawled out to the west.

For those who went on to the Missouri in June, the last leg of the journey was almost a picnic after what they had already endured. Though they had violent storms, there was sun between them, the roads had dried out, the grass was knee-high to their animals. And on sunny slopes women and girls walking after the wagons found the grass roots reddened with wild strawberries, and picked delicious bowlsful. They met the Pottawattamie, exiles like themselves, deprived of their lands and on their way to Indian Country beyond the Missouri, camped on the Nishnabotna. Some of the halfbreeds among them were educated and cultivated people; there were friendly sessions in which Indian and Mormon exchanged opinions of the United States. And finally, without real strain, they passed through the romantically roughening country and came to the bluffs and spread their camps along Indian Creek and Mosquito Creek to wait while Brigham arranged their next move. By June 22 there were five hundred wagons and nine of the Twelve Apostles on the bank of the Missouri. The rest of the Mormon people, up to about 14,000 of them, were either on the road or still in Nauvoo.

On April 30, while the Camp of Israel was engaged in building Garden Grove, the Nauvoo Temple had been privately dedicated, with Brigham's brother Joseph officiating. The next day it was publicly dedicated by Apostle Orson Hyde. Only a few of the ranking hierarchy were in attendance: in addition to Hyde and Joseph Young, there were the trustees of Church property, Joseph L. Heywood, Almon Babbitt, and John S. Fullmer, and Wilford Woodruff, recently returned from an English mission. A mere straggling remnant of leaders, making a token dedication before a remnant congregation of a temple already given up and posted for sale; and now all those able to move could leave.

Woodruff, pious, methodical, superstitious, accident-prone, had a faculty for seeing the hand of God in the slightest incident, the lucky accident, the sickness that was healed, the bone that knitted, the fall that did not kill. On the road to the Missouri he would be elected to fill an empty seat among the Quorum of the Twelve Apostles, and in 1887 he would become the sixth president of the Mormon Church, the president who under pressure from the United States finally renounced polygamy in 1890. He was one of those who departed Nauvoo at the lucky time and had a prosperous trip; not leaving for good until May 26, he reached Mt. Pisgah on June 15, having spent less than three weeks on the trip that had taken Huntington, Stout, Clayton, Markham and the rest three months. And as with Woodruff, who suffered not the slightest hardship except to have his father's legs run over by a loaded wagon, an incident that added one more to his collection of miraculous providences, so with others. Norton Jacob, departing Nauvoo with his family on May 28, spent a while on the Iowa shore breaking his oxen to the yoke and did not finally start west until June 17. They arrived at Council Bluffs on July 24 without accident or even much bad weather. And for Irene Pomeroy and her husband, brother, and mother, the four hundred miles from Nauvoo to the Missouri were one long pleasure excursion.

Irene's urgings had persuaded her mother into joining the Gathering, and Ursulia Hascall arrived in Nauvoo with her twelve-year-old son Thales in late April. Once she made up her mind to throw in her lot with the Saints, Ursulia proved herself as cheerfully pious and practical as her daughter. She wasted no lamentations on lost Nauvoo, for she had never struck root there. Full of the adventure of her voyage from Boston to New York, New York to New Orleans, and New Orleans to the city of Joseph, she looked forward to more of the same. When she landed, she saw the ferries loading with team after team to cross to the Iowa shore, and all her care was of preparations to join them. She found Irene laying up sup-

plies in a way to gratify all her housewifely instincts; her letters
back to New Salem are full of lists and inventories: what they ate,
what they were preparing, what Francis Pomeroy, now working
on a steamboat, brought them when his boat passed Nauvoo every
week. A hundred pounds of nice sugar, a box of raisins, pork and
ham and dried fish and veal, coffee, tea, powder. When they started
west they were going to have two yoke of oxen, two cows, four
sheep. Ursulia's principal reaction to Nauvoo, cracking with tension and in the process of being sold out for ten cents on the dollar and invaded by property-hungry Gentiles, was a gentle wonder
at how many locks of Joseph Smith's hair her friends seemed to
have been able to clip from his martyred head and enclose in lockets.

A complacent, gossipy, lively woman with a cornpopper mind,
an interest in anything that moved, and a vitality even greater than
that of her daughter, she could put behind her anything done and
past—anything, for example, such as her husband, a hard drinker
and something of a skeptic with regard to Mormonism. He had
elected, instead of joining up with the overland trek, to sail with
Samuel Brannan's shipload from New York on February 4; his
rather vague intention was to rejoin his family wherever the Saints
finally settled. He would not make it. Companions would bury him
in the Nevada desert months later, and Ursulia would mourn him
comfortably and hope that his soul was saved (there was always
the promise given Irene in her patriarchal blessing) and go on with
her life.

The Pomeroys, Ursulia Hascall, and young Thales left Nauvoo
on May 30. "Had as good a wagon as any of them," Ursulia wrote
her sister back in New Salem, and with relish she went on to tick
off their outfit. It may be taken as representative of what the best
equipped Saints started west with, and it actually exceeds Parley
Pratt's ideal:

> ... three yoke of oxen with flour enough to last us one year,
> ham, Sausages, dry fish, lard, two cans hundred pounds of sugar,
> 16 of coffee, 10 of raisins, rice with all the items we wish to
> use in cooking. I will describe our waggons and tent as well

as I can. . . . The waggon is long enough for both our beds made on the flour barrels chests and other things. (Thales and I sleep at the back end, and F. and Irene at the forward end while we were travelling if we camped too late to pitch our tent.) It is painted red. It has eight bows eighteen inches apart, a hen coop on the end with four hens, we had two webs of thick drilling. We put on one cover of that, then three breadths of stout sheeting over that and then painted it, the heaviest showers and storms does not beat through only a few drops now and then. Our tent is made of drilling sixteen breadths in the shape of an umbrella. A cord three feet long on the end of every seam and a pin on that to drive into the ground. The pole in the middle that holds it up carries it three feet from the ground, then a breadth of sheeting put on the edge to let down in cool weather and fasten with loops and pins in the ground.

Francis Pomeroy, who had been a sailor, was a good provider, and had the benefit of good steamboater's wages. He spoke Spanish, learned during two years of a shipwreck in Peru, and he would later prove very useful in dealing with the New Mexicans the Mormons encountered. Both he and his brother-in-law Thales Hascall would have respectable careers as frontiersmen and scouts in southern Utah and northern Arizona. Now and later, in fact, this whole family demonstrated a practical good sense that let them all but create their own good luck, and their journey was very different from that of William Huntington with his empty grub box and his borrowed team, or that of Hosea Stout's sick and miserable family.

Leaving Nauvoo at four in the afternoon on a warm summer day, they ferried the Mississippi and rolled on three miles, fed the oxen, made a late supper on bread and milk and pie, went to bed in the wagon, and "never slept better." Next day they joined up with a company of fifty that included the Farrs, old friends from New Salem, and others nearly as well provided as themselves. The lists and inventories and menus continue to fill Ursulia's letters—the coffee for breakfast, milk and hasty pudding for dinner, the fat calves that the company killed every now and then and divided up, the "old fashioned soups with a light crust." Entirely without incident or even discomfort, this fifty which had left a full two months behind the Camp of Israel caught up with it at Council Bluffs ("you can find it on the map") and pitched their tents with the rest of Zion to await the completion of a ferry boat. Two weeks later they were across and settling down for the winter, briefly at Cutler's Park and finally at the place they called Winter Quarters.

"I feel as if I narrowly escaped from Babylon with a mighty effort," Ursulia wrote, and ended her first letter from the wilderness with another housewifely inventory, this one of the native resources of the Missouri: "there is no end to them black walnuts in abundance hundreds of bushels of grapes orchards of wild plumbs, fifty bushels in a place, you never saw anything better [to] make pies and preserves." Well looked after by her competent son-in-law, Ursulia could view the coming winter with more equanimity than some. But one feels that she would have managed equanimity under any circumstances. She had a knack for making the best of things. If it had hailed stones as big as baseballs she would have come out from shelter wondering if it wasn't a good time to make up a nice freezer of ice cream.

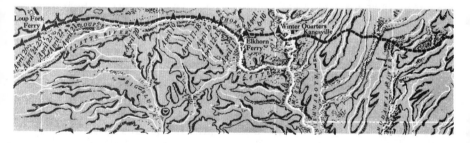

5

We Wept When We Remembered Zion

From the time when the Mormons yielded and agreed to leave Nauvoo, Brigham Young had kept before him the desirability of an uninterrupted, controlled hegira clear to the mountains. Security, policy, and hatred of the Gentiles all suggested that the Saints should stick together and go a long way. But now in the summer of 1846, the advance guard only as far as the Missouri after four months on the road, the Mormon people strung out sick, undernourished, and exhausted across the whole state of Iowa, and the chances of a prosperous journey westward growing shorter by the day, Brigham and the Twelve had some hard choices to make. If, as appeared probable, Mr. Polk's war with Mexico should turn the Rocky Mountains into United States territory, it might be necessary to find another destination. Even if it did not, it was clear that all could not be taken across immediately, and equally clear that few wanted to stay within reach of their enemies. So when Brigham reiterated his plan to send a party of young, vigorous pioneers, unencumbered by families, to prepare the way and select a stopping place, he found himself facing disagreement even among the Twelve. When he suggested that the Twelve themselves should lead the pioneers, he fired the apprehension of those who would not only be left behind, but left leaderless. The terrible road across Iowa had killed so many and left so many exhausted and ill that their spirits could not be revived. They dragged around with dysentery and "phthisis" and the malaria that came on in the "sickly season" of late summer. Lorenzo Young's wife Harriet was a chronic invalid, Eliza Snow and Sister Markham were up one day and down three, Hosea Stout's family had hardly enough well to care for the dying, William Huntington had a chronic and abysmal cough. There were few at Garden Grove, Mt. Pisgah, or Miller's Hollow in anything like condition to travel, and few enough in condition to stay. Some of them argued, with a rebelliousness that Brigham was never to encounter again in all his years as leader of the Church, against his plan to split them by sending off a band of pioneers.

But if they stayed, where would they stay? Brigham had written from Sugar Creek asking permission of the Governor of Iowa to cross his state and plant temporary settlements. (Permission would come in September, when the settlements were already planted.) Now he diplomatically buttered up the Pottawattamie, who had temporary right to the land on the east side of the Missouri, and he also cast his eye across the river at the Indian Lands. Over there, where white settlers were barred, there were no Gentiles except a few traders, agents, and missionaries to be potential enemies of the Saints. But the Mormons were likewise prohibited from settling there, even temporarily, and to go ahead and do so could involve them in difficulties with the federal government.

Some sort of solution might be forthcoming from Washington, where Jesse C. Little, President of the Eastern States Mission, was busy offering President Polk the services of the Mormon people and delicately hinting that if the United States would not help them they might have to turn to the British in Oregon. The Mormons, Little had been instructed to say to Polk, were available for building roads or bridges, establishing ferries, transporting troops or supplies, and even for fighting. Actually, when Brigham's time of decision came on the Missouri, Polk had already made up his mind, and on June 12 Little and Thomas L. Kane had left Philadelphia to carry to Gen. Stephen Watts Kearney in Fort Leavenworth instructions about enlisting some Mormons. But Brigham did not know this, and while he struggled with his logistical problems and brought more and more Saints up to the Missouri shore, still on Pottawattamie lands but facing the empty Indian Lands across the river, rumors multiplied.

Along the four hundred miles of the Mormon road, every new company and every courier from Nauvoo blew a grain or two of information into dust devils of hearsay. And what was true for the Mormons, who after all were in close contact with one another, was even more true for the Gentiles, who had no such direct lines of communication and neither means nor will to correct rumors. During the summer of 1846 Fort Leavenworth and the Missouri outposts heard that the Mormons were fortifying themselves somewhere up the river and preaching "Jewish powwow" to the Indians, that they were distributing arms and inciting the tribes to a holy war, that they were on their way to Oregon to join forces with the British. No one knew exactly where they were or what they were doing; therefore they seemed doubly dangerous.

The Mormons themselves could not in good faith have denied everything that was in the wind about them, for so far as the ordinary Mormon knew, they *might* be on their way to ally themselves with the British in Oregon. Wilford Woodruff, fresh from Nauvoo and not too distantly from England, and hence to be listened to, met William Clayton returning through Mt. Pisgah on June 28, and gave him the latest: the British were interceding strongly with the United States in behalf of the Saints, and were at the same time preparing for war. A fleet was on its way around Cape Horn, 10,000 troops had been dispatched to Canada, British agents were working quietly among the Indians and also among the slaves in the South, arming and preparing them for an uprising against the Americans. (*O daughter of Babylon, who art to be destroyed, happy shall he be that taketh and dasheth thy little ones against the stones!*) Woodruff said that the Missourians, not knowing what the Mormons

might be up to, were moving in panic back from the frontier. Just
the other day they had sent a committee to spy out the extent of
the Mormon armament and fortifications at Mt. Pisgah.

That last item had a core of fact wrapped in a blanket of somewhat paranoid speculation. There had been a "committee" that
passed through Mt. Pisgah on June 26, but it had not come to spy
out Mormon cannon that still technically belonged to the state of
Illinois. It was composed of Capt. James Allen and an escort of three
dragoons, and it came from Fort Leavenworth to ask Brigham
Young to furnish five hundred Mormon volunteers to march against
Santa Fe and southern California with General Kearney's Army of
the West. This was no Missouri spying expedition, but James K.
Polk's means of insuring the loyalty of the Mormons who might
otherwise be an embarrassment running around in territory still
technically Mexican. Perhaps it was also his way of easing the national conscience for what the nation had permitted to happen to
American citizens on American soil. Though it was unmistakably
a demonstration of Polk's political realism, it looked like the payoff
in Brother Brigham's campaign of offer and hint and veiled threat,
and it came just in time.

Not that many Saints understood at once the implications of Captain Allen's errand. For one thing, they were remembering: the
next day, June 27, would be the second anniversary of Joseph Smith's
murder. So when someone reported uniforms approaching Pisgah,
there was instant alarm. Women rounded up children and herded
them to shelter, men reached rifles out of wagons, Huntington and
Rich and others went out stiff-legged to confer with the strangers.
Allen turned out to be a pleasant enough young man. His errand
was for Brother Brigham, but he would appreciate a chance to
speak of it to the people here. Huntington called them together and
they listened, but their mood was a compound of indignation and in-
credulity. After all it had failed to do to protect them or reimburse
their losses; after telling them, as President Van Buren had once
told Joseph's emissaries, "Your cause is just but I can do nothing
for you," after permitting bloodthirsty mobs to drive them from

their homes and kill their leader, the United States had the gall to
come asking for volunteers to help it fight the war it had started
with Mexico.

The Mormons saw it, with Woodruff, as a pretext to spy on them,
or as a plot to lure away their best and strongest and leave them at
the mercy of their enemies. Huntington, after Captain Allen had
finished, stood up and "followed him with an adress by way of
commendation or as the old proverb says answering a fool according to his folly." Then he gave him a letter to Brigham and sent
him on toward the Missouri, while the Pisgah camp buzzed about
the "heartless demand" or exploded in scornful laughter.

Hearing the story two days later, on the road between Pisgah
and Council Bluffs, Hosea Stout was not one of the laughers. On
the night of June 25 his son Hosea, still sick with whooping cough,
had been soaked by rain that beat through the wagon cover: they
had found him lying in water with his eyes glazed and his lips enameled with fever. On June 28 he died, the second of Stout's sons
to die on that Iowa road, and was buried on a hill beside an infant
of John Smith's. That evening, into their camp near the Pottawattamie village, a Mormon brought news of Captain Allen's visit. "We
were all very indignant at this requisition, viewing it as a plot to
bring trouble on us," Hosea wrote in his journal. "In the event we
did not comply with the requisition, they would have a pretext for
denouncing us as enemies of the country. If we did comply, they
would then have 500 of our men in their power to destroy as they
had done our leaders at Carthage. . . . General Rich sent me word
by Brother Wright to keep a sharp lookout for Captain James Allen, so that he did not get any knowledge of the public arms which
I had."

If there is a trace of paranoia in the judgment, we should hardly
be surprised. Hosea had earned his right to paranoia.

One day behind the captain, Wilford Woodruff took the road
for Council Bluffs. On the way he met Parley Pratt, returning to
Pisgah to raise there a hundred volunteers to join the advance party
to the mountains. Brigham had won his argument, convinced the

Twelve that most of the Saints must winter on the Missouri or in Iowa, and persuaded them that five hundred young and vigorous men should go ahead to explore, plant way stations, and locate sites for colonies, perhaps even on the coast if the mountains proved inhospitable. Hearing Pratt's news, Woodruff hurried ahead, wanting to be part of the advance party; but on July 4 he encountered Brigham, Heber Kimball, and Willard Richards returning in haste to Pisgah. They had talked with Captain Allen, wrung an extra concession or two out of him, and then accepted Polk's terms; and now they were hurrying back to supplement Pratt's call for volunteers to the mountains with a call for volunteers to Santa Fe. For however preposterous and insulting Polk's request might look to the man in the mud, to Brigham the government's demand was a godsend, a solution to at least the most pressing problems. Having for reasons of morale encouraged his people's hatred of the United States, he was now taking his two ablest counselors back to help persuade the Saints of their patriotic duty.

Some orthodox histories say that Brigham at once found among his steadfast people the volunteers their ungrateful country called for—simply asked and saw the firm chins rise, the resolute figures step forward. The fact is that he asked from Miller's Hollow through Mt. Pisgah to Garden Grove, and in every place got mainly shuffling feet and downcast mulish looks. Parley Pratt's call of a day or two before had raised, out of Mt. Pisgah's undernourished and malarial population, seventy-one men willing to go to the mountains; Brigham's plea to march with Kearney got at first only a handful. Yet Brigham knew that sending five hundred men with Kearney would be far easier and cheaper than sending them as pioneers, and might be nearly as helpful to the Saints as a whole. Not only would the army furnish their food and transportation to California—where there was still a good chance the Saints would settle—but the volunteers would be allowed to take along as "laundresses" a certain number of women, and they would be dismissed in California at the end of a year's enlistment with the privilege of retaining their arms. Furthermore, they would draw pay all that time in cash, and cash was the rarest of all commodities on the frontier. Nevertheless Brigham had a hard time persuading men who had perhaps already lost a wife or child, and who would now have to leave their families to the care of others, that they should go marching in a Gentile war. He counseled and exhorted, wheedled and thundered, said he would draft old men and women if the young men did not come forward. In the end, not in the three days that some Church accounts mention, but in three hard weeks of recruiting, he raised in the camps of Zion five companies totaling just over five hundred men.

One of those who witnessed, and indeed had an important part in, the raising of the Mormon Battalion was Thomas Kane of Philadelphia. The brother of the Arctic explorer Elisha Kane, and son of the attorney general of Pennsylvania who was a political ally of President Polk, young Kane had by chance wandered into one of Jesse C. Little's conferences of Philadelphia Saints in May. Touched by what he heard of Mormon wrongs, his interest and sympathy stirred, he took Little home with him and enlisted the elder Kane's help in Little's mission to Washington. Eventually young Kane got Brigham's envoy clear to the President, and in most of the histories Kane and Little are credited with gaining Polk's qualified aid, though DeVoto has pointed out, from the evidence of Polk's diary, that a week before he officially yielded to Little's pleas Polk had instructed General Kearney to enlist a few Mormons. That word was already on its way to Fort Leavenworth when Little and Kane set out for there from Philadelphia with more specific orders on June 12. They arrived in Leavenworth in time to talk with Kearney, who was about to start west with his cavalry; and they left Leavenworth for the Mormon camps just a little after the departure of Captain Allen.

So now, on Allen's heels, came this Philadelphia aristocrat, susceptible and poetic and tempted out of sheer sympathy to share Israel's exodus, and with all the capacities for disseminating what DeVoto calls "the best propaganda the Church ever had." When the Mormons were being reported mainly in scarehead rumors, he lived among them, was desperately ill among them, was healed by them, perhaps was baptized into their church, certainly was given a patriarchal blessing by John Smith.* Though he spoke as a non-Mormon, he spoke from intimate knowledge and a friendly point of view. It was he who, out of misinformation or out of a desire to speak well of a wronged people, started the historical non-fact that the Battalion was recruited in three days, and it was he who, in a lyceum lecture later published as a book understandably cherished among the Saints, painted such touching pictures of abandoned Nauvoo and of decent godly people suffering in the wilderness that for almost the first time Gentile eyes grew wet with guilt and loving kindness.

For Kane, the Battalion requisition "could not have been more inconveniently timed"—a judgment which does not agree with Brigham's, though it was probably the opinion common among the Saints. Many of the young men were off seeking work in Missouri, pretending apostasy or hiding their Mormonism; some were about to set out with pioneer companies west of the river. All were needed to take care of the helpless and sick. Even the young men were by no means hearty, and nearly a third of the entire Mormon Battalion would have to be invalided off to Pueblo by the time the marchers reached Santa Fe. There simply were not five hundred men in all the host of Israel in shape to go soldiering, and to that extent Kane was right. But his sympathetic account does neglect what was to Brigham the central issue: that without this windfall of Polk's "demand" the Mormon people would face the winter lacking nearly every sort of supplies, and could look forward to a scarecrow march to the mountains in the spring. The Mormon Battalion, which did very little to break the Mormon Trail to the Great Salt Lake Valley, went a long way toward making it possible.

Its departure also provided Kane with one of the most touching scenes in a book which consistently presents the Mormons as kindly, generous, and long-suffering. As much as any homespun settler along the Mormon Road through southeastern Iowa, Kane was impressed by the Mormon love of music and the habit of dancing away troubles in a cotillion. By catching the Mormons at their most resili-

* He had another in St. George, Utah, in 1873.

ent and most charming activities, he reinforces our perception that these were not isolated drifters, certainly not frontier scum, but a people in movement, a community and even a culture on the march —by all odds the most civilized element on that raw frontier. Music was their gift and their blessing, an expression of their oneness in the hostile wilderness.

> Some of their wind instruments, [Kane wrote] ... were uncommonly full and pure-toned, and in that clear, dry air could be heard to a great distance. It had the strangest effect in the world, to listen to their sweet music winding over the uninhabited country.... It might be when you were hunting a ford over the great Platte, the dreariest of all wild rivers, perplexed among the far-reaching sand bars, and curlew shallows of its shifting bed—the wind rising would bring you the first faint thought of a melody; and as you listened borne down upon the gust that swept past you a cloud of dry sifted sands, you recognized it—perhaps a home-loved theme of Henry Proch or Mendelssohn. Mendelssohn Bartholdy, away there in the Indian marches!

Captain Pitt's Brass Band was certainly one of the most significant group-baptisms of Mormonism's early years. The Saints could hardly have survived the exodus without the cheer it brought them. And when they gathered in Council Bluffs to bid the Battalion goodbye, it was characteristically with a dance that they did it, just as every departing Mormon missionary to this day is given a farewell dance in the ward house. Their party, said Kane, revealed the fact that they had known better times: men and women had sold their trinkets and jewelry to get this far, and now watchpockets were innocent of chains, and ears showed no earrings and fingers no rings. The white stockings were darned, the lawn or gingham gowns faded with much washing. But waists were slim and feet were light, and when the Twelve led out in a great double cotillion,

> they did dance! None of your minuets or other mortuary processions of gentles in etiquette, tight shoes, and pinching gloves, but ... French fours, Copenhagen jigs, Virginia reels, and the like forgotten figures executed with the spirit of people too

happy to be slow, or bashful, or constrained. Light hearts, lithe figures, and light feet, had it their own way from an early hour till after the sun had dipped behind the sharp skyline of the Omaha hills. Silence was then called, and a well cultivated mezzo-soprano voice, belonging to a young lady with fair face and dark eyes, gave with quartette accompaniment a little song, the notes of which I have been unsuccessful in repeated efforts to obtain since—a version of the text, touching to all earthly wanderers:

> By the rivers of Babylon we sat down and wept.
> We wept when we remembered Zion.

Leaving their families on that note of exile and grief, the soldiers were ferried across the Missouri from Point aux Poules and started on foot for Fort Leavenworth, four companies of them on July 20, the fifth two days later. A group of them, from the Sick Detachment sent to winter at Pueblo, would enter Salt Lake Valley with the pioneers almost exactly a year later, and the remainder of the Sick Detachment would make it to Zion shortly afterward. A few of the others, after walking all the way from Fort Leavenworth to San Diego and thence up the coast to Sutter's Fort, would come over the Sierra eastward as part of the guard escorting John Charles Frémont back to the States to stand trial, and would meet their fellow-Saints of the main 1847 emigration east of Fort Laramie. Still others, after heroic journeyings, discoveries of gold in Sutter's millrace, and other adventures, would cross the deserts and mountains to Salt Lake, or go all the way eastward to the Missouri again, to pick up the families they had left behind them when Brigham recruited them into the army. They are plentifully worth our attention but they are not our concern except as we meet them on the trail.

And as their pay made possible the development of Brigham's plans, one of the first things he did after the Battalion marched away was to send Parley Pratt in their wake to collect and bring back their advance pay. Pratt, leaving one trouble in order to deal with another, was on his way to England with Apostles Orson Hyde and John Taylor, to straighten out the mess that had been made of the English mission by the speculations and malfeasance of its head, R. Hedlock. Pratt's family, "dwelling in tents and wagons on the west side of the Missouri," would have to look after themselves, with help from neighbors, relatives, friends, and the watchful bishops. On July 31 the three apostles caught a ride downriver on a flatboat belonging to some Presbyterian missionaries, who were abandoning their mission on the Loup Fork because of the raids of the Sioux. At St. Joseph the missionaries landed, selling their boat to the Mormons, who went on to Fort Leavenworth. There Pratt was able to collect a substantial contribution from the just-paid Battalion members (by his own account, five or six thousand dollars of the $21,000 that would be their year's pay), with which he made a forced ride back to Council Bluffs. Thus, little more than a month after Captain Allen came seeking volunteers, the benefits began to accrue to the Saints, already sickening in the malaria season. Brigham devoted the Battalion money to buying wagontrainloads of supplies at wholesale prices from St. Louis; and if, as some Saints complained, the pay of individual soldiers did not come back to serve their immediate families, but was spread over the whole camp or even appropriated by Brigham and other leaders for their personal comfort, those were the murmurings of proto-apostates. Arbitrary or not, fully equitable or not, Brigham's use of the Battalion money, then and later, was probably calculated to keep the whole people alive if anything could, though he was not the man to submit to any audit of his books. As for Parley Pratt, once he had delivered the money and said a fresh goodbye to his pinched family, he drove across country to Chicago, took a steamer across Lake Michigan and the railroad to Boston, and caught up with the other two apostles in time to board ship with them for England. Not all the volunteering that winter was done by soldiers.

Something more than cash had meantime accrued to the Saints through Captain Allen's recruiting. Instead of jumping at Allen's proposals, Brigham had feigned reluctance, saying that the withdrawal of five hundred men would stall the Mormon people on the Missouri, among their enemies. He wanted permission to winter

on the safe west bank, on Indian Lands. Allen, believing that he
had no alternative if he was to raise his force, granted the permission—which was not his to grant, but was properly within the juris-
diction of the Bureau of Indian Affairs. Brigham did not wait to
question Allen's authority. He at once began moving people, wagons, and cattle across the river, crossing people and wagons on the
ferry that the Saints had completed on June 29, and swimming the
stock, of which according to Kane there were 30,000 head. The
by-passed Indian Bureau would catch up with Brigham, and protest
his settlements on Indian Lands, and question his insistence that they
were only temporary, and eventually in 1848 force him to abandon
them and move the remaining Saints back across the river. But for
the time being he had a sort of permission to get out of reach of the
Gentiles, and he made full use of it. With Big Elk of the Omahas,
and the French and halfbreed *engagés* of the American Fur Company around Sarpy's post at Bellevue he held a conference and
smoked the pipe, and got Omaha agreement to let the Saints stay
two years in exchange for instruction in farming and help against
their enemies the Pawnees. If the price turned out to be a little higher
than that, and if Omaha and Oto made themselves nuisances begging and stealing in the Mormon camps, and if on occasion the
enemies of the Omahas raided and killed them almost in the streets
of the towns, those were merely inconveniences to a people who
had experienced the greater destructiveness of the Gentiles.

Brigham had not yet relinquished his hope of sending out a significant advance party during the current year. He had men out
on the Elkhorn, thirty miles west, cutting timbers and setting piers
for a bridge,* and on July 22, the day the last company of the Battalion set off for Leavenworth, 150 wagons started for the Elkhorn
to catch up with the hasty George Miller and James Emmett, already well out into the Platte valley. About August 1 they found
the Miller-Emmett group camped on the west bank of the Loup
Fork near modern Fullerton, Nebraska, and while they were all

---

* Thomas Kane describes it as a bridge, but it seems to have turned out to be
permanent log abutments for a ferry.

there counseling about their next move, a courier came from Brigham on August 8, instructing them to go no farther that season, but to organize themselves into a branch of Zion and sit tight for the winter. Exploration of the country along the Loup Fork revealed no highly desirable wintering site, and that whole region was made dangerous by the Pawnees; and so this party, some of whom had already spent one isolated year away out on the Big Sioux in 1845, accepted the invitation of two Ponca chiefs and went nine days' journey northwest to the mouth of the Niobrara, where they holed in. Characteristically, Miller's decision to winter among the Poncas took him far out of the line that Brigham would later pursue; Miller had a gift for diverging from Brother Brigham.

So now the Saints all along a road hundreds of miles long must manage to survive through the winter in whatever shelter they could throw together and on whatever food they could find, and they must manage to bring to them the stragglers still in Nauvoo. Those on the Missouri and the Papillon and in the roadside camps in Iowa were in a condition that was difficult and that gradually became terrible; those still caught in Nauvoo or laboring along the beginning of the road were in a condition terrible from the start.

Franklin Dewey Richards was one of the bright young men of Mormonism, intelligent, devoted, somewhat frail, well-connected through his uncle, the Apostle Willard Richards, and at twenty-five clearly marked for leadership. He was from Berkshire County, Massachusetts, his wife Jane from New York State. In intelligence and education they were both representative of the better class of early Mormons. Both had a history of spitting blood; both credited the priesthood with making them well through faith. Jane had been baptized by her brother in midwinter, through a foot of ice, and from that time forth was troubled no more by the consumption. Both sides of the family had taken part in the Gathering and walked most of the roads of the driven faith. Jane's family had been two hard years, because of illness, in getting across New York and the Middle West as far as Nauvoo. In 1838 Franklin, on his way to gather to Far West, had crossed the Alleghenies on the day his brother George was shot down in the blacksmith shop at Haun's Mill, and he had arrived in Far West just in time to be driven out of it again with the rest of the Lord's people. The four years of the married life of this young pair had been broken by several missions lasting months. Brought back to Nauvoo by the news of Joseph's death, Franklin had worked on the temple and by harsh economizing had managed to build a small two-story house for Jane and his daughter Wealthy Lovisa. It was completed in March, 1846, and they lived in it two months—Jane and Wealthy Lovisa downstairs, the second wife, Elizabeth McFate, upstairs. In May, unable to sell it, Franklin traded the house for two yoke of oxen and an old wagon, and they crossed the Mississippi to start west in the wake of the Twelve.

Their outfit was minimal. Besides their team and wagon they had two cows, a few portable pieces of furniture, a trunk of clothing, and a few provisions, chiefly breadstuff. Just before they left, a friendly neighbor gave Jane Richards a pound of tea, and that small gift probably did more than anything else except her faith to keep her alive for the next months.

For six weeks they camped on the Iowa shore trying to get better prepared, but by the time they started, about July 1, their supplies had dwindled rather than grown, and someone had stolen one yoke of their oxen. And they got only as far as Sugar Creek, a bare seven miles, before word came back from Brother Brigham calling Franklin to a mission in England.

It strikes us, at our remove in time and belief, as incredible. Jane Richards was pregnant, eight months along. Elizabeth McFate, a pretty girl of seventeen, was tubercular and also pregnant. Moreover, Jane had not accepted polygamy without misery and doubt, and had told her husband that if she found she could not stand it she would leave him. She did not blame Franklin, who was obeying counsel, and she did not blame Elizabeth, whom she liked. She simply did not know whether or not her own faith was strong enough to stand it. Now at the very beginning of their dubious and ill-prepared journey Franklin was called away, to be gone at least a year, perhaps more. He did what any good Mormon would have done. He prayed over his problem, and then he went. The family, driven by a teamster named Philo Farnsworth, started on.

In place of the interminable cold rains that had afflicted the Camp of Israel, they had summer heat, violent storms, and the sickly season. From the first the Lord laid His heavy hand on them, testing them. Elizabeth had chills and fever, Wealthy Lovisa took sick with one of the ambiguous ailments that had already lined that road with graves. Their food was mainly milk and cornmeal. Starting so late, they had none of the wild strawberries that had reddened the wheels of earlier wagons, and such other wild fruits as the creekbottoms provided were not yet ripe. Having no hunter, they enjoyed no prairie chickens or wild turkeys. With their one poor team they made slow time, and when Jane was brought to bed with the pains of childbirth three weeks after Franklin's departure, they were still less than sixty miles from their starting point.

The child that she bore in a dreary rain (it is almost as if the Lord demanded the most lugubrious of settings for these events) lived an hour. Unable to get a fire going, and without decent food, they rested three days and went on, carrying the tiny wrapped corpse because Jane wanted it blessed and buried by the priesthood. Rain gave way to sun; across the prairies the intense muggy heat pressed on them until they panted, drenched and suffocating, under the wagonbows.

And more than merely heat, for if the story that Jane Richards later told was true, they would have shortly been driven out of the wagon by the gagging, loathsome, impossible stench of the little decaying corpse. It is hard to believe that Jane Richards did not mis-speak; but she says that three weeks—*three weeks!*—after its death they brought the baby into Mt. Pisgah where it was decently, but one would think hurriedly, buried. Peaked and pale, little Wealthy Lovisa was brought to the elders, and Huntington, Rich, Willard Richards, and Samuel Bent prayed over her, anointed her with consecrated oil, rebuked the illness, laid hands on her. But none had the confidence to promise that it was the will of the Lord she

should live; and she did not rise from their ministrations, as so many
in Mormon folklore do, and go about her business in perfect health
and strength. She remained weak and feverish, Elizabeth continued
to have her malarial bouts that rendered her helpless, Jane was too
weak to walk. Farnsworth put them into the wagon and they went
on.

Somewhere on the road between Mt. Pisgah and Council Bluffs
Brother Brigham, hearing about her condition, suspended some business or other and came back to see about her. He said that if he
had known her situation he would never have sent Franklin on a
mission—a kind of semi-apology, or acknowledgment of fault, that
he did not customarily make. He told her that if anyone could be
said to have come up through tribulation, she could; he also told
her that when she got to the Missouri she was not to wait in line
but to go straight aboard the ferry, no matter how many wagons
were waiting.

She did as he told her, his word was good, they were given priority across the ferry and on the other side were met by Jane's
mother. If not safe, they were at least comforted. Then on the way
to Cutler's Park, where many Saints were camped, Wealthy Lovisa
wished aloud that she had some potato soup. There was not a potato
in the wagon. But just before Cutler's Park there was a squatter's
cabin, and beside it a thriving potato patch. Mrs. Snyder, Jane's
mother, went to the door and begged a few potatoes to gratify a
dying child. The woman of the place snarled at her from the doorway, "I wouldn't give or sell a thing to one of you damned Mormons." They drove on.

At Cutler's Park they still had to live in the wagon, for Jane's two
brothers, who might have built them a cabin, were both sick. Jane
herself, though she now began to be able to walk around, had no
rest from looking after the others. With her husband's second wife
she had developed an honestly loving relationship. In their months
of sharing a husband, and in their weeks of sickness and exhaustion
on the road, they had had only one harsh moment. On that night
Elizabeth started to get out of the wagon barefoot and Jane remon-

strated with her, fearing chills or snakes. Out of the tension of the trip, out of their sorrow and strain, Elizabeth snapped, "Who does that concern the most?" and put her bare feet down on the ground. But that was all. Now she was too ill to be anything but gentle in response to the gentleness shown her.

Gentleness would not save her, any more than the laying on of hands and the prayers of the elders would save Wealthy Lovisa. On a night when both of Jane's brothers were prostrated with fever and Elizabeth was screaming in delirium in the tent, Wealthy Lovisa died beside her mother in the wagon. Elizabeth, dwindling with tuberculosis and the compounded scurvy that they called black canker, would last until the following March. Franklin Richards, thousands of miles away in London, months away by mail, would much later receive a letter telling him of the death of his infant son, and months after that another telling of the death of his daughter, and months after that another still, informing him of the death of his second wife. When Jane got her first letter from him in April, 1847, he had not yet learned of even the first death. At the moment of writing, he was tending his brother, ill with smallpox. So to the destruction of all her immediate family Jane Richards was able to add worry about the health of her husband, with no way of knowing whether the brother had died, whether Franklin had caught smallpox from him, whether Franklin himself might have died. But by that time she was too numb to feel. "I only lived," she told one of H. H. Bancroft's interviewers years later, "because I could not die."

6

ΤΙΤΙΤΙΤΙΤΙΤΙΤΙΤ

Poor Camp

ALMOST DAILY, as wagons in tens and fifties straggled in from the east, or riders on fast horses passed on their way to report to the Twelve, they had word from Nauvoo. Some of it cheered them. For instance, on a Sunday in mid-August, while Brigham, Willard Richards, George A. Smith, Orson Pratt, Lorenzo Young, and others of the priesthood were visiting bedridden William Clayton in his tent, the tent flap lifted to admit a surprise: Porter Rockwell, that long-haired, cold-nerved instrument that Joseph had created, scout and messenger and, on at least two occasions up to that point, avenger. He had spent a good part of the summer in jail, but when his trial came up there was no one to accuse him, and he was released. One can imagine why no one wanted to point the finger at Rockwell. He was surely as dangerous a man as existed on the whole frontier, and all the more fearsome because he worked in silence, on orders or what the Gentiles thought were orders, and not for his own purposes but for the Church. He was tireless, strong, a dead shot—and moreover blessed by Joseph with the promise of invulnerability. They welcomed him with joy. The man who would become the murderer of many men joined the rest of the brethren in laying hands on Clayton and rebuking his sickness in the name of the Lord, President Young being mouth.

If Porter's trial had come up a month later, he might have found enemies bold enough to accuse him. The Mormons who had remained in and around Nauvoo had excited Gentile wrath by planting crops, in evident repudiation of their agreement to move as soon as grass grew and water ran. By September the violence which had begun as threats and night-riding had matured as "posses," "wolf-packs," whippings, and finally a full-scale invasion of the Saints' once populous city, inhabited now by the poorest, feeblest, and sickest of the Mormons plus a sizable body of Gentiles who had bought up Mormon property and moved in. Property now threw them on the side of those whom a few months before they had perhaps helped to displace.

The wolfpacks converged on Nauvoo with artillery and anywhere from 1,500 to 2,500 men. Their leaders, who were militiamen and preachers and thus usurped the airs of both legality and righteousness, were quarreling among themselves over authority, but they were united in their lust for violence. The state stood by helplessly; the federal government, then and later, did nothing. The thousand or so men, women, and children inside the city, of whom perhaps 100 to 150 were capable of war and of whom many were Gentiles, threw up barricades and planted crude mines in the roads, and made cannonballs out of an old steamboat shaft. Their resistance was heroic, hopeless, and absurd. After several days of wild shooting, sneaking, and scrambling that resulted in three Mormon deaths and an unknown number of casualties among the attackers, peacemakers met under a white flag and the Mormons agreed to clear out at once. By the evening of September 17, jeered, harassed, beaten, possessing only what they could hastily tie into bundles, the last of the Saints crossed the Mississippi. The next day the mob expressed its mind by throwing out the Gentile residents too, and settled down to drink and fight and burn and deface and defile with the single-minded enthusiasm of Moslem troops shooting the faces off statues in a captured temple of the infidel.

As early as September 15, not yet knowing of the siege but well aware of the growing threat of violence, Brigham had sent ten wag-

ons back along the Mormon Road to assist the last refugees from
Nauvoo. On September 24, Daniel Wells and William Cutler, riding hard, brought word of the city's fall, arriving at a time when
the camps around Council Bluffs were hit with rumors of further
trouble there. It was said that a United States Marshal from Missouri
was on his way with a warrant for the arrest of the Twelve; men
heard that the Secretary of War had instructed the Indian Agent
to evict all Mormons from the Pottawattamie lands by April 1, 1847.
Both rumors, as it developed, were untrue. The United States Marshal from Missouri was one of those embodied fears of persecution
that haunted the Mormon mind. And there was no immediate danger that the Saints would be thrown off the Pottawattamie lands,
for the long-awaited permission to make temporary settlements
there had finally come through. What was actually under question was the settlements across the Missouri; the Bureau of Indian
Affairs did not acknowledge the authority of either Captain Allen
or Chief Big Elk to grant the permission they had given. Brigham,
by now having possession, simply sent out Hosea Stout's police to
establish a picket guard, and sat tight. As a Yankee guesser, he would
probably have guessed that the Saints would be pretty hard for the
government to move.

But the stragglers from Nauvoo were another matter. When the
refugees were driven to the river and into skiffs and flatboats, the
rescue wagons that left the Missouri on September 15 had not yet
reached Mt. Pisgah. They would be joined by other wagons from
Mt. Pisgah and Garden Grove as soon as the news of disaster reached
those settlements. But meantime the victims had neither food nor
shelter nor transportation nor assurance of safety from violence.

Often it is not safe to take a Mormon report of any part of the
persecutions at quite its face value. The testimony of a victim is inclined to be self-righteous. But there can be no palliation of the
actions of the Gentile mobs at Nauvoo. These were the border scum
at their drunken and violent worst. And so we may as well let
Thomas Bullock tell it as it happened to him, and as he later wrote
it in a letter to Franklin Richards, off in England.

Winter Quarters, Camp of Israel
Omaha Nation

Beloved Franklin:

In the month of August, 1846, I was taken very sick with the ague and fever, and soon after my wife and four little children were taken with the same disease. In this condition we continued until the 16th of September. On that day a friend, George Wardell, packed up my goods on two wagons and removed them to his house to be out of danger from the cannon balls, which were flying about too thick for anyone to feel anyway comfortable. He located us behind his house out of danger. As I did not see this battle, I don't write much about it. But I know for a whole week the roar of cannon and the sharp cracking of rifles kept us in awful suspense and anxiety.

Our devoted city was defended by about one hundred and fifty poor, sickly, persecuted Saints, while it was cannonaded by from fifteen hundred to two thousand demoniacs in the shape of men, who had sworn to raze our temple to the ground, to burn the city, ravish our wives and daughters and drive the remainder of the people into the river. With what desperation our little band fought against such an overwhelming horde of desperadoes, I leave you to judge. My flesh seems to crawl on my bones at the remembrance of those scenes. On the 17th of September, two thousand men with five hundred wagons marched into the city. Such yelling and hooting I never heard before from civilized men, nor even from the wild savages...

While the leaders were haranguing their mob followers at the rope walk, by Hibbard's, such an awful and infuriated noise I never before heard, though I was in Warsaw street, more than a quarter of a mile from the scene. We expected an indiscriminate massacre was commencing. Myself and others who were sick were carried by friends into the tall weeds and into the woods, while all who were able to do so hid themselves. Many crossed the river leaving everything behind them. As night approached we returned to our shelter. But, O God, what a night to remember!

The next morning at nine o'clock saw me, my wife, my four children, my sister-in-law Fanny, my blind mother-in-law, all shaking with the ague in one house, only George Wardell to do anything for us, when a band of about thirty men, armed with guns, with fixed bayonets, pistols in belt, the captain with sword in his hand, and the stars and stripes flying about, marched opposite my sheltering roof. The captain called and demanded that the owner of the two wagons be brought out. I was raised from my bed, led out of doors, supported by my sister-in-law and the rail fence. I was then asked if those goods were mine. I replied, "They are." The captain then stepped out to within four feet of me, pointed his sword at my throat, while four others presented their guns with bayonets within three feet of my body, and said, "If you are not off from here in twenty minutes my orders are to shoot you." I replied, "Shoot away, for you will only send me to heaven a few hours quicker, for you may see I am not for this world many hours longer." The captain then told me, "If you will renounce Mormonism you may stay here and we will protect you." I replied, "This is not my house; yonder is my house," pointing to it, "which I built and paid for with the gold I earned in England. I never committed the least crime in Illinois, but I am a Mormon, and if I live I shall follow the Twelve." Then said the captain, "I am sorry to see you and your sick family, but if you are not gone when I return in half an hour, my orders are to kill you and every Mormon in the place."

But Oh, the awful cursing and swearing these men did pour out! I tremble when I think of it. George and Edwin drove my wagons down to the ferry and were searched five times for firearms. The mob took a pistol, and though they promised to return it when I got across the river, I have not seen it to this day. While on the bank of the river I crawled to the margin to bid a sister who was going down to St. Louis goodbye. While there a mobber shouted out, "Look! Look! there is a skeleton bidding death good bye." So you can imagine the poor, sickly condition of both of us.

On Wednesday, the 23rd of September, while in my wagon on the slough opposite Nauvoo, a tremendous thunder shower passed over which drenched everything we had; not a dry thread left to us; the bed a pool of water, my wife and sister-in-law lading it out by basins full, and I in a burning fever and insensible, with all my hair shorn off to cure me of my disease. Many had not a wagon or tent to shelter them from the pitiless blast. One case I will mention. A poor woman stood among the bushes, wrapping her cloak around her three little orphan children, to shield them from the storm as well as she could through that terrible night, during which there was one continued roar of thunder and blaze of lightning while the rain descended in torrents.

The mob seized every person in Nauvoo they could find, led them to the river and threw them in. I will mention one individual case. They seized Charles Lambert, led him to the river and in the midst of cursing and swearing one man said, "By the holy saints, I baptize you by the order of the commanders of the temple," plunged him in backwards and then said, "The commandments must be fulfilled, G—d— you, you must have another dip." They threw him in on his face, then sent him on the flat boat across the river, with the promise that if he returned to Nauvoo they would shoot him . . .

A little while after the evacuation of Nauvoo Thomas Kane, recovered from his long illness and entrusted by Brigham with the task of trying to gain Washington's permission for temporary Mormon settlements on the Indian Lands, came back along the Mormon Road across Iowa. He must have met and talked with messengers and perhaps even the first miserable refugees, and he certainly knew before he arrived on the Mississippi what had happened to Nauvoo: the road would have been boiling with that news. But for literary and perhaps propaganda reasons Kane chose to report his visit as if he were a stranger to Mormon affairs, to describe the stricken city as it might have seemed to some sensitive and uninformed traveler. One can forgive him the literary flourishes and the mystery with which he invested the emptied countryside and the silent town, for only by the exercise of his literary gifts could he possibly have communicated the nightmare incredibility of the sack of the greatest city in Illinois by a graceless mob.

He was at pains to point the contrast between the slovenly Iowa countryside, "marred without being improved" by the "careless hands" of borderers, and the city he could see across on the Illinois shore, "glittering in the fresh morning sun, its bright new dwellings, set in cool green gardens ranging up around a stately dome-shaped hill which was crowned by a noble marble edifice, whose tapering spire was radiant with white and gold." Around that city he saw the "unmistakable marks of industry, enterprise, and educated wealth," the evidences of "fruitful husbandry." But when he crossed the river he landed on a deserted shore. No one was in sight, the streets were empty, the houses silent, the fields deserted. He found blacksmith shops whose fires, though cold, were laid ready to be kindled, and carpenters' workbenches still smelling of fresh shavings, as if the carpenter had only stepped out for an hour. He walked in gardens among marigolds and heartsease that still looked tenderly kept, and in graveyards whose mounds had been sodded only a little while ago, and through orchards whose apples hung unpicked. Through the stillness of the dead and deserted city he came finally to the temple, and there he found arms stacked in the yard and rough men sleeping and drinking and spitting. Walking past their curious stares, he entered the temple and saw its great baptismal font on its twelve marble oxen: it was green with vomit and urine. Upstairs the rooms were strewn with broken bottles and the debris of a long carouse, and the steeple stairs had been violated by defecations and crude deliberate filth.

It is an affecting and disgusting picture, and one suspects that in spite of its artificially created mystery and its calculated suspense it is not untrue in its details. But when to his picture of the debased city he added an account of what had befallen the inhabitants, Kane tripled his effectiveness as a propagandist for the Mormon side.

He crossed the river and made his way (he says, though it probably didn't happen in this order) to the place where 640 destitute refugees huddled on the Iowa shore near the present town of Montrose. There he saw (if indeed he saw, though if he didn't he almost certainly could have) a man dying by the light of a tallow candle in a paper funnel shade.

> Over his head was something like a tent, made of a sheet or two, and he rested on a but partially ripped open, old straw mattress, with a hair cushion under his head for a pillow. His gaping jaw and glazing eye told how short a time he would monopolize these luxuries, though a seemingly bewildered and

excited person, who might have been his wife, seemed to find hope in occasionally forcing him to swallow awkwardly measured sips of tepid river water. . . . Those who knew better had furnished the apothecary he needed, a toothless old baldhead, whose manner had the repulsive dullness of a man familiar with death scenes. He, so long as I remained, mumbled in his patient's ear a monotonous and melancholy prayer, between the pauses of which I heard the hiccough and sobbing of two little girls who were sitting upon a piece of drift wood outside.

Enhanced or not by a literary impulse, that was how death could have come to what the Mormons learned to remember as the Poor Camp. So far as I know, there has never been a census of deaths in that pitiful straggle of huts and tents on the Iowa shore, but every evidence indicates that death must have been appallingly frequent. These were the lame, the halt, and the dying, the aged and infirm, the chronically ill. They were also the least well-equipped of all those who left Nauvoo: they literally had nothing but the clothes on their backs. Without statistics on their suffering, we may judge that suffering to have exceeded anything that happened to the others. The rest of the Mormon people, themselves no strangers to suffering, freely handed the Poor Camp the palm.

They sat there in the late September sun and rain, sunburned by day and chilled by night, malarial, hungry, without adequate shelter, while the wagons labored eastward to help them. By now the Mormon people had become experts in rescue. Both their peculiar difficulties and their peculiar solidarity encouraged situations in which the hand of brotherhood had to be stretched out to the persecuted, the unfortunate, or the belated. Through the entire history of the Mormon Trail, rescue is a major theme; and some of the noble moments of Mormon history have been those in which the safe risked their safety to help the endangered. The wagons began reaching the Mississippi during the early days of October. By October 9 the survivors were loaded for the return journey that would distribute them among friends and relatives hardly better off than themselves. But on that morning of October 9 they had evidence that other eyes than those of their fellow-Saints were on them.

"These signs shall follow them that believe," Joseph Smith had said, opening his people's minds to the possibility of divine intervention and the evidences of God's care. Now as the wagons drew up in line preparatory to starting for Garden Grove, God vouchsafed one of His signs, as miraculous as the visitation of seagulls that in 1848 would save the crops of the infant colony in Utah. We may again observe it with Thomas Bullock, who was himself not without literary flourishes.

> But hark! [he wrote to Franklin Richards] what noise is that? See! The quails descend. They alight close by our little camp of twelve wagons, run past each wagon tongue, when they arise, fly around the camp three times, descend and again run the gauntlet past each wagon. See! the sick knock them down with sticks and the little children catch them alive in their hands! ... One descends upon our tea-board in the midst of our cups, while we were actually around the table eating our breakfast, which a little boy eight years old catches alive in his hands. They rise again, the flocks increase in number, seldom going seven rods from our camp, continually flying around the camp, sometimes under the wagons, sometimes over, and even into the wagons where the poor sick Saints are lying in bed; thus having a direct manifestation from the Most High that although we are driven by men He has not forsaken us ...

Others might interpret these as quail exhausted by flying across the wide river, or as a flock of passenger pigeons alighting at their accustomed roosting place to find it encumbered by the Poor Camp, but to the Saints they were a miracle as authentic and incontrovertible as the quails and manna that saved the Children of Israel in the wilderness. On the last day of the Nauvoo anguish, bare hours before the rescue wagons moved out westward with the last of the tribe of Joseph, the Lord sent them His sign, so that when they started, even these started in hope. *At even ye shall eat flesh, and in the morning ye shall be filled with bread.*

7

∏∏∏∏∏∏∏∏∏∏∏∏∏

All Is Well

As early as august, while Thomas Kane was still desperately sick and being cared for by Mormon women on the Little Papillon, and while at Brigham's request medicines were being rushed from Leavenworth to save this friend for whom, presumably, the ministrations of the priesthood would not work, there was a demoralizing wave of sickness through the Mormon camps. Kane reported that in the camp which was building the bridge across the Elkhorn, more than a third were down at once, and that burial parties could not keep up with the deaths: he speaks of mass burials in trenches, and of women sitting in the doorways of tents keeping the flies off the faces of dead children whose bodies had already begun to decay. What was true on the west side of the Missouri was at least as true on the Pottawattamie side, and possibly—though there is less documentation in this case and though the dry plains were always healthier than the riverbottoms—among the three wagontrains under George Miller and James Emmett, out on the Running Water. From the time the Mormons gave up all thought of proceeding to the mountains, and began digging in for the winter, they worked against sicknesses so pervasive and violent that they amounted to a plague.

Since there were no trained physicians among them, and since to the priesthood with its dependence on consecrated olive oil and the laying on of hands all illness was the work of evil spirits, there is no way of determining exactly the nature of their ailments. Certainly a good part of what laid them low was the abiding curse of the Midwestern frontier, the fever-and-ague that was estival-autumnal malaria. Certainly too, though the Mormons were better organized and cleaner than most frontier communities, there would have been plenty of dysentery of the virulent kind that all but prostrated Francis Parkman out along the North Platte that same summer and fall. If there was no typhoid, there should have been, for they drank creek water and had only the most primitive notions of public sanitation. It is hard to take public health measures when the germ theory of disease has not yet been proposed, and when you would not accept it if it had. Exposure and malnutrition encouraged tuberculosis, pleurisy, asthma, croup, whooping cough, the common cold. Smallpox they happily escaped, and cholera, a killer in the Platte valley in the emigration years, hit them not at all in 1846 and only relatively lightly later, for the riverboats that brought the disease from the Gulf stopped at Independence or St. Joseph, and the Oregon- and California-bound wagontrains that carried it on into the plains traveled the south side of the Platte. Strains and injuries, ax-cuts and falls and broken bones, they sustained their share of, and especially on the trail, men and boys were often afflicted with boils.

Run-down as they were, they seldom had the satisfaction of dying from a single uncomplicated illness. Even in mid-summer their fevers were often accompanied by symptoms of the scorbutic disease that they called black canker. And as autumn tipped toward winter, as the cottonwoods went yellow and then bare, as the wild grapes and the wild Pottawattamie plums passed, and they fell back on cornmeal and flour from Brigham's mill, and on potatoes and turnips if they had any, and on occasional beef or pork or mutton from the slaughterhouse that Lorenzo Young maintained more as a charity than as a business, and on the infrequent civilized treats that the more affluent could buy at the American Fur Company posts at Pointe aux Poules or Bellevue, then the symptoms of scurvy and pellagra became more pronounced and their combined sicknesses more deadly despite the fact that the malarial symptoms waned. Scurvy added to their headaches, colds, toothaches, phthisis, and pleurisy the weight of a progressive, hopeless exhaustion. Their faces, already sallow, grew sallower. Their gums softened, their teeth loosened, they suffered from dizzy spells and night blindness and were scoured by the bloody flux, and they died like the May flies whose bodies used to stink up the summer backwaters at Nauvoo, and which are still, along the Mississippi, known as Mormon flies.

Jane Richards, skinny as a stick but apparently unkillable, spent that winter learning to love Elizabeth McFate's child in place of her own two dead ones, and taking care of the dying Elizabeth. When she went out along the beaten, dog-yellowed snow paths of Winter Quarters she had a choice of two dresses—an old gingham wrapper and a best black silk. The first was altogether too disreputable to wear in public, the second was altogether too showy. Like a survivor in a destroyed city, she went out often to scrounge wood or a cup of flour, or simply to seize an hour's comfort by some friend's fire; and she alternately offended herself with her own elegance and was brought close to laughter by the absurdity of the balls of ice frozen along the hem of her skirts. Late that winter she traded Franklin's violin to a nephew of Brother Brigham's for a gallon of wine; and as a pound of tea, disapproved by the Word of Wisdom, had sustained her on the bitter road across Iowa, so this sipped and cherished wine, likewise disapproved, may have given her enough vitamin C at a critical time to save her life.

Those whose husbands or brothers brought supplies back from trading or working trips into Missouri, and those who had had sugar for preserving wild plums and grapes, and those who had managed to make and keep a little cider, a little vinegar, a crock of pickles, fared better, but few fared well. Back in Mt. Pisgah Zina Huntington Jacobs had seen her husband Henry Jacobs sent on a mission, and at the end of summer found herself with only her father for a protector. Brigham was up ahead, on the Missouri, with his hands and his house more than full. Zina's brothers were scattered—two still in New York State on missions, John back in Nauvoo working, Dimick off marching with the Mormon Battalion. The sickly season came on, and "death invaded our camp. Sickness was so prevalent and deaths so frequent that enough help could not be had to make coffins, and many of the dead were wrapped in their graveclothes and buried in split logs at the bottom of the grave and brush at the sides." Shortly it came William Huntington's turn. He had never been well since he brought his hacking cough into the camp that would become Mt. Pisgah. Now he sickened, sank, and in eighteen days was dead. Having proved his faith first with his security, then with his property, and finally with his life, he was buried in the growing cemetery on the hill overlooking the middle fork of Grand River, and Zina, gathering together her few belongings and her two young sons, made her way to Winter Quarters and was taken by Brigham into his family. A little over a year later, when Henry Jacobs returned with an unauthorized second wife and was cut off from the Church, Zina became in fact as well as in name one of Brigham's wives.

Eliza Snow, not yet given Brigham's protection, was still living with the Markhams, and in the constricted darkness of a 12 by 12 cabin could lie awake at night and hear Brother and Sister Markham fiercely quarreling and threatening to leave one another. Patiently Eliza settled down to her winter's work of composing obituary poems. She recorded in verse the death of Elder William Green, the death of Eliza P's child, the death of her own mother; she memorialized the three dead children of Wilford and Phoebe Woodruff, the daughter of Robert Pierce, Brother Luke Johnson's companion Susan, the children of Franklin and Jane Richards. When she was not writing poems or attending funerals, Eliza participated in the acts of neighborly kindness at which Mormon women have had few equals, and sat in on many a good session when one of the sisters burst out in tongues and others leaped up to interpret. The ladies had some gossip to spread and discuss, for early in the fall two young men had to be given eighteen lashes each for the crime of adultery; and Peter Haws, he of the coffee-throwing daughter, was accused of selling whiskey to the Indians; and several times there were raids on the Omahas by one or another of their pressing enemies; and talk went that John D. Lee was in bad with Brother Brigham, and then that John D. was strong enough but that Hosea Stout was in bad. The Lion of the Lord had the constant burden of small as well as large decisions. There were quarrelings over precedence and authority in the artillery company of the Nauvoo Legion, and there was trouble getting volunteers to stand guard all night in any weather for the safety of Israel, and murmuring about the diversion of the Battalion's advance pay (by now Lee and Howard Egan and James Pace had gone to Santa Fe and picked up a second installment) to buy wholesale supplies in St. Louis. There were apostasies, and sneakings-off to Missouri, and rumors of bogus-making. The ladies were human and female. Gossip gave an air of community stability to the cramped and dismal huts of Winter Quarters, and kept their spirits up.

Grim, suffering, much hated, Hosea Stout went about his business as Captain of the Guard. It was he who ordered the young adulterers whipped, after first scaring them to death with the threat to shoot them. It was he who, in order to discover if the roughhouse gang had confederates, buckled on his guns and took two of his policemen and walked the length and breadth of the camp, speaking everybody fair. At once the word flashed through the town that he was hunting more men to whip, and by the surliness of their greetings or the show of weapons they made, Hosea estimated the men he had to deal with.

It was Hosea who had to discipline delinquent policemen and guards, search the wagons of suspected thieves, ride patrol through country where the Indians were reported to be rising, examine into rumors that the Missourians were raising a force or that army horses had been seen downriver. He kept his ears open for the grumblings of rebels and apostates, and informed Brigham so that rebellion could be nipped in the bud. He was never truly in bad with Brother Brigham, for Brigham found him too useful: to the extent that Zion was a police state, Hosea was its enforcement arm. But Hosea was in bad with many, and he himself had his passionate dislikes, one of whom was William Clayton. Toward spring, apparently because Clayton had been careless about his police duties, he assured Clayton that he would kill him as soon as the Twelve started west, and it is a testimonial to Brigham's complicated relationship with his people that he did not rebuke Hosea for the threat, but at the last minute took Clayton along with the pioneers to keep him from harm. In the intervals between his watchful and suspicious duties, Hosea had been building a 12 by 12 log cabin. Nine and a half months after he had ferried his family across from Nauvoo, beginning so unluckily that some of them were shipwrecked on an island in the February cold, he moved the survivors once more under a roof. The survivors were few. His son Hyrum had died in Garden Grove, his son William Hosea between Mt. Pisgah and Council Bluffs. His wife Marinda had died in childbirth, along with her child, in Winter Quarters on September 26. His wife Lucretia had run away. Lonely, secretive, harsh, self-righteous, inwardly anguished, Hosea made note of present uncertainty and past disaster in his journal:

> Often have I lain and contemplated my own sickness and feeble situation without food for myself and family and death staring me in the face. I could only contemplate what would become of them in case I was called away. How often have I beheld my family—one by one—yielding up the Ghost, warning me of what may follow. How often in sorrow and anguish, I have said in my heart: "When shall my trials and tribulations end?"

To which the answer was, not yet.

And so through that long winter of shortage, hardship, Indian scares, army scares, Missouri scares, gossip, rumor, petty crimes, sickness, and apostasy, while the rank and file fought to survive and the leaders dealt with the Indian Bureau or umpired disputes between the Otos and the Omahas or protected both from the Pawnees. So through days of labor and nights when groups of them, families or whole wards, celebrated birthdays or anniversaries with

cotillions danced to the music of the Quadrille Band. Faith and the
solidarity of family and Church gave them strength for endurance
and survival.

In Mt. Pisgah, Charles Coulson Rich had succeeded to the presidency of the local council after the death of William Huntington,
and he in turn was succeeded in March by Lorenzo Snow, when
Brigham called Rich to Winter Quarters to help organize pioneers for the mountains. With the coming of winter the whole town
had moved into the riverbottoms, better sheltered and with handy
wood and water. August had been their worst time, during the
epidemic of malaria when half the camp had either been scorching
in fevers as high as 106 degrees or bathed in the profuse sweats of
utter weakness, and when deaths had been as frequent as sunsets.
Now in the winter, even with the black canker and pneumonia
and other possibilities, they were healthier, and their gardens had
borne so plentifully that Snow was able to send a wagonload of
produce to Brigham as a Christmas present. They made strenuous
efforts at self-sufficiency. The same Yankee practicality that had
taught Mormon women to churn their butter by the rocking of a
wagon on the road, or raise their bread in transit so that it could be
popped into an earthen oven almost as soon as they stopped, led
them to utilize every trade and skill they possessed. Rich, who was
a cooper by trade, supervised the making of tubs, barrels, churns,
and baskets that they sold wherever their wagons went trading;
and during the winter Lorenzo Snow sent back to Ohio agents who
raised nearly $700 of relief money among sympathetic Gentiles
there.

They praised God and they worshipped Him in their own peculiar ways. "Man is that he might have joy," Joseph Smith had
taught them. Having had a gift for enjoying life, he would have
responded to a party given that winter at the house of Lorenzo
Snow. Lorenzo's sister Eliza describes it: The house was 15 by 30,
dirt-floored, dirt-roofed, turf-chimneyed. In it lived Lorenzo, his
four wives, and several children. (Lorenzo, something of a phi-
losopher and a man of the world, a graduate of Oberlin, had not

been a marrying man until Brigham advised him that marrying
was his duty; then he took two wives, and shortly afterward two
more.) For the party, the Snows had sprinkled the dirt floor with
straw, draped the log walls with the sheet-casings of featherbeds
that had long since been traded for food, and lighted the single
room with tallow dips stuck in hollowed-out turnips. Having no
band in Pisgah to make them music, they made their own: the
entertainment consisted of songs, recitations, toasts, riddles, and
prayer. The refreshments were a dish of succotash. It was a party
that some of the participants remembered all their lives as the gayest
in their experience.

Near the end of the year, the Winter Quarters census showed
3,483 persons, of whom only 502 were men. About 138 other men
were absent on trading trips or herding Israel's thousands of cattle
"down to the rushes" in the Missouri bottoms. The town was divided into wards (the Mormon term for a parish) and had built a
log council house for meetings. It was, thanks to Hosea Stout's
basilisk prowling, well policed. Its inhabitants lived by the grace
of God and the skin of their teeth. By spring, they and their counter-
parts in Mt. Pisgah and Garden Grove were a hard core, tested and
tempered by tribulation and shared hope, as tough and durable a
people as this republic has ever produced.

Some of them were even well and cheerful. In April, 1847, just
before the pioneer party was to start west, Ursulia Hascall wrote
her brother back in New Salem, and all the difficulties of the winter
had touched her enthusiasm no more than a snowflake douses a
church fire. Francis Pomeroy, Irene's husband, was going with the
pioneers; the women would go with the main emigration later in
the year, with young Thales Hascall as their teamster. Thales,
Ursulia said, was almost a man at thirteen. "He has grown tall and
stout, his flesh is hard and health good." Already he and Francis
had begun to make that transition to cowboyhood that so many
young Mormons made at the edge of the wilderness. The thousands of cattle down at the rushes were more and more valuable
to them as they had to adopt nomadic ways. According to Thomas
Kane, "the manliest, as well as the most general daily labor, was

the herding of cattle." Young Thales, not harmed but only hardened by a winter beyond the Missouri, had only one regret: he wished a friend from Massachusetts could come out and go hunting turkeys, prairie hens, geese, ducks, and possibly deer and buffalo with him. As for the rest of the family, Ursulia reported them with her usual complacency. One can imagine her with her hands folded across her stomach:

> We have lived in our log cabin through the winter very comfortably. We have a brick chimney and hearth (two thirds of the people have them made of sods and they do very well) a window with four lights of glass 10 by 12, gave eight cents a light, the furniture consists of sacks barrels chests trunks and two wild bedsteads with curtains from eaves to floor, my chest for a table, We have had plenty of provisions except vegetables, we have had beans enough and some potatoes this spring there is abundance of wild onions and artichokes first rate, there is a store opposite to us [the American Fur Company post at Pointe aux Poules] with every necessary, English and west Indies goods, coffee sugar, saleratus all fifteen cents per pound. First best sugar house mollases one dollar per gallon, I think we shall get along first rate . . .

Ursulia would always get along first rate. Thanks to the providing of Francis Pomeroy, his forethought, his good teams and his ample supplies, the Hascalls and Pomeroys would continue to escape the malnutrition and disease that pulled others down. And anyway, in a people remarkable for their capacity to survive, Ursulia had a special knack for survival. She could have existed, if she had to, in places and on food that would have let others starve. She could see plenty in a barren prairie. She would have learned the Omaha trick of robbing the nests of field mice of their hoards of wild wood-pea seeds. And with death all around her, the graveyard full and hardly a cabin without its victim, she retained her cheerfulness. Her catalogues sound sunny even when they are catalogues of death:

> I suppose you have heard of the deaths in brother Ponds family. The children are all dead but Elizabeth and Loenza, when they were on the way here they turned from the main

road into a settlement where he and Samuel could earn two
dollars per day with their teams. It proved to be an unhealthy
place, They were all taken sick and they came away as soon as
they could, but they were unable to take care of themselves
on the road and suffered for the want of care, Lowell died before they arrived, the rest lived to get here and then dropped
away one after another, Sister Pond has not recovered and I
fear she never will, Brother Ponds health is very poor. Sister
Clark died on the way here. She wore herself out with hard
work I think, I never saw a female that could live and do as
she did, The children came on with P. Rockwell they have the
first rate families to live in. Hiram lives in the same family with
Emiline. She thinks them the best people in the world. She is
as happy as a queen, has everything to eat, drink wear. She in-
structs the children has the care of their clothes and does as
much or as little as she pleases.

Ursulia teaches us, as do Eliza Snow's sessions of tongues and
gossip, Hosea Stout's grim round of duties, and Lorenzo Snow's
makeshift good cheer, how so many managed to last through to
face 1847 and the journey to Zion.

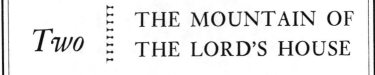

Two THE MOUNTAIN OF
THE LORD'S HOUSE

Brigham Young

1

TTTTTTTTTTTTTT

Rendezvous on the Elkhorn

THE 1847 TREK of the Mormon pioneers from Winter Quarters
to the Salt Lake Valley must be the most extensively reported event
in western history. Of the 148 people who started, at least fifteen
kept faithful journals, either personally or by proxy, and nearly
as many more later published reminiscences or letters. It is true that
some of the original journals, notably those of Brigham Young,
Heber C. Kimball, George A. Smith, and the official historian,
Thomas Bullock, have never been made freely available to scholars;
but excerpts from them all appear in the *Journal History* as well as
in the day-by-day reconstructions published in the Salt Lake
Tribune on the fiftieth and hundredth anniversaries of the pioneer
journey, and an edited version of Kimball's was published in 1882.
Though it might be interesting to compare this with the original,
the chances are it would yield little that is not already known, for
Kimball's journal was largely kept for him by William Clayton, and
Clayton's own journal is so voluminous that he can hardly have
given Brother Heber many observations that he did not also retain
for himself.

Besides the partially known journals of Apostles Young, Kimball,
and Smith, we have fuller records by three other apostles, and one
by a man who became an apostle later. Of the journal of Apostle

Wilford Woodruff there is a published, but edited, version. From Apostle Orson Pratt we have a series of letters published in the *Millennial Star* in 1849–50. The original journal of Apostle Amasa Lyman, kept for him by Albert Carrington, is available intact, and since Carrington also kept the diary of George A. Smith, we may assume that the Smith diary is a paraphrase of this. The journal of Erastus Snow, who became an apostle along with Lorenzo Snow, Franklin Richards, and Charles Coulson Rich soon after the settlement of the valley, has been twice published.

From these, as well as from the unexpurgated journals of the rank and file, it seems clear that the records withheld from outside eyes by the Church Historian's office have not been held back for any valid security reason—we already know, from many points of view, everything that happened on that trip. The motive seems instead to be a combination of the usual Mormon caution about exposing intimate history, and the even more usual myth-making and whitewashing impulse of the hierarchy. Though there were some pretty hard cases among the 1847 pioneers, there were no incidents that discredit anyone; the worst one can imagine is that some of the leaders wrote with too forceful a gift of tongues. Leaving Nauvoo, for instance, Willard Richards had reported Heber Kimball's characterization of a Strangite as "not worth the skin of a fart"—the sort of talk not unusual in both Heber's mouth and Brigham's. Nevertheless a later and more proper generation of hierarchs has pretended that the 1847 leaders spoke always with the tongues of angels and prophets, and that the pioneer company was composed of 148 stalwart, disciplined Saints each of whom combined the qualities of zealot, frontiersman, and good soldier. In the myth, they can hardly be told apart.

Actually, they were as humanly various as any company. Besides the hard cases, whose presence is mentioned gingerly if at all, there were three Negro "servants," technically baptized but doctrinally of a secondary status as Church members because of God's curse on the sons of Ham, and there was an indeterminable number, reported variously as anything from two to six, who were not

members of the Church at all. From these minority groups we have
no journals or reminiscences, and they figure importantly in the
history of the trip only on one occasion when Brigham chose to
include them among the scapegoats in a withering sermon. Still,
their presence gives a variety to the historical journey that is not
there in the mythical one. And the everyday humanity of the pioneers glances out again and again from some of the records that it
has not been thought necessary to withhold or edit. Some of these
chroniclers we have met before this, on the sad road from Nauvoo:
Lorenzo Young, Norton Jacob, Appleton Harmon, and, above all,
William Clayton. Others are new to us: William Empey; James
Smithies; Levi Jackman; Lorin Farr, a friend of the Hascalls' and
Pomeroys' from New Salem; John Brown, who had converted most
of the Mississippi Saints including the three Negroes who went with
the pioneers; Harriet Decker Young, Lorenzo's wife, and Ellen Sanders Kimball, a wife of Heber's. Howard Egan also gives us occasional details, but his journal is less useful than it might have been if
he had not, on busy days, cut corners by copying verbatim from the
diary of his friend Clayton.

It is not for the events of the journey that we go to them, for
the events have been reiterated in a thousand retellings, they are
made manifest in stone and bronze in Mahonri Young's "This Is the
Place" monument, they are annually acted out before filled foot-
ball stadia in Pioneer Day pageants. What we get out of the journals is people. From Wilford Woodruff, that gullible Connecticut
Yankee who had been a mighty proselytizer in England, who had
presented a specially printed *Book of Mormon* to Queen Victoria,
who had survived a hundred accidents and been visited by a thousand prophetic dreams, we learn to expect the portents and miraculous providences in which he specialized, but at least once he will
astonish us by reaching into his buggy and unlimbering his English
fishing gear and becoming perhaps the first fly-fisherman in the
history of the Rocky Mountains. From Orson Pratt, as absent-
minded as scholars are supposed to be, we may anticipate mainly
latitudes, longitudes, and temperatures: he went across the plains

with his eye glued to an artificial horizon and his wet finger up to test the wind. From Albert Carrington, eventually to become one of the Twelve but in 1847 a young clerk, we are certain to learn the color, friability, and mineral composition of every rock and ledge between the Missouri and the Wasatch. Someone at Dartmouth had inoculated him with geology, and the trail brought it out of him as a poultice draws an infection. Some of the rank and file, notably Levi Jackman and Appleton Harmon, will light their sober and dutiful narratives with occasional "literary" responses to scenery, and Lorenzo Young, Jackman, Harmon, James Smithies, and William Empey are all blessed with an orthography that is so phonetic it clears the head like menthol. William Clayton is his old clerkly self, bitching secretly; and Thomas Bullock, recovered from the fever and ague that had sent him out of Nauvoo on a stretcher, will improve certain camps by planting three grains of corn so that following companies of Saints can have the gladness of encountering those familiar and symbolic blades far out in the wilderness.

The journey these travelers record was no such desperate flight as the exodus from Nauvoo, for these were picked men, well-supplied, well-armed, and well-led; and for at least the first half of the journey they had only three women and two children to hamper them. Forms of trouble that afflicted some wagontrains even unto death—Indians, weather, poison water, dry *jornadas*, lack of feed—were for them no worse than annoyances. The Mormon pioneers lost more days to the Sabbath than to any hazards of the trail.

Whatever the variants of the myth may say, their story is not a story of hardship. It is a story of organization, foresight, and discipline. "I will do the scolding to this camp, no other man shall," Brigham told them on May 23, out along the North Platte. But that was only a reminder. They knew well enough who their leader was, had known it since the days following Joseph's murder, and only the normal temptations of the trail led them into temporary lapses of discipline. As for the rules by which they traveled, those had been given them by the Lord, in the first and only revelation that

Brother Brigham ever had. He announced it at the Council House in Winter Quarters on January 14, 1847, as "The word and will of the Lord concerning the Camp of Israel in their journeyings to the West." As practical a piece of exposition as the Lord ever issued, it was actually a restatement and corroboration of a pattern long since created by Joseph, and tested on more than one Mormon march.

The Lord directed the Saints to organize themselves into tens, fifties, and hundreds; to make preparations and gather supplies; to choose a group of pioneers to go ahead with plows and get crops into the ground. He recommended the widowed and fatherless to the care of those able to look after them, told them to cease drunkenness and the speaking of evil, urged them to praise the Lord in dance and song, and reassured them that their enemies were in His hands. And He stated yet once more the theme that had already endowed Mormonism with so much backbone: "My people," said the Lord through the mouth of Brother Brigham, who did not pretend to be a prophet but admitted to being a Yankee guesser, "My people must be tried in all things, that they may be prepared to receive the glory that I have for them, even the glory of Zion, and he that will not bear chastisement is not worthy of my kingdom."

Presumably Brigham selected the pioneers partly for their ability to bear chastisement, though surely such frontiersmen as Porter Rockwell and Howard Egan were also picked for their capacity to dispense it if need be. Significantly, Brigham did not ask for volunteers, as he had done the summer before when he hoped to send a party to the mountains, and he did not contemplate a company so large as five hundred. For one thing, Mormon numbers as well as resources had shrunk. Of the 25,000 people who had attended April Conference in Nauvoo in 1845, about 3,500 were in Winter Quarters and possibly twice that many more were scattered from Garden Grove to the east bank of the Missouri.* Of the Emmett-

* Superintendent Thomas H. Harvey of the Indian Bureau estimated 10,000 Mormons on both sides of the river in December, 1846.

Miller company, most had been called back to Winter Quarters by the Twelve; a few, including Miller, had rebelliously refused to come, and had been cut off from the Church at the end of February. Five hundred men and a few women were with the Mormon Battalion or in its Sick Detachment at Pueblo. Scores were dispersed through Iowa and Missouri working as rail splitters, gristmill hands, or herders. Hundreds had apostatized, hundreds were dead. The Mormon migration when it finally started across the plains was a more modest operation than the one that had been contemplated from Nauvoo, but there were few left who were weak in the faith. Nevertheless, considering the depletion of their numbers and the scattering of their men, the removal of another five hundred of the hardiest might have left the Missouri River settlements unable to maintain themselves. And anyway there was no need of so large a company as five hundred. Twelve times twelve was a more resounding and Biblical number, and it could do anything that the advance company would have to do.

One of the last acts of the Twelve in 1846 had been a meeting to discuss the organization of the pioneers. "The word and will of the Lord" followed two weeks later, and thereafter individuals began to be "called," as if to a mission. Norton Jacob, as an artillery officer in the Nauvoo Legion, got his call about March 1, and for a month all his care was preparation—arranging with Joel Ricks over in Iowa to board his family and lend him a team, arranging for equipment and supplies, repairing his wagon, fighting for teams to draw the cannon that was shortly consigned to his charge. The same pattern applied to others throughout the settlements. On March 12 Charles Coulson Rich, whose organizational sense Brigham respected, was called from Mt. Pisgah to help with the preparations, though he would not go out with the pioneers. The Twelve would go with the advance party as a matter of course, except for Parley Pratt, John Taylor, and Orson Hyde, who were still straightening out the mess in the English mission. Brigham's brothers Phineas and Lorenzo got their call, along with dependables such as Stephen Markham and Albert P. Rockwood, and less-dependables such as

John Pack, whom the Legion had refused to re-elect as major because they thought he had shown the white feather in Nauvoo. Under these leaders were steady men such as Francis Pomeroy, and hard-core veterans of the Missouri drivings, and a good many hard-muscled youths. Men going with their own outfits selected wagon-mates; the more opulent lined up young and reliable teamsters for their extra wagons; the cattle were brought in from the rushes. As Winter Quarters shook itself free from long paralysis, housewives thinned the blood of their families with sulphur and sorghum, and yearned for the first wild greens, the first pieplant. Men shuffled wives and children into new combinations of dependence and responsibility, and traded and borrowed and sold to fit themselves for the plains.

But it was not easy, in a place living so close to the bone, to get even twelve times twelve men equipped. On March 26 Brigham had the old temple bell rung to call the people together, and blistered them for their covetousness in not giving more freely to outfit the pioneers. Time was getting short. In order to reach the mountains in time to plant crops, and in order to get ahead of the Oregon and California emigration, they would have to leave before grass. He told them on March 29 to hold themselves ready to go as soon as the prairies dried. On that day Norton Jacob managed to sell his cabin for enough cloth and powder to do him, but he still had no teams for his cannon. As late as April 5, when Heber Kimball started six teams toward the rendezvous at the crossing of the Elkhorn, thirty miles west, Jacob still had only three horses and two sets of harness, despite the exhorting of the Twelve.

None of the hierarchy left with the first wagons, for April 6 was the anniversary of the founding of the Church seventeen years before, and the date of the annual spring Conference. In their last official act before departure the Twelve called for the "sustaining" of all the quorum except Lyman Wight, once a great fighter beside Joseph but now on the way to apostasy; and all of the High Council except Bishop George Miller. At that Conference, finally, Heber Kimball put the screws on the congregation until he got enough horses, harnesses, and feed to take care of Norton Jacob's cannon.

There was no big parade of departure, nothing at which women and children could line up and wave handkerchiefs. As far as the Elkhorn they dribbled and trickled off a few wagons at a time and by several routes. Though Levi Jackman, arriving at the Elkhorn on April 6, found four teams already there ahead of him, it would be another nine days before most of the pioneers were assembled.

Brigham and others of the Twelve started on April 7, but as they camped at the big Mormon farm west of Winter Quarters, word came that Parley Pratt had arrived from England, and they returned to hear what Parley had to tell, and to leave instructions about the big company that he and John Taylor would lead out later in the summer. On April 9 the Twelve started again, only to be intercepted by the message that Taylor had now arrived, bringing scientific instruments for Orson Pratt and $2,000 in gold raised among the British Saints. Again they returned, and at this last moment Brigham improved the occasion by telling first Thomas Bullock and then William Clayton to rise up and come along. Presumably he called them both because there would be work for good clerks, but almost certainly his choice of Clayton was motivated partially by his desire to save him from the basilisk ill will of Hosea Stout. Brigham spoke to Clayton at eleven in the morning; at two that afternoon Clayton had his trunk in Heber Kimball's carriage and was on his way. On April 15, the last group of wagons rafted the Elkhorn and joined the main camp on the bank of the Platte, about three miles below the site of modern Fremont, Nebraska.

Even yet there would be some comings and goings and last-minute errands, and at least one pioneer was still to come in. But essentially they were assembled. Thanks to the stubbornness of Lorenzo Young, they would not in the end total twelve times twelve, for Lorenzo had insisted on taking along his asthmatic wife Harriet and her two children, Isaac and Sabisky. Failing to move him, Brigham had decided to take one of his own wives, who happened to be Harriet's daughter Clarissa Decker, and he allowed Heber

Kimball to select one likewise—that same Ellen Sanders who had brought Clayton news of the birth of his son on the road from Nauvoo. Outside of these three women and two children, who in all the journals are mentioned only three or four times and might as well have been invisible and insubstantial, they numbered exactly 144 men and boys, seventy-two wagons, ninety-three horses, fifty-two mules, sixty-six oxen, nineteen cows, seventeen dogs, and some chickens. It sounds like a dog's dream, that trip; but the journals don't mention the dogs much either.

It was not quite a village on the march, as later wagontrains of Saints would be, but in its organization it was incomparably Mormon. Simply as Saints, they were members of either the Aaronic or the Melchizedek priesthood, their spiritual affairs controlled by the Twelve and the High Council, their material affairs looked after by the bishops and their counselors. Their first camp, between the Elkhorn and the Platte, saw them organized into tens, fifties, and hundreds and assigned a regular rotation of leadership on the road, so that no one group of wagons had to break trail or eat dust every day. On April 16, going on three miles to where the city of Fremont now stands, they completed an entirely separate military organization, with Brigham as general and Stephen Markham as colonel, and set up a schedule of guard duty. Still later they designated committees for lining out the trail, and committees of mounted and pedestrian hunters. So many overlapping structures of authority might have created confusion except that whenever a man felt a conflict among his spiritual, his military, and his trail duties, he could always go to the source of all his obligations, Brother Brigham, and have his difficulty resolved.

Their precautions, as summarized in the camp rules that Brigham laid down, were elaborate, even fussy. Once they started, every man was to walk beside his wagon with his loaded gun in his hand or within reach. They were to rise by the bugle at 5:00 A.M. and be ready to pull out at 7:00, with dinner ready-cooked so that the noon halt would not take more than an hour. Wagons were to travel in close order, and no man was to go more than twenty rods from camp without permission (that rule was fractured early, the first time some adventurous youth wanted to climb the bluffs to see ahead). At night wagons were to be corralled, tongues pointing outward, left hind wheel of each wagon interlocked with the right front wheel of the next, and when necessary the animals were to be kept inside the circle. At the 8:30 bugle every man was to retire to his wagon to pray, and at 9:00 all should be in bed and all fires out. The trail would loosen these rules, but not undo them entirely; and they constituted a norm to which at any emergency the train could return.

Their outfits varied with the wealth and power of the owners. Some men, such as Clayton and many of the young teamsters, might have nothing but a box or trunk of clothes and a rifle. The independent wagons carried everything that their owners had thought they would need or had been able to assemble, but even those outfits were often skimpy. The leaders, however, went as patriarchs. The inventory that Howard Egan made of Heber Kimball's layout indicates not only the care that went into their preparations, but the profound difference in economic status that already existed between Mormon leaders and the Mormon people:

> Teams belonging to H.C. Kimball: Horses 5, mules 7, oxen 6, cows 2, dogs 2, wagons 6. List of provisions: Flour 1228 lbs., meat 865 lbs., sea biscuit 125 lbs., beans 296 lbs., bacon 241 lbs., corn for teams 2869 lbs., buckwheat 300 lbs., dried beef 25 lbs., groceries 290¾ lbs., sole leather 15 lbs., oats 10 bus., rape 40 lbs., seeds 71 lbs., cross-cut saw 1, axes 6, scythe 1, hoes 3, log chains 5, spade 1, crowbar 1, tent 1, keg of powder 25 lbs., lead 20 lbs., codfish 40 lbs., garden seeds 50 lbs., plows 2, bran 3½ bus., 1 side of harness leather, whip saw 1, iron 16 lbs., nails 16 lbs., 1 sack of salt 200 lbs., saddles 2, tool chest worth $75, 6 pair of double harness worth about $200,... Total [value] $1592.87½.

It is a significant list. They went to discover and possess the Promised Land with their assets well concentrated in the hands of the hierarchy and itemized down to the last half-cent, but also with a

strong sense of solidarity and a considerable patriarchal responsibility of the leaders toward the led. According to a practise common during the time of the eviction from Nauvoo but later allowed
to lapse or decline, many of the lesser men were officially "adopted"
by individual leaders, and looked upon themselves as virtual members of their families.

They were in the broad sunken floodplain of the Platte, called
by the Indians the Nebraska, or Shallow Water. From their April
16 camp they could look back and see the Y of greening cottonwoods where the Elkhorn flowed down to the junction of the
rivers. A level crest of cedar-dotted bluffs shut off the east, but westward the Platte valley stretched without obstruction, level as a
floor, a highway ten to fifteen miles wide. They knew that it went
that way for hundreds of miles, clear to the mountains. Frémont's
Report called it 1,330 miles from the Elkhorn to Bear River Bay
in Great Salt Lake, and for almost half that distance the Platte or its
northern fork would have graded their road for them up the im-
perceptible slope into the West, with no more problems than
occasional quicksand fords or steep crossings of creeks, an occasional heavy slough, an occasional pull over bluffs that crowded in
to the river's edge.

The first part of their road some of them knew, and at least two
of them knew the road up the other side of the Platte nearly as far
as Fort Laramie. The Emmett-Miller party had gone this way as
far as the crossing of the Loup Fork, a little over a hundred miles
from Winter Quarters, and one of their own company, James Case,
had worked for a while at the government station near the Pawnee
Mission there. Another of their company, John Brown, had the
summer before led nineteen wagons of Mississippi Saints out the
Oregon Trail almost to Fort Laramie before turning off to find
winter shelter at Pueblo. Howard Egan, going to Santa Fe to collect an installment of the Battalion's pay, had also traveled part of
the Oregon Trail the autumn before. Also they had Frémont's
Report and Hastings' *Guide,* and they knew, as borderers, much

of the lore of the Oregon Trail, which would parallel their own
road across the river, after coming into the Platte valley at the head
of Grand Island. Though the main emigration, starting as it did from
Independence or St. Joseph, had always gone up the south side, there
was nothing difficult or unknown about the north side except the
details of fords, water, and campsites, and the question of where
to get across the Loup Fork. The general problem was profoundly
simple. You went up the Platte valley.

It was hardly quite wilderness. And yet the Missouri River, thirty
miles behind them, marked what was called the Permanent Indian
Frontier, and on their whole journey to the Great Salt Lake they
would come upon only three white habitations, one of them abandoned: the Pawnee Mission, evacuated the last autumn because of
Sioux raids; Fort Laramie; and Fort Bridger. Of Indians they would
meet first of all the Pawnees, notorious as thieves, blackmailers,
and occasional murderers, and the terror of the dwindling and
demoralized Otoes and Omahas; then the Sioux, warlike and numerous, as fearsome to the Pawnees as the Pawnees were to the
Omahas of Big Elk; then the Crows and the Shoshones, deadly
enemies, hunting the Black Hills and the Wind Rivers; and finally
the Utah Indians, an unknown quantity.

It was a journey big enough and portentous enough to start
young blood pumping, and with enough dangerous possibilities so
that most of them at first took their elaborate system of guards and
passwords very seriously. The coasts of the Nebraska closed off the
East and the known, but at sunset the West opened up in wide
wings of pink and saffron that paled to a cold green through which
they looked ineffable distances. The bugle blew. They went to their
wagons and prayed, or wrote hasty last letters to their families. The
fires died, they crawled into their blankets or under a buffalo robe.
The footsteps of the guard passed, they heard the crop and jingle
and blow of picketed horses. And they heard the night wind, blowing eastward from unimaginable Canaan, and the lonely sound of
the Platte, whose waters had come all the way from the Wind River
Mountains, talking to itself among its sands.

Except for the prayers, which were probably devout, they would have felt as all felt who ever prepared to start up that trail. It was impossible that anyone should lie in April, 1847, at the beginning of the Platte valley road, with the entire West open and the start only one sleep away, without feeling anticipation tighten his skin in gooseflesh.

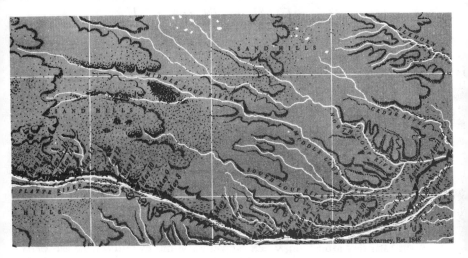

2

The Endless Platte Valley

THEIR FIRST DAY'S TRAVEL, on April 17, was an inauspicious seven miles against a bleak northwest wind. The next day, Sunday, they rested to complete their military organization before entering Pawnee country, and on that day they sent back a casualty. He was Ellis Eames, once a fiddler for dances in the Nauvoo temple, now spitting blood and according to Amasa Lyman disheartened by his sickness. Howard Egan thought him weak in the faith. History does not tell us which was right. His decision to quit was sudden, for on Saturday afternoon, when Newel K. Whitney and other visitors from Winter Quarters turned back, and when Porter Rockwell, Jesse Little, and Jackson Redden, or Redding, started for town to pick up some presents that Thomas Kane had sent for the Twelve, Eames made no move to accompany them. But the next day he caught a ride with some of Sarpy's wagons coming down from the Pawnees with robes and peltries. Truly ill or only weak in the faith, he has the distinction of being one of the very few of the 149 who started from the Missouri who failed to make it to the Great Salt Lake.

On April 19 they had an acquisition, a somewhat dubious one, to make up for him. Rolling briskly in pleasant weather up the valley, they had covered fifteen miles by the noon halt. Just as they were starting again they were overhauled by Rockwell, Little, and Redding, who had made their round-trip ride of more than a hundred miles in a day and a half. They brought the gifts from Kane, everything from patent life preservers, stop compasses, and vials of gun cotton to a supply of fine brandy, which the Twelve and a few other favored ones promptly retired to sample. But they also brought along a man who was now apparently joining them for the first time. His name was Thomas Brown, sometimes listed as Nathaniel Thomas Brown, and he hardly matched the godly character of the expedition. Norton Jacob, Amasa Lyman, and Erastus Snow all mention his arrival; Snow calls him "the notorious Tom Brown," and for cause.

He was wanted for the robbery-murder of a German named Miller, on the Iowa side of the Mississippi across from Nauvoo. His knife had been found in Miller's chest. His companions or dupes, two brothers named Hodges, had already hanged for the crime, but Sheriff William Bonney, who would later draw Tom Brown's outlaw portrait in *The Banditti of the Prairies*, wanted Brown too —wanted him worse than he wanted any other badman. But Brown had evaporated, perhaps into the Mormon sanctuary that the Gentiles were so sure existed. At any rate here he came in the company of Rockwell and Redding, neither of whom was lily-white in the eyes of the law. It is permissible to speculate that Brown wanted to come with the pioneers because the law was beginning to sniff uncomfortably close to his coattails. But why was he permitted to come? To help him escape the Gentile sheriff? Quite likely. To add firepower? Possibly. To remove him from Winter Quarters, where he might cause trouble, and keep him among men who could handle him? Perhaps. They knew perfectly well who he was, and there is no question that he was a member of the Church.

There would be no trouble with Tom Brown, at least on the way out, for Brigham's authority extended even over such hard cases as he. But once Brigham's personal authority was removed, and Brown started back from the Salt Lake Valley under Norton Jacob's captainship, Jacob would find him unruly and profane, and almost as soon as he reached the Missouri, Brown would get himself shot to death in a brawl in Council Bluffs and save Sheriff Bonney the cost of a hanging. As a member of the pioneer party, men such as Tom Brown must always have been a pebble in the shoe of Mormon piety, a grain of that violent outlaw individualism so common on the frontier and so infrequent among the Saints. Brown was as different from a truly Mormon man of violence such as Porter Rockwell as a barroom tough is from a police sergeant or a public executioner. There was really no danger in taking him along. If he had made trouble, Rockwell or another would certainly have "cut him off," in Brigham's favorite phrase, "just behind the ears," —would have cut him off cheerfully and unquestioningly despite any considerations of personal friendship. So now, whether for friendship's sake, or to keep an eye on him, or to make use of his special talents, Rockwell enlisted him among the mounted hunters and scouts.

For four days they made nearly twenty miles a day, with no excitement and with only routine discomforts and accidents. William Clayton was having a bad time with an ulcerated tooth until Luke Johnson yanked it for him. James Case, cutting cottonwoods for browse, felled a tree on one of his oxen and knocked the ox's eye out of sight into its socket, but in ten minutes the eye swam up into view again as good as ever. Passing the "new" Pawnee village near the mouth of the Loup Fork (modern Columbus, Nebraska) they resisted the Pawnees' attempt at blackmail, giving only tightwad amounts of tobacco, powder, lead, salt, and flour, and when the outraged chief refused to shake hands at parting they braced for trouble. That night Brigham asked for extra volunteers to stand guard and got a hundred takers, "amongst whom," said William Clayton waspishly, "were all the Twelve except Dr. Richards." In shifts of fifty, they shivered through a night of icy wind and rain, but saw no Indians.

Angling up along the Loup Fork hunting for the Emmett-Miller company's ford or ferry across that swift and quicksandy stream, they crossed Looking Glass and Beaver Creeks and came to the mission on Plum Creek, abandoned the fall before. It was untouched, its hay stacked inside neat rail fences, but the Sioux had burned both the government station a quarter of a mile below and the "old" Pawnee village four miles beyond. Because James Case had been fired from the government station when it was discovered he was a Mormon, Brigham permitted the pioneers to take iron, plows, wagonboxes, and other plunder, all solemnly credited to Case's account. From the mission they took only hay, as being expendable. The rawhide ropes they found around the corrals at the burned Pawnee village they appropriated on the principle of finders-keepers. There was no point now in placating the Pawnees, but in his care not to lift anything from the mission, and in his orders that men taking iron or other items from the government station keep strict account of them, Brigham acknowledged the fact that this was not a trip of passage, but the beginning of a road. Other Mormons, thousands of them, would pass this way, and should not be embarrassed by litigations or hostilities aroused by acts of the pioneers.

The Loup Fork had already diverted them forty miles or more, and they were twenty airline miles north of the Platte. Crossing the Loup to get back to the main valley was their first major difficulty. West of the burned Indian town, at modern Fullerton, Nebraska, they attempted rafting but found the river alternately too swift and too shallow. Luke Johnson, Orson Pratt, John Pack, Wilford Woodruff, and William Wordsworth tried fording, angling upstream along a bar. True to his accident-prone bias, Woodruff got in trouble, mired his team in the quicksand, and had to have his load transferred to the leather boat, the "Revenue Cutter," that they carried on a wagonbed. That was the first of a hundred times that the Revenue Cutter served them well. In the course of their journey it would be ferry, pulpit, and butcher wagon, and it would give them an advantage over every Gentile train they met on the road.

The Cutter got the five mired men across the stream, but then they found themselves marooned on the Pawnee side while the

camp made up on the other. To protect them, Brigham crossed five
more men, but the only incident of an uneasy night involved not
Indians but Brigham's own horse, which was tied too short and
choked himself to death. At meeting next day, Sunday April 25,
Brigham gave the guards such a thunderous scolding for their care-
lessness that he later felt to repent his harshness a little, and jokingly
appointed Henry Sherwood of the High Council Chief Grumbler
for the party. And that, noted Norton Jacob, put a crimp in the
style of Solomon Chamberlain, who had been bucking for the job.

They had been alarmed by the rumbling sound their wheels made
on the quicksand bottom, but they soon discovered that after a few
wagons had passed the quicksand packed down and they could
cross without trouble. Past their first real obstacle, they spent a
pleasant evening looking at the moons of Jupiter through Orson
Pratt's telescope, and appointing hunters both horse and foot. It
was the truest testimonial to their discipline that when they did
meet the buffalo, the non-hunters stayed in line, quivering but
obedient, while the favored ones, plus the Twelve, chased up and
down in that most intoxicating of all sports.

For the angling stretch from the Loup back to the Platte they
were breaking road, for Miller and Emmett had turned north from
the old Pawnee village to the mouth of the Niobrara. The dry,
scabby, roadless country at once gave them proof that it was Pawnee
territory. On the morning of April 26 the guards scared off with
gunfire six Indians who were sneaking up on the horses. A day later,
Pawnees got away in broad daylight with two horses, and the day
after that, Tom Brown, Rockwell and others had a brush with
fifteen Indians who fired at them without doing damage. Their
bad luck was compounded when John Brown, pulling his coat out
of a wagon, caught it on the hammer of his rifle, which went off
and broke the leg of Joseph Matthews' horse—the fourth good horse
to be lost in four days.

Their course was now south, sometimes even a little east. In unseasonable heat (Pratt's thermometer on April 27 registered 86 degrees) they moved on under a hanging curtain of dust and on the

twenty-eighth crossed a little stream and rocked down once more into the valley of the Platte. The grass was coming on. The valley was an even green fabric threaded by the quick channels of the river, all of it treeless except for a thin fringe of cottonwood along the banks and the green irregular beads of islands protected from the annual grass fires. They did not know it, and their journals reflect it only in half-comprehended observations, but they had come into the West. Their crossing of the Loup Fork was almost directly on the 98th meridian, that all-but-mystical line at which begins another climate, another flora and fauna, another ecology, another light, another palette, another air, another order of being. The "poor and sandy" country they had just crossed, the antelope that Woodruff shot on April 27, the first prairie dog town and the first lizards, the increasing number of wolves—these were all symptoms. So was the tendency of the dry wind "to make sore lips, parched up and feverish." So was the general "shrinking up" that they noticed; even Clayton's portable writing desk was splitting with the dryness. As they turned upriver on an Indian trail that showed occasional tracks of wagons, with Grand Island on their left, bluffy with timber, across the braiding channels of water and sand, they passed their first alkali flats and tasted that bitter dust, and saw the white rumps of many antelope coasting away ahead. Westward there was no timber at all except on the island. The grass now was a variety new to them, the short curly kind they called buffalo grass.

The weather turned from sudden heat to sudden cold by the time they reached Wood River, now a station on the Union Pacific and all through the emigration a favorite stopping place for wagon-trains. Their camp on April 30, twenty miles farther on, was their first night in the incontrovertible West, for there for the first time they had to dig for drinkable water, and there for the first time they burned the fuel that "to save a hard word" was called buffalo chips. The western climate explained those too; anywhere in a wet country they would have remained cow pies. Novelty inspired their inventiveness. Heber Kimball constructed a fire pit made of three holes connected by draft tunnels, Luke Johnson devised a buffalo-skull chimney. Then on May 1 they encountered the source of those most useful chips and skulls, that universal provider and basic resource, giver of meat and thread and glue and leather, food and house and fire, that heroic excitement, that object of passion and reverence, that very symbol of the West, the buffalo himself.

Discipline kept them moving while the inexperienced hunters galloped and panted after the game, but every journal lifts to the encounter and counts the bag, not always to the same total. Apparently they killed twelve. Jackman reports that the camp looked like a meat market—and none too soon either for such as Jackman and his wagonmate Lyman Curtis, who had been living on corn-bread and water porridge and the occasional buffalo-fish they seined out of sloughs.

Made cautious by the smoke of burning prairie ahead, Brigham ordered a day's layover for blacksmithing and general repairs, during which many plainsmen in the making tried their hands at raw-hide halters and lariats. He read the camp rules over with vigor, and he had the cannon fired off just to let any passing Indians know they had one. A reconnoitering party sent on ahead found camp-fires still smoking, and William Empey was sure he saw a band of four hundred Indians hiding in a gulch. Others were of the opinion he had seen a band of antelope, but there was no question that there were Indians hunting the buffalo all around them, and when the camp started again on May 4 the wagons went four abreast for quicker corralling in an emergency.

They met no emergency. Instead, across the Platte on the Oregon Trail which had come down to the river opposite Wood River, they saw wagons, and one of the wagoners, fording to talk, presented them with a dilemma. He was Charles Beaumont, a halfbreed in Sarpy's employ, sixteen days out of Fort Laramie with ox teams. He advised the Saints to cross and take the road on the south side, which was good and hard, empty of Indians, and with good feed. The ford here (they were just above the site that would soon be Fort Kearney) was easy, only knee deep and with a good bottom. For several reasons they seriously considered taking his advice.

The road up the north bank was unknown to them, and threatened by Indians and grass fires. They could see the prairie burning for miles, and feed for the next days was certain to be short. If they crossed now they avoided at a stroke all the awkward possibilities. On the other hand it weighed on all of them, as a sacred responsibility, that they were "making a road for thousands of Saints to follow." They did not want to expose themselves or those Mormons who came later to the Oregon and California companies that traveled the south bank. Moreover, this ford might not be easy in all seasons. Companies meeting it during the summer rise might find it impassable, and so have to pioneer their way up the north side encumbered by all their women and children.

Two men sent across to check on Beaumont's words found the ford easy and the road on the other side hard and good, as he said. Nevertheless the Mormons voted to continue as they had started: separateness was in their institutions and their blood, and might as well be in their roads too. They gave Beaumont the sugar and coffee he and his men craved, and accepted his offer to carry letters back, and then they rolled on, to camp on Clear Creek on burned-over ground where the buffalo chips were still smoking and there was no feed whatever.

All the next day a strong wind from the south fanned the burning grass, forcing them to keep to windward, along the river where the going was soft and miry. After twelve to fourteen miles by their guesswork reckoning they met a wall of fire spreading from bluffs to river and had to turn back to camp on an island. Though they had already fed all the corn they could spare, their animals were failing. They began to wonder if they had been wrong to reject Beaumont's advice. But in the night the Lord sent a shower that doused the burning prairie, and with a hard drive the next day they got beyond the burned country and into good grass again. Their route was so alive with buffalo that they had great difficulty to keep their cattle from mixing with the wild herds. In one chase after some oxen that Erastus Snow had allowed to escape, Brigham lost what Lorenzo Young spelled as his "spiglace." Promptly he forgot his appointment of Sherwood as Chief Grumbler. He lit on Snow and gave him a chastisement that a half dozen journals record. Snow himself ruefully set it down as "a regular built dressing . . . In attempting to exonerate myself from blame I drew from him a severer chastisement . . . the first I have had since I have been in this church, which is nearly fifteen years, and I hope it may last me fifteen years to come." Fortunately for Brother Snow, Porter Rockwell rode back and found the lost spyglass, and Brigham's wrath, which was often lasting, cooled down. But that scolding was a demonstration that this was indeed a peculiar people. In any other wagontrain, such a scolding of a grown man, and a prominent man at that, would have meant rebellion and probably violence. Here it meant meek submission, for even when he exploded about a piece of personal property Brigham spoke as the Lion of the Lord.

From the beginning of the trip, William Clayton's clerkly nature had been offended by the discrepancies among their guesses of the day's mileage. He was one who liked precision—and also he wanted to prove that his own guesses were more accurate than those of some others. As one of the expedition's clerks, he was supposed to keep a careful record of distances, camping places, water, timber, and grass, and he thought that everyone except himself overestimated. On the third day out from the Elkhorn he had consulted with Orson Pratt about possible ways of rigging cogs to a wagon hub so as to measure distances accurately, and he had brought up the idea several times since without getting any action. On May 8 he undertook to justify himself without the aid of science. He measured the wheel of Heber Kimball's wagon and found it to be fourteen feet eight inches in circumference, a wheel that to his astonishment made exactly 360 revolutions to the mile. So he tied a rag on a spoke and all that day walked beside the wheel and counted the rag every time it came around. When they stopped after ten miles, he added his measured distance to his estimate of their previous mileage, and put up the first marker on the Mormon Trail: a cedar post on which he had written in pencil, "From Winter Quarters, two hundred ninety-five miles, May 8, '47. Camp all well. Wm. Clayton."

His total measured mileage for that day was eleven and a quarter miles plus twenty revolutions. Inquiring around, he found that some had guessed the day at as much as fourteen miles. So when they moved on next day to hunt better grass, even though it was Sunday, he counted revolutions again, and at the end of the day put up a second post with a board on it, this time not neglecting the proper credits: "From Winter Quarters three hundred miles, May 9, 1847, Pioneer Camp All Well. Distance according to the reckoning of Wm. Clayton." To make the credit line all the more necessary, Willard Richards chose that camp as the place to leave a letter for the following company, inserting it in a sawcrack in a piece of wood and mounting it on a prominent post. *His* distance from Winter Quarters was 316 miles.

That was the day they came to the junction of the north and south forks of the Platte, and bent northwestward to follow the more northerly stream. Clayton was still doggedly counting revolutions, but by now Orson Pratt had at Brigham's order put his mind to the "roadometer" that "Clayton and several others" had been suggesting, and Appleton Harmon, a good mechanic, was starting to whittle the cogs out of a piece of wood.

It is a long walk up the dusty Platte valley, whether one is counting revolutions of a wheel or merely plodding. The valley grew drearier and dustier; it had for many miles been entirely treeless. Feed was poor, the weather changeable, the ground littered with the bones of countless buffalo, some of which evidently had been driven by Indians over the bluffs. Here and there they saw human bones among the others, the unhistoried leavings of accident or war. Endurance and tempers were strained. Both Clayton and Woodruff reported ambiguous vivid dreams, Thomas Tanner and Lorin Farr had hard words because Tanner, of the guard, arrested Farr for talking after bugle. William Empey reports that on May 11 Sylvester Earl and Zebedee Coltrin had to be separated. Coltrin, Empey said, "has done all the Rangling in the camp," and was universally held to be a "quarles some man." Not everyone, it seems, could scold with Brigham's authority or impunity.

For Clayton the days now were easier. Appleton Harmon had finished the roadometer and installed it on a wagon hub. It operated as an endless screw, six revolutions of the wheel turning the screw once, and the screw in turn acting upon a wheel of sixty cogs, one full turn of which would equal a mile. But within two days Clayton's joy in the accomplishment of his idea had soured. "I discovered that Brother Appleton Harmon is trying to have it understood that he invented the machinery to tell the distance we travel, which makes me think less of him than I formerly did. He is not the inventor of it by a long way, but he has made the machinery, after being told how to do it. What little souls work."

The valley of the North Platte had narrowed, with bluffs that several times came to the water's edge and forced them, double-teaming, over hard climbs before they could get back to level going. Feed was better and the buffalo fatter, but they were troubled to come upon recent Indian kills and to see the tracks of moccasins —Sioux from the fact that they were pointed and shaped to fit right and left foot. On Sunday May 1, Appleton Harmon added a second gear to the roadometer so that it would count miles as well as revolutions, and Clayton put up another signboard, 356¾ miles from Winter Quarters, and Richards left another letter protected from the weather in a wooden case. Brigham unlimbered his tongue against the mounted hunters for not helping to scout out a way for the wagons, and against the captains of ten for murmuring when they got only fore-quarters of buffalo. The first and second hundreds were bickering about priority on the trail, which was the worst they had met, until Brigham announced that anyone who held up the procession would be penalized by bringing up the rear, in the dust. Dr. Richards, ever willing to find work for William Clayton, proposed to him that he assemble data for a new map of the route, supported by Orson Pratt's observations, which they had found often in disagreement with Frémont's. As if to give them

an accurate starting-place for their scientific data, they pulled opposite a cedar island and recognized the wooded coulee across the
river as Ash Hollow, a landmark on the trail to Oregon. And as if
to make science more difficult, the rain-swollen second screw of
the roadometer broke, so that Clayton had to start keeping track
of miles again, and Harmon to renew his whittling.

Even with the passing of a landmark that assured them they had
been making progress, that Platte valley was of an endless, weary
length. Every mile Clayton recorded had to be ground out through
sand or soft sloughs or over gravelly bluffs, 360 slow turnings of the
wheel for every slow mile. The incontrovertible West that they
had entered opposite Grand Island was more incontrovertible now.
They killed rattlesnakes and raided eagles' nests in the bluffs, dug
wolf pups out of dens in the slopes, were so badly fooled by the
clear air that they repeatedly shot at buffalo well out of range, found
bones of great beasts "turned into solid hard stone, which proves
that the atmosphere is pure and the country would doubtless be
healthy." Romantic castle-like formations began to lift ahead of
them, and their farmer eyes were astonished at the raw confusion
of "rocks, gravil and sand jest as it hapned." New plants sprouted
from the arid earth—Indian soap weed, or yucca; prickly pear; Old
Man weed. Across the North Platte they could sometimes catch a
glimpse of the ruts that were the trail to Oregon.

The newness perked them up and tempted them into horseplay.
They christened Solomon Chamberlain "the most even-tempered
man" because he was the worst crab in camp; they held a mock
trial of James Davenport "for blockading the highway and turning
the ladies out of their course." We are left to imagine what Davenport might have been doing in the road. On Sunday, May 23, climbing the bluffs to see Chimney Rock, which Port Rockwell had reported to be visible from there, Nathaniel Fairbanks was bitten by
a rattlesnake, and the rest of them brought him in just in time to
run into a brisk sermon by Brigham on the subjects of profanity
and general horsing around. But he praised them in general, because "no one had refused to obey his counsel on the journey," and

the meeting actually added to rather than diminished the hilarity of the camp because Brother Heber, having his hat blow off while he was praying, refused to interrupt his conversation with the Lord and in consequence had to chase his hat for three-quarters of a mile.

So far they had met only two Sioux, a man and his wife, both definitely friendly. Now they encountered thirty-five of them—magnificent, clean, well-dressed, noble-looking, many cuts above the demoralized Omahas or the thievish Pawnees. The Saints were universally impressed, extended overnight hospitality to the chief and his wife, and gave them a thrill by letting them observe the moon through Pratt's telescope. In the morning there were more visits, some trading, much handshaking. "Truely gentlemen and ladies," said Levi Jackman, and Thomas Bullock wrote the chief a "recommend" to go with his letters from Papin and other Fort Laramie traders. Seven years hence, an incident involving a lame Mormon cow would precipitate the so-called "Grattan massacre" and send these Indians into abrupt bloody war, but now all was geniality and good will. Stephen Markham traded a used-up mule for an Indian pony, bade his Indian friends goodbye, and hitched the pony in with his team. By the time the spooked team had run itself out (they went by Woodruff's carriage "like electricity," he said) they were opposite Chimney Rock.

For the Saints, as for every traveler who passed it, Chimney Rock was a principal milestone. Its inverted funnel, in sight for more than forty miles, was the true indicator of the higher, drier country, not yet mountains but the beginning of the roughening of the plains. Though it was only 425 miles from Winter Quarters by Clayton's reckoning, they chose to regard it as a sort of halfway mark. After days and weeks of the monotonous Platte valley with only the level coasts of the Nebraska along the skyline, they thought the scenery around Chimney Rock the most romantic and sublime they had ever seen; and what Levi Jackman called the Scotch Bluffs had "the sam apearance of decyed magnificence." Full of euphoria, Bullock planted three of his grains of corn at that campground, hopeful of demonstrating the fertility of the soil. Their evenings now were lively—no retirement to prayers at 8:30 and fires out at 9:00. The fiddles and jew's-harps were out, men danced together, Heber Kimball had to rebuke some card players and protest against a spirit of levity.

Then on May 29, Brigham's wrath boiled over. They had stopped for the weather, which was wet and cold. About half past ten in the morning Brigham had the leather boat drawn to the center of camp and had the bugle blown and the roll called. Nathaniel Fairbanks was still recovering from his snake bite, and Elijah Newman was likewise sick; two were out hunting. The rest were there, to be slowly and methodically skinned alive. Brigham reminded them of the sacrifices they had all agreed to make, and of the sobriety proper to men who held the priesthood. Instead of sobriety, what did they have? "When I wake up in the morning, the first thing I hear is some of the brethren jawing each other and quarreling because a horse has got loose in the night. I have let the brethren dance and fiddle and act the nigger night after night to see what they will do ... Well, they will play cards, they will play checkers, they will play dominoes, and if they had the privilege and were where they could get whiskey, they would be drunk half their time, and in one week they would quarrel, get to high words and draw their knives and kill each other ... Do you suppose that we are going to look out a home for the Saints, a resting place, a place of peace where they can build up the kingdom and bid the nations welcome, with a low, mean, dirty, trifling, covetous, wicked spirit dwelling in our bosoms?"

With an unfailing instinct, even while he blistered them he allowed them a half-alibi, he suggested scapegoats. "I understand that there are several in this camp who do not belong to the Church. I am the man who will stand up for them and protect them in their rights. And they shall not trample on our rights now ... They shall reverence and acknowledge the name of God and His priesthood, and if they set up their heads and seek to introduce iniquity into this camp and to trample on the priesthood, I swear to them, they shall never go back to tell the tale."

Rough words, the blunt ruthlessness of a man now so far from external controls that he could speak his mind plainly. If they didn't like his attitude, he said, they could turn around and go back—not exactly a tempting notion nearly five hundred miles out in the Indian country. He told them that he refused to proceed so long as the camp retained its present spirit. He told them he wanted them to get ready for meeting in the morning, instead of lying around playing cards. He guessed that fasting and prayer wouldn't do any of them any harm. Then he called the roll of the High Priests, and the Seventies, and the Bishops, and the Elders, and the Quorum of the Twelve, all the interlocking directorates of Mormon organization, and asked them in turn if they were ready to cease their wicked nonsense and get in line. Every hand went up. The spirit of revival began to work in them. Heber Kimball and Orson Pratt bore their testimony, and Wilford Woodruff reminded them what had happened to Zion's Camp when it was marching against Missouri and fell into quarrelsome ways. Stephen Markham rose and confessed his guilt and begged forgiveness, weeping like a child. All around the circle of wagons, hitched up for travel but still wheel-locked, men's cheeks were wet with the ecstasy of self-blame. When they were dismissed, and started to roll, there was no swearing at mules or oxen, no laughter. "It truly seemed," said William Clayton, "as though the cloud had burst and we had emerged into a new element, a new atmosphere, and a new society."

The cleansing lasted. During the morning, the Twelve and nine others "clothed" and retired from camp to go through some of the holier rituals, with Carrington and Porter Rockwell standing guard. At three they broke their fast on boiled beans and sea biscuit, and the rain, which had held off to let the priesthood complete its meeting, began to come down hard. But that night, as the rain tapered off, the moon swam out, and shining over the misty river produced a perfect lunar rainbow—an omen, a bow in the firmament, the Lord's promise that He accepted their offering of a contrite heart. These signs shall follow them that believe.

When they rose next morning they saw the early sun pink on

a snowpeak far to the west: Laramie Peak, the first of the mountains. On June 1 they drew up opposite the ruins of old Fort Platte, at the mouth of Laramie Fork, and set up their forges to reset tires and reshoe animals while Brigham and the Twelve went down to visit the trader Bordeaux at Fort Laramie, two miles west.

By their several reckonings they were anywhere from 522 to 554 miles from Winter Quarters, and in better health than when they started. Their casualties had been only four horses lost to accidents or to the Pawnees. Spiritually they were as a new-washed garment, in the best possible shape to confront the temptations of Fort Laramie and the polluting influence of the Gentile trains that they might meet from here on. Brother Brigham had been well-advised to deliver his purifying sermon just before they were due to make renewed contact with Babylon.

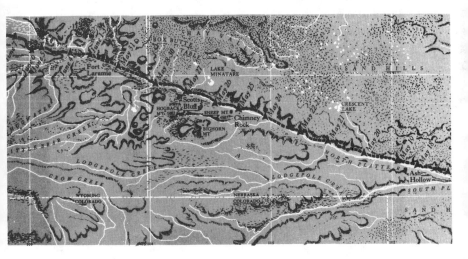

3

The Dreary Black Hills

MODERN PILGRIMS FROM THE EAST, even some who can distinguish Ohio from Iowa and both from Idaho, are likely to be a little confused about whether or not Fort Laramie on the Overland Trail is the same place as Laramie, the home of the University of Wyoming; and even if they know that the fort is a hundred-odd miles northeast of the city, those who read trail history may be confused by pioneer references to the Black Hills, and vaguely imagine that the trail ran so far north that it touched the southern end of the Black Hills of South Dakota. It did not. The Black Hills of South Dakota are 150 miles from the track of the western wagons. The Black Hills spoken of in overland journals are the Laramie Range, which runs southeast to northwest between the 105th and 107th meridians, roughly parallel to the course of the North Platte, so that to travelers approaching Fort Laramie it showed ahead and to the left.

Some men may labor all their lives in a region, as did Father De Smet, and leave hardly a mark on the map. But the obscure French Canadian called Jacques La Ramée, by the simple expedient of getting himself killed by Indians on a remote Rocky Mountain stream, left his name on the stream, on the mountains out of which it flows, on the highest peak of that range, on the high plains that reach southward from the range, on a county, and on a city—and on the most important way station in all the West. It was one of the great fixed points of the later fur trade, in the heart of the Sioux country, on the way to the Shoshone country, linked to Bent's Fort (Pueblo) by a well-traveled trail along the Laramie Fork and the Chugwater, linked to the lower Missouri posts by the great highway of the Platte valley.

Established in 1835 by William Sublette, it was first called Fort William for its builder. In 1841 the log fort was rebuilt of adobes on almost the same site and renamed Fort John, for John Sarpy, whom the Mormons knew as the friendly bourgeois of the American Fur Company post at Bellevue, below Winter Quarters. But not everyone called it Fort John. Most knew it as Fort Laramie, and literally everyone who traveled the Overland Trail knew it. Whether bound for Oregon, California, or the valleys of the mountains, whether traveling south bank or north, they had to come up the trough of the North Platte, and just at the bottleneck where the river emerged from rough country into the comparative open, there sat the fort on its barren gravel flat within a bright swift curve of the Laramie Fork, two miles above its junction with the North Platte.

Emigrants coming up the south bank forded the Laramie Fork to reach the fort, those coming up the North Platte forded or ferried the North Platte, depending on the season and the stage of water. From Fort Laramie onward to beyond South Pass, a distance of three hundred miles, the country cramped the several streams of the emigration into a single channel, at least at first. After 1850, when a way was opened along the north bank of the North Platte between the mouth of the Laramie Fork and the so-called Last Crossing (modern Casper, Wyoming), some trains, especially Mormon trains, elected to by-pass Fort Laramie. Their reasons were various—hurry because of lateness on the trail, fear of contamination by Gentile companies, unwillingness to pay bridge or ferry charges, or plain well-organized bull-headed self-sufficiency. But most, after weeks of plodding up the hot, dusty, treeless, brain-baking Platte valley, found the attractions of companionship, news, trail information, gossip, trade, repairs, and Taos Lightning more than mortal flesh could resist even if it wanted to.

At various times there were rival trading posts along the same bottleneck. Sybille, Adams and Company built Fort Platte at the mouth of Laramie Fork in 1840 or 1841, but abandoned it in 1845. Throughout the 1850's, fly-by-night traders set up shop in huts and dugouts in the stretch between Scotts Bluff and Laramie Fork —and for that matter all the way along the trail as far as the Green River—to sell basic supplies, principally whiskey. But whatever these blood brothers to the gas station and motel and snakepit keepers of our modern western highways may have offered the Indians, they provided inadequate and undependable services and second-rate company to the wagontrains, and except in emergencies were not likely to cut seriously into Fort Laramie's business. Once Fort Laramie became a military post in the summer of 1849, it had all the more advantage over the competition. In the five years following the June day in 1847 when the Mormon pioneers drew up opposite Fort Platte's adobe ruins, nearly 150,000 people would pour west up the two branches of the trail, and nearly all would go directly past Fort Laramie, and nearly all would stop.

The pioneers had no intention of not stopping. They wanted trail information and they wanted news of their Pueblo contingent, composed of the Mississippi Saints that John Brown had taken over there in the fall of 1846 and the Sick Detachment of the Battalion. They got their news before they could form camp. Two horsemen hailed them from across the deep, swift-flowing river. Brought over in the Revenue Cutter, they turned out to be Brother Robert Crow and his son-in-law George Therlkill, who had come over from Pueblo with fourteen others of the Mississippi Saints under the guidance of a mountain man named Lewis Myers, and who had been waiting here for two weeks to make their long-delayed union with the Camp of Israel. They brought word of four deaths among the Battalion boys—deaths that had to be attributed either to a failure of their faith, since Brigham had promised that not one of

A PORTFOLIO
of MORMON TRAIL ENGRAVINGS
by
FREDERICK HAWKINS PIERCY
and
THOMAS MORAN

In the summer of 1853 the English artist Frederick Hawkins Piercy accompanied a company of Mormon converts from Liverpool to New Orleans, up the Mississippi to Nauvoo, and west along the Mormon Trail to Salt Lake City (See Part II, Chapter 7). His sketches were published in *Route from Liverpool to Great Salt Lake Valley* in 1855. In 1873, twenty years after Piercy and four after the completion of the transcontinental railroad, the noted landscape painter and illustrator Thomas Moran traveled west along the route from the Missouri to Salt Lake City, sketching the still-unaltered landmarks of the Trail for William Cullen Bryant's "coffee-table" book *Picturesque America*, Volume II, 1874.

These two series of pictures, reproduced as steel and wood engravings, offer the best record of what the travelers along the Trail saw, and how it impressed them.

Carthage Jail (Piercy). From its upper window Joseph Smith fell wounded, to be propped at the well curb and finished with a volley. By his death the Mormon exodus was made inevitable.

Nauvoo Temple (Piercy). Seven years after their flight the Nauvoo Temple, profaned by mobs, fired by an arsonist, damaged by storms and partly wrecked as a safety measure, was already a grandiose ruin.

Kanesville (Piercy). Across Iowa's dolorous miles, enduring snow, sleet, rain, mud, rattlesnakes, dysentery, scurvy, and bitter death, the fleeing Mormons came to the end of the first leg of their journey on the east bank of the Missouri at Kanesville, now Council Bluffs.

Winter Quarters (Piercy). Kanesville was evacuated by the Mormons in 1852. Winter Quarters, across the river, had been cleared by government order in 1848. Piercy found it gone back to grass, its last cabin in flames.

Mormon Ferry (Piercy). The Mormon ferry linking Kanesville and the Indian Lands, later Nebraska, was for a full generation of Saints their gateway into the wilderness, the true beginning of the road to Zion.

Elkhorn Ferry (Piercy). Elkhorn Ferry, rendezvous for scores of Mormon wagon trains: the camp for checking outfits, girding loins, saying prayers: last chance for the faint-hearted to turn back: the jumping-off place.

Chimney Rock (Piercy). The fabled landmarks made tourists out of pilgrims, bad poets out of good diarists. Chimney Rock might beckon on the horizon of a slow train for nearly a week.

Scott's Bluff (Piercy). By Scott's Bluff they had penetrated into a new world of strange forms, strange colorings, parching air, deceptive distances: buffalo country, horned-toad country, wolf country—the authentic West.

Fort Laramie (Piercy). Fort Laramie in the Y of the rivers, where plains broke into mountains: bastion of the fading fur trade, major supply post on the Trail. Comforting themselves, they called it halfway.

Laramie's Peak (Piercy). Landmark for many miles in advance, dominant feature of what the emigrants called the Black Hills, Laramie Peak in the Laramie Range marked the beginning of the mountains, the end of the relatively easy Platte River road.

Independence Rock (Piercy). Carved and painted with ten thousand names famous or lost, Independence Rock marked the end of another segment of the Trail, the segment of alkali sinks and poison creeks, and the beginning of a difficult love affair with the Sweetwater.

Devil's Gate (Piercy). Where the Sweetwater, scorning an easy corner, had cut Devil's Gate through the Rattlesnake Range, there would be men and boys at evening rolling rocks off the cliffs or firing guns for echoes.

Church Butte (Moran). On the west side of South Pass, past the crossing of the Green and the crossing of Ham's Fork and the several crossings of Black's Fork, Mormon trains made a habit of stopping at Church Butte, a landmark visible for several days, a good place to let the kids try their climbing skill.

Fort Bridger (Piercy). Built by Jim Bridger in 1843 and operating as a meager supply station and blacksmithing service station for Oregon, California, and Utah wagontrains until the Mormons bought it in 1853, Fort Bridger was a ramshackle station in a beautiful, well-watered setting when Piercy came through. In 1857 the Mormons burned it to delay the advance of Johnston's army, and in 1859 the army, forced to winter there, rebuilt it.

Castle Rock (Moran). From Chimney Rock and
Courthouse Rock onward, the erosional forms of the
dry country had amazed travelers with their resemblance
to human architecture. Those forms came to a climax
in Echo Canyon, the first stage of the passage through
the Wasatch, where nearly every diarist saw fortresses,
castles, battlements, and ruined cities, and marked them
for the attention of later travelers so that they became
looked-for tourist attractions.

Monument Rock (Moran). Another architectural monument, idealized by a great romantic painter.

Witches' Rocks (Piercy). In Weber Canyon, one of the two routes into the Salt Lake Valley, the architectural broke into the fantastic. Piercy's drawing, rendered as steel engraving, saw the Witches' Rocks more or less realistically.

Witches' Rocks (Moran). Moran, an idealizer of landscape, reported
them in this wood engraving in gothic and heightened forms.

Devil's Slide (Moran). The Devil had a good deal to do with the making of the West, if we may believe the West's place names. Devil's Gate, Hell's Half Acre, Devil's Slide, punctuate the mountain section of the Trail. This volcanic dike in Weber Canyon is still something tourists pause to wonder at. So did the Mormon wagons. So did the railroad tourists of 1873.

Weber River—Entrance to Echo Canyon (Moran). Here, almost within shouting distance of the Valley, wagon trains made a decision, whether to go down the difficult rock-and-tree-choked canyon of the Weber or whether to turn left along the difficult tree-choked way to the head of Parley's Canyon and down Parley's and across the hard slopes of Big Mountain and into Emigration Canyon and so to safety in Zion.

A Kanyon in the Rocky Mountains (Piercy). It was a particular trial to travelers along the Mormon Trail that its most difficult mountain section came at the very gates of the valley. Wagons, animals, human spirits, were at their lowest ebb when they came to the hardest trial.

Great Salt Lake (Piercy). At last, "like Moses from Pisgay's top," they looked upon a desert valley rimmed with mountains, watered by quick streams flowing into a Dead Sea: sanctuary: the promised land: Zion.

Salt Lake City in 1853 (Piercy). "And the solitary place shall be made glad for them, and the desert shall rejoice and blossom as the rose." The city of the Saints as Piercy saw it six years after its founding.

the faithful would die, or, more darkly, to the persecutions and calomel of the army doctor. Other news was that the Sick Detachment would be paid off in a few days at the end of their year's enlistment, and intended coming on through Laramie to catch up with the pioneers.

Of the Mississippi Saints, who with their hunter Myers brought the total company to 152 men, eight women, and five children, none was particularly noteworthy unless it was George Therlkill. Without knowing it, he had already fumbled his way into history, for in Pueblo, while recovering from a mauling by a grizzly the autumn before, he had so annoyed young Francis Parkman with his insistent quizzing that Parkman in a fit of Brahmin distaste wrote him up as a sample of the loutishness of western emigrants. But Therlkill was destined to get into the record in a sadder way. Less than three weeks after their arrival in the Salt Lake Valley, his three-year-old son would drown in City Creek, and would fill the first white grave in Zion.

Leaving the brethren to reset tires and repair chains and wagons, and to satisfy their sightseeing itch with the ruins of Fort Platte or with the search for Indian beads on the "pis aunt's houses," Brigham took the Twelve and a few others to visit the fort. They found it in charge of James Bordeaux while the bourgeois, P. D. Papin, was off taking furs and robes to Fort Pierre. Bordeaux, who had already seen many kinds of people pass under Fort Laramie's adobe walls, and would see many more, was friendly and informative. They would find the north bank road impassable for wagons after four miles, and should therefore cross here: he would ferry them for twenty-five cents a wagon, or rent them his flatboat for fifteen dollars. On this side the road was good, though rough in places where it cut across the apron of the Black Hills. They did not need to fear the Sioux, who would not steal on their own land, but the Crows only three weeks ago had got away with the fort's entire horse herd, stealing them under the noses of the guard within three hundred yards of the walls. He offered blacksmithing service, and was impressed to hear that they already had three forges of their own going. His stories of the disorderliness of some Missouri trains, especially the one led through last year by their old enemy Lillburn Boggs, gratified them. Diplomatically, he made them feel what in fact they were—disciplined and well-behaved—and demonstrated what has become a truism since: that no one is so popular among the Saints as a Gentile who expresses a good opinion of them. All the journals that mention Bordeaux mention him with special approval.

Ending this pleasant visit, the party piled into Bordeaux' flatboat and had a swift boatride down to the junction. The next day, June 3, they sent Apostle Amasa Lyman and three companions to Pueblo, to meet and guide the people there, and between rains began ferrying the river, making a contest of it between the first and second hundreds. They were good at such team sports: the winners averaged a wagon every eleven minutes. And they had need of haste, for just as rain stopped them for the day, riders came up the trail who said they had personally counted five hundred wagons close behind, and had heard that there were 2,000 within a few days. The Gentile emigration was catching up.

Not eager to share the trail with Gentiles, or to have Gentiles get ahead and use up the grass, the Saints were ferrying again by 4:30 the next morning, but Brigham delayed them by walking to the fort for another conversation with Bordeaux, and it was noon before they were on the road. Most of them had seen no more of Fort Laramie than they could glimpse passing by, and they had formed no deeper acquaintance with the fort's French Canadian population than to observe that "thoes jentle men has got squass for their companions," as William Empey wrote in a mood of calculated neutrality. But they had learned that a mountain man (that would be Miles Goodyear, whom they would meet in person on the Bear River Divide) had squatted in the Bear River Valley (Weber Valley, the site of modern Ogden) and was raising crops there. They had gathered data for the use of later companies, including for some reason a solemn measuring of the ruins of Fort Platte. Their wagons were in good repair and their animals rested.

Harriet Young had been able to bake up bread and pies, the ladies had picked some nice messes of greens, everybody had brought his journal up to date, and many had written letters. The plains half of the trip was over, now for the mountain half.

Their first night's camp was in the pleasant cottonwood-shaded bottoms near what later came to be called Register Cliff, one of those "frontier post-offices" where hundreds of emigrants scratched their names and the date of their passage. Since no diarist mentions the cliff, it had evidently not yet achieved fame. Their second day out, June 5, they crawled up over the bluffs west of modern Guernsey, Wyoming, where today's tourist may see the trail rutted nearly four feet deep in the soft rock, and as they were nooning at the warm spring which Frémont had noted, they were passed by an Oregon company that had left Independence on April 22 and was pushing to stay ahead of everything on the road. Next morning another Oregon train passed them, and there were murmurs and dark looks, for in this company were some recognized Missourians. But segregation was impossible, for water and camping sites were scarce, and at Cottonwood Creek (the Hermann Ranch) the Saints found themselves corralling only a little beyond this second Oregon company. For all their mutual suspicion, there was some hobnobbing. Some of the Missourians had heard about the roadometer, and came over to inspect it. Burr Frost, one of the Mormon blacksmiths, got some credit in heaven by setting up his forge and repairing a carriage spring for one of them.

Having left the river valley just beyond Register Cliff, they were now cutting across rough country on a road full of cobblestones and interrupted by numerous tributary streams. For the sake of the Saints coming after, though it must have exasperated them to be aiding the Gentiles too, they put road gangs to work throwing rocks out of the track and digging down the steepest pitches and leveling approaches to fords. Clayton was putting up signposts every ten miles now, and noting the campsites, which along this stretch were generally good. Every tributary creek provided clear water, wood, good grass, sometimes fishing. At Horseshoe Creek, where a few years later the notorious Jack Slade would run a stage station, the smell of crushed mint perfumed the whole camp. It was considerably different from the Platte valley. The darkly timbered Laramie Range along the southwest showed them patches of snow.

On La Bonte Creek (modern Douglas, Wyoming) they met some traders, friends of Lewis Myers, who agreed to carry letters back and who said they had left a bullboat hanging in a tree at the Last Crossing, seventy miles ahead, which the Saints might have. By now the Missouri companies were several miles in advance of the pioneers. To beat them to the crossing, Brigham sent on nineteen wagons and about forty men with the Revenue Cutter. Shortly afterward, four men on horses and mules passed, riding hard. The Saints did not know it, but one of the mules had been stolen from their brethren in Pueblo.

On that populous road, hard-riding horse thieves were only a momentary diversion. They took more interest in a toad encountered by Brigham and Heber, which had horns on its head, and a tail, and did not hop but crawled like a mouse. Like the long-tailed deer the hunters were now bringing in, like the innumerable crickets, the bunch grass, the tall sagebrush, that horned toad was part of the new mountain ecology. So were the bright silvery fish that William Clayton and others caught in Deer Creek, at whose mouth they came down again into the valley of the North Platte. These were grayling, Rocky Mountain herring. They so intrigued Clayton that he rose at four to try for more of them, and "the calm, still morning with the warbling of many birds, the rich grass, good streams, and plenty of timber" made him homesick for England. He was not alone in his pleasure. Erastus Snow and Thomas Bullock record Deer Creek (the site of modern Glenrock, Wyoming) in superlatives, and Albert Carrington, who found a bed of stone coal in the bluffs, thought it the best place for a settlement between the Missouri and South Pass.

But if their pleasure in that well-watered glen indicated the shadow of a temptation, a feeling that perhaps here was that valley of the mountains they were in search of, the fact that it was absolutely athwart the trail, and that the trail crawled with Missouri wagons, would have quickly squashed any brief wistful dream of settling. When they caught up with two Missouri companies which had camped to ferry the river twelve miles below the usual ferry at Last Crossing, Thomas Bullock thought the brawling and swearing from the Missouri camps abominable, and the noise ten times that made by the Saints. Nevertheless, even here the trail promoted a certain fraternization. Stephen Markham talked of the Missouri troubles with the father of one of the guards who had let Joseph Smith escape from Liberty Jail, and who had been ridden to death on an iron bar by his fellows for his softness. Dark, half-pleasant reminiscences of old violence, a sharing of memory with this man whose son had suffered death for his kindness to the prophet. Not quite fellowship, but something short of hostility, with suspicion temporarily allayed. A Missourian gave Porter Rockwell part of a snowball he had brought down from the hills. We can hear their wonder. Snow in June!

Testing the river every so often for ferrying or fording places, they went on another dozen miles until, about 3¾ miles above modern Casper, they came up with their advance party, camped near two Oregon trains. They had not found the mountaineers' bullboat, but their own Revenue Cutter, which would carry 1,500 to 1,800 pounds, had turned out a gold mine. They were busy ferrying Missourians for $1.50 a load payable in flour at Independence prices— that is to say, at $2.50 a hundred rather than at the ten dollars it would have cost at Laramie. The whole operation looked like another of those manna-droppings by which the Lord was accustomed to help them along. Wilford Woodruff so interpreted it, but he was in a mood of thanksgiving and faith anyway, because he had just been bitten on the knee by Brother Brigham's horse. The horse's teeth had gone to the bone through three layers of clothing, one of them buckskin, but the leg had not been bitten off, and so the incident qualified as one of Woodruff's remarkable providences, and went down in the book with his long list of falls, shootings, near-drownings, and sicknesses unto death.

Travelers late in the season often found the North Platte here clear and shrunken and shallow enough to be waded, but in June it was a hundred yards wide and fifteen feet deep, with a current strong enough to roll a swimming horse. (It did in fact drown Myers' buffalo horse.) The Revenue Cutter could carry the wagons' loads, but the wagons themselves were a problem. While some of the Saints brought down poles from the mountain and worked at making rafts, others experimented with swinging wagons across the river on a long rope tied to the opposite bank. Two wagons tied together keeled over on striking the far shore, breaking the reach of one and the bows of the other. Four lashed together proved to be stabler, but too heavy to handle. One alone, with an outrigger of poles to steady it, was caught by the current and the strong southwest wind and rolled over and over. The best system appeared to be ferrying one at a time on a clumsy raft. A backbreaking day of that, up to their armpits in icy water, and they had crossed only twenty-three wagons. It rained and hailed on them, and the wind blew. The river was rising so fast they were afraid of being held up for days; and thinking of themselves, they also thought of the great company crowded with women and children who would soon follow them. Brigham put a crew to hewing two long dugout canoes from cottonwood logs and planking them over to make a solid ferryboat.

By the time the ferry was nearly done, all the wagons had been laboriously rafted over. There were 108 Oregon wagons on the south side of the swollen river frantic to cross, and rumor said there were a thousand more between there and Fort Laramie. To Brigham's practical mind, when manna was falling a wise man spread a blanket. The Mormons fell to and worked all night to ferry the Gentiles for a fee, and when it was time to start on, on June 19, Brigham delegated Thomas Grover and eight others to stay behind, improve and operate the ferry for the Gentile emigration, help the Sick Detachment and the main Mormon company across, and then either come on or return to Winter Quarters, as seemed best. One of the buffalo hunters named Eric Glines, either because he was eager to stay and wait for his family on the river or for some more private reason, wanted to join the ferrymen. Brigham told him he had no counsel of that kind. Glines said he would stay anyway. The diarists shake their heads over him, but strangely, Brigham did not blast him or coerce him. Perhaps he did not want at that time to make an issue of discipline; perhaps he was in a mellow mood because of the $400 worth of supplies that luck had dropped into their wagons and because of the control that the providential ferry had given them over this part of the trail. Glines stayed, the company went on.

Now the long and mainly useful intercourse with the Platte came to an end. For more than six hundred miles from the Elkhorn they had been either on or within a few miles of that dreary but indispensable river. Its valley had been their road, they had drunk its muddy water when they had to, its cottonwood islands and its driftwood had fed their fires. Now they parted from it, the river bending southwest and the road keeping on, to climb over some high bluffs and then swing south along the long laborious edge of Casper Mountain, still unnamed. As if to dramatize the end of the happy symbiosis of river and road, the country grew arid and forbidding, and their camp that night, in a sagebrush pocket surrounded by cliffs, with one poisonous creek coming down from the southwest and another only less tainted from the north, and nothing to burn but sage, was the worst of the whole trip so far. The smell of the poison creek and the swamp it created was nauseating, the mosquitoes rose in millions from the disturbed mud, the cattle had to be watched constantly to keep them from miring down in the stinking sloughs.

They would learn, and their guides and experienced wagonmasters would warn later comers, that the fifty miles between Last Crossing and the Sweetwater were the worst stretch of trail between the Missouri and the Salt Lake Valley—would kill more cattle and sicken and depress more people and collect more abandoned equipment than any comparable reach of road. Except for one good but miry spot at Willow Springs, campsites were few and bad: if there was good water, there was no wood or grass; if there was grass, there was bad water, or none. Even after the road topped the summit of "Prospect Hill"—a spot that Brigham remarked would be a fine place to set up a summer mansion and keep tavern—and showed them the Sweetwater Mountains across a broad irregular plain, the road was rougher than it looked from a distance, and for the last ten miles before Independence Rock was very heavy, and unpleasant with the smell of the alkali lake it crossed. Lorenzo Young and others gathered pailfuls of the efflorescent white bicarbonate of soda—"saleratus"—for the women to try out in baking, but it made bread of a suspiciously green cast and had to be used in moderation. The water that sat on these glaring flats in shallow lakes tasted not very salty, but "sickly," and was said to be poisonous, and to "burst" cattle that drank it. For lack of anything better, the cattle of more careless or more uninformed trains than theirs did often drink it, and all during the years of the emigration this part of the trail was marked by hundreds of cattle carcasses, bloated and loathsome, or scattered by wolves, or dried to racks of hide-covered bones.

They were in the very midst of the Gentiles, with Oregon companies before and behind. John Brown and Wilford Woodruff, going ahead to hunt a campsite, saw six men who acted strangely and who (they concluded afterward with the sublime Mormon belief in persecution) were decoying them away from the one good spot. The pioneers did, as a matter of fact, find and stop at that spot, but Brown and Woodruff rode on too far, and had to spend the night with a Missouri company whose "men, women and children were all cursing, swearing, quarreling, scolding and finding fault with each other and other companies." Woodruff blamed their quarrelsomeness on the fact that they came from Missouri; he should have blamed most of it on the fifty miles of trail they had just come over.

In the morning the two climbed Independence Rock, next to Chimney Rock the most famous natural landmark on the trail, and from that dome of gray fissured granite took a wide look at the

surrounding country. East, south, and southwest was the toss of
buttes and ridges that they called the Sweetwater Mountains but
that is actually half a dozen small ranges. Directly west six miles,
the Sweetwater broke through the pillars of Devil's Gate; around
the end of the ridge through which the river had cut they could
see the glint of water and green meadows along the foot of the
Rattlesnake Range beyond. Far to the west were other mountains,
a wild waste. The scenery they had thought romantic and wonder-
ful around Scotts Bluff was nothing to this. Here the distances were
enormous and empty, the air had a mountain keenness, the sun a
bite, the shade a coolness almost chilly. The colors of the earth were
gray and faint green and toned white and the mirage blue of the
saleratus lake.

While they were up on top, a party of Missourians came to the
foot of the rock and dug a hole and buried somebody. They noted
the name later: Rachel Morgan, aged twenty-five—one of the fleet-
ing identities, casualties or casual passersby like the names scratched
and painted all over the rock, who by their lives or deaths turn
topography into human history. When they had added their own
names to the rock, and prayed—"the first Latter-day Saint[s] that
ever went onto that rock or offered up prayers according to the
priesthood"—Woodruff and Brown rode on to take a look at Devil's
Gate and then returned to Independence Rock in time to meet the
nooning pioneers.

Briefly they were all tourists. At summer solstice on that high
place they clambered around the dome of Independence Rock or
kicked stones off the cliff of Devil's Gate into the river or fired off
guns in the gorge to start the echoes. Also they put up more signposts. At Devil's Gate they were 50¼ miles from Last Crossing and
175¼ from Fort Laramie. But one development must have given
William Clayton a slight heartburn. At the request of Willard Richards, a distinguishing brand was burned onto each board so that
later companies could identify the Church's authentic signs. The
brand they selected was the initials W.R.

For five days they played musical chairs with the Sweetwater, which though a bright pounding stream, cheerful to camp by and lined with good grass, was a difficult highway because of its many fords and its steep, narrow tributaries, which forced them several times around through the hills to the left. Their ambition to get ahead of the Missouri companies could not be realized; even when they rose early one morning without the bugle in order to get the jump, the Missourians went past them while they were yoking up. The road was heavy, and even good outfits felt the strain. Lorenzo Young broke an axle and was rescued by a Missourian and never thought to invoke the ghost of persecution; others broke traces and had to "whang them up." But there were compensating wonders. Coming out onto the south side of the Sweetwater valley after one detour, they saw break into view northward the great snowy chain of the Wind Rivers. Groves of aspen appeared on the hills, the near distance was always marked by the white rumps of antelope. At the corner where the Rattlesnake Range turned north they passed the Ice Spring mentioned by Frémont, and satisfied themselves that down under the sulphur-smelling bog a foot or so there was clear and sweet-tasting ice.

Crossing and recrossing the Sweetwater, leaving it and finding it again, they climbed higher, following swales and pulling the humps when they had to, until they surmounted what would come to be called Rocky Ridge. The Sweetwater had become a narrow, tumbling, ice-cold creek fringed with willows. The nights were very cold, and one noon they rested between five-foot snowbanks and mats of wild strawberry in bloom: they picked flowers with one hand and snowballs with the other. That was the day the repentant Eric Glines caught up with them, and on that same afternoon Orson Pratt and some others, hunting the exact summit of the characterless pass, crossed over and camped at Pacific Springs, two miles onto the western slope, in company with some Oregon men returning to the States. With one of them they sat talking a long time around the fire.

The casual contacts of the road had made the Saints acquainted before this with traders and mountain men—Sarpy, Lucien Fontenelle's halfbreed son Logan, Bordeaux, Prudhomme—but this one, as if South Pass marked a human as well as a drainage divide, was of another and larger breed. He had been in these mountains since 1822, beginning as an Ashley man, companion of such heroic names as William Sublette, Jedediah Smith, Thomas Fitzpatrick, Jim Bridger, Jim Clyman, Jim Beckwourth, old Hugh Glass, and later of Joe Walker, Joe Meek, Kit Carson, Bill Williams. He had known them all, and he knew the country from South Pass to the Oregon and California shores as well as most. He had circumnavigated Great Salt Lake in a bullboat with Bridger, he had made rendezvous on the Green and in Cache Valley and on Bear Lake. His name was Moses, known as "Black," Harris, and he was their first authentic information on the Promised Land. On everything but Cache Valley his report was pessimistic, but they drank in his words anyway, because he had been there. As if he recognized the significance of his role, he left his companions to go on to the States alone, and turned back with the main body of the pioneers when it rocked over the pass next day and on to a camp on the Dry Sandy.

The day was June 27, 1847. Exactly three years before, at a little after five in the afternoon, the overcast sky had parted and a beam of light had glared down on a scene of blood in the yard of Carthage jail. A barefooted, black-faced militiaman with his bowie raised to cut off the head of the dead prophet had been transfixed by that sudden brilliance. His knife arm fell, the muskets of four others who had just fired into Joseph's body dropped from their hands, the mob that seconds before had been furious with bloodlust broke and fled in terror from its work. A sign.* Now the Lord, who had started the pioneers west on the anniversary of Joseph's founding of the Church, took them over South Pass into the country of sanctuary on the anniversary of the martyrdom. It was Sunday, and many would have preferred to stop for fasting and prayer, but

* This story, which appeared shortly after Joseph's death, was printed in Nauvoo and repeated as fact to more than a generation of Mormon children. Brigham H. Roberts, the historian of the Church, later went through the court records and concluded that it was essentially fiction, but it was believed unquestioningly by all the faithful of the Migration years.

the necessities of their journey weighed on them, and their competition with the Gentiles forced them to a day of fifteen miles and a camp with little grass on a creek so thirsty that only by digging in its bed could they find water.

But the day after that, as if to mark the beginning of their separation from the Gentiles now that they had crossed out of the United States, they came after six miles of easy sagebrush slope to a parting of the trails. The right-hand fork went on westward to the Big Sandy, and from there jumped off through broken country on a forty-three mile waterless *jornada* to the Bear River, where it met the older trail between Fort Bridger and Fort Hall. That way, which was known as Greenwood's or Sublette's Cutoff, went most of the Oregon- and California-bound trains. Those who preferred the longer drive to the dry *jornada*, or who had been taken in by Lansford Hastings' promotion of a short cut to California around the south end of Great Salt Lake, took the left-hand fork to Fort Bridger. Being bound vaguely for the Great Salt Lake country, the Mormons turned left. Shortly after fording the Little Sandy they met George Albert Smith, who had been scouting ahead, riding back in company with three strangers. One of the strangers knew more about the country than Black Harris, perhaps more than any man alive, for he was Jim Bridger, Old Gabe himself. He said that if they would turn aside and camp, he would spend the night with them and tell them what they wanted to know.

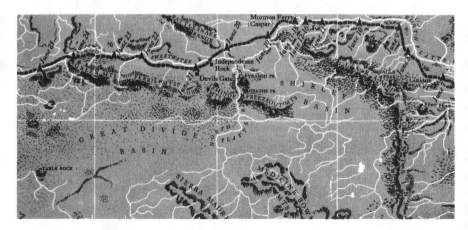

4

⊤⊤⊤⊤⊤⊤⊤⊤⊤⊤⊤⊤⊤⊤

"Like Moses from Pisgay's Top"

CONSIDERING THE EXPERIENCE Jim Bridger was to have with the Mormons later, he would have done well to direct them as far from his own post on Black's Fork as they could travel in a month of good weather. For however friendly here on the Little Sandy, the people with whom Bridger spent a long gabby evening were like no people he had ever seen in all his long experience on the frontier. They followed a pillar of fire and cloud, they went to inhabit Canaan according to the Lord's promise, and any Canaanite should have taken warning, remembering the Lord's words:

> And I will send hornets before thee, which shall drive out the Hivite, the Canaanite, and the Hittite, from before thee. I will not drive them out from before thee in one year; lest the land become desolate, and the beast of the field multiply against thee. By little and little I will drive them out from before thee, until thou be increased, and inherit the land.... Thou shalt make no covenant with them, nor with their gods. They shall not dwell in thy land, lest they make thee sin against me ...

Still, in 1847 Bridger had a few years left before the Mormons could multiply and inherit the land, and he had probably not read Exodus recently, or kept up with frontier gossip about the group

methods of the Saints. He was friendly and expansive, unaware that
these were the people who would buy him out or crowd him out,
whichever was indicated.

Mormon legend has it that Bridger so scorned the Great Salt Lake
country that he offered to give a thousand dollars for the first bushel
of corn they raised there. It would have been a rash statement, for
when a Mormon community wants to prove something to the Gentiles it can grow corn in a cement sidewalk. But like many stories
of the trail, the story of Jim's offer is somewhat stretched. Bridger
actually took a more favorable view of the Bear River Valley than
Black Harris had, he thought the Utah Valley a very likely place
for a settlement, and he gave them a good report of the valley of
the Sevier and of the country along the eastern rim of the Great
Basin for two hundred miles south of the Salt Lake. He expressed
doubt about the Salt Lake Valley only because he thought the nights
might be too cold for the maturing of corn. The discontent they
felt at his information reflected more bewilderment than disappoint-
ment. For the knowledge in Old Gabe's head was too broad to be
handily condensed, or perhaps they had primed him with too much
tongue-loosener, or perhaps their extraordinary attentiveness, with
three trained clerks keeping minutes and a dozen other men taking
notes, led him into expansiveness. From whatever cause, his specific
information on the country they wanted to know about was half
lost in a rambling discourse that covered the whole West from the
Pima country to Oregon. Clayton, who set down pages of Bridger's
answers to their questions, concluded that "it was impossible to
form a correct idea" of either the route or the country "from the
very imperfect and irregular way he gave his descriptions," and
that "we shall know more about things . . . when we have seen the
country for ourselves." Since Bridger was bound for Fort Laramie,
they got him to carry a letter to Thomas Grover at the ferry, and
themselves rolled on, more confused than enlightened, toward Fort
Bridger.

Two days into the land of promise, they saw little that was prom-
ising. Pilot Butte and then Church Butte, well-known landmarks,

were on their left, to the southeast. Far to the northwest the three Tetons lifted their pure needles, and the "Utah" or "Bear River" mountains—the Uintas—were a snowy crest along the south. But the country they traveled through was "hard-faced," its soil "as hard as cast iron" and barren of anything but sage. For lack of a campsite with grass and water they had to drive 23¾ miles, the longest day's travel yet, before they corralled by moonlight on the bank of the Big Sandy.

For some, that day was not only the longest but the most excruciating, for a sickness had come among them about the time they reached South Pass. It announced itself with a blinding headache, which was followed by severe pains in the joints and spine, by high fever, and often by delirium. For lack of a more precise name they called it mountain fever, and laid it to the sharp mountain alternations of heat and cold, or to the saleratus they had scraped up and used in baking, or to the inhalation of alkali dust. There is no telling exactly what it was. Altitude sickness does not seem likely, for even on the pass they were only at 7,550 feet (7,085 by Orson Pratt's barometer), and they had reached that moderate elevation by very gradual stages. Some historians, including Dale L. Morgan, believe it to have been Rocky Mountain spotted fever, or some related tick fever. No one in the pioneer company, and few later, died of it, but the joint pains and headache made riding the jolting wagons a torture. John Fowler arrived at the Big Sandy out of his head; several others were down, by morning several more. It was a blessed relief to the sick ones when at noon on June 30 they reached the Green River three miles above the mouth of the Big Sandy and found that the river was too high for fording, that the Missouri companies ahead had turned loose their rafts to prevent their use by the Saints (persecution again), and that they would have to wait until they could build rafts of their own. They were still building them when three travelers rode in from the west. With their arrival, two of the three prongs of the Mormon migration had made contact after nearly seventeen months.

For one of the three was Samuel Brannan, who had sailed from

New York on the same day, February 4, 1846, when Charles Shumway had led off the flight from Nauvoo. By way of the Horn and the Sandwich Islands, Brannan's company had reached San Francisco Bay on July 29, 1846, to find that the Bear Flag Revolt had made the sleepy settlement of Yerba Buena an American town. Without fully intending to, the Mormons had reinforced its new character; Brannan had established there the first newspaper on the coast, the *California Star*, and now he came eastward overland to persuade Brigham to bring all the Saints to California.

Having plans of his own, Brigham was not much impressed by Brannan's promotion of California; he knew Brannan of old as an unreliable enthusiast. But he and the rest listened eagerly enough to some of the news that the three brought. They heard that Addison Pratt, serving a mission in the Society Islands, had baptized 3,000 natives. That impressed the thoughtful and the zealous with the comforting assurance that even in its hegira, the Church had not forgotten the Gathering, but was fulfilling itself as a world religion. Something else that impressed them was the story Brannan brought of the Donner-Reed party whose trail the pioneers would follow from Fort Bridger to Salt Lake. Brannan had passed through the camps and seen the grisly remains just being uncovered by the spring thaw, and had talked with survivors, including the ghoul Keseberg, and had heard of a Mormon woman, Mrs. Murphy, once a resident of Nauvoo, who had been eaten. The journals are full of moralizing I-told-you-so's. Traveling with the quarrelsome Gentiles, Mrs. Murphy had obviously been an apostate, and her fate and theirs demonstrated a gruesomely satisfactory form of retribution. "These are the men," wrote Norton Jacob, "that have mobbed and killed the Saints!"

Despite his role as California booster (the second of the species; Lansford Hastings was the first) Brannan got nowhere with Brother Brigham, who disregarded the story that John Sutter would welcome a Mormon colony as he disregarded the ambiguous word of Black Harris and Jim Bridger on the Salt Lake country. And he wanted all the Saints together. To prevent any possibility of their being misled by rumors or uncertainty, he sent his brother Phineas back with four men in the Revenue Cutter wagon, to meet and guide the main company. But they had hardly started recrossing the Green when thirteen members of the Mormon Battalion rode up, and now the third prong of the migration had rejoined the main force. The thirteen were in pursuit of the horse thieves who had passed the pioneers just west of Fort Laramie. They said that forty-three wagons and about 140 men of the Battalion were not far behind, having already crossed the ferry at Last Crossing.

They had no way of knowing exactly where the main company under John Young, John Taylor, and Parley Pratt might be (on July 4 it had just made it back to the Platte valley after the cross-country drive from the crossing of the Loup Fork), but after the Battalion boys had been welcomed with hosannahs, one of them expressed such a powerful yearning to see his family that he turned around with Phineas Young and started back. It is one of the astonishing things about this emigration that men trailworn after hundreds or thousands of miles on their own legs could turn and retrace their route for other hundreds of miles as casually as they might go back a little way for something forgotten.

From the Green the pioneers went on across twenty choking, waterless miles to Black's Fork. Next day they shortly crossed Ham's Fork, then Black's Fork again. The grass improved, they saw wild-flowers and flax, and when the water of the creek took his fancy as looking trouty, Wilford Woodruff got out the artificial flies he had brought from his last mission in England and tried a little casting, "the first time I ever tried the artificial fly in America or ever saw it tried. I watched it as it floated upon the water with as much intent as Franklin did his kite." He caught twelve of what they called either "spotted trout" or "salmon trout," which would have had to be the cut-throat species native to the waters of the Rockies —trout which showed their romantic readiness by rising to lures tied thousands of miles away for other varieties of the genus *Salmo*, and which after this auspicious beginning would be furnishing sport for thousands of other fishermen until crowded out by the more

easily propagated rainbow and eastern brook. Woodruff with his
fancy tackle, and others with plebeian worms, kept catching messes
of them while they were camped on one of the several channels
of Black's Fork, in good grass and timber, a half mile beyond the
double log house, pole stockade, and cluster of Shoshone lodges that
constituted Fort Bridger.

The thief wanted by the Battalion detachment, a mountain man
named Tim Goodale, was camped among the Shoshone lodges,
though his men had gone on to Oregon. But on Brigham's advice,
the warrant carried by Sergeant Tom Williams for Goodale's arrest
was not served. For one thing, what would they do with a United
States prisoner if they had him? For another, Brigham could not
have wanted to sow any trouble along the trail that the later company might have to reap (*I will not drive them out from before thee
in one year . . . By little and little I will drive them out . . .*). Only
when the Saints were secure in their mountains would Brigham
show a hard hand. When Williams seized a horse from Goodale
to compensate for the mule Goodale's men had stolen in Pueblo,
Brigham made him give Goodale a receipt, just as he had made the
Saints keep account of the plows and old iron they picked up at
the government station back on the Loup Fork. His warning against
too much fraternizing with the Gentiles at Fort Bridger was hardly
needed, however, for the temptation to trade at Bridger prices was
not irresistible. They had thought Black Harris a robber to ask three
dollars for a pair of buckskin pants back on South Pass; here the
same pants were six.

Through July 7 and 8 they rested in the good grass of that pleasant mountain valley, reset tires, washed clothes, fished, and cast their
thoughts ahead. By Clayton's reckoning they were 397 miles from
Fort Laramie, 919 from Winter Quarters. Lansford Hastings' *Guide*
said it was only about another hundred miles to the Great Salt Lake
Valley. The roadometer would clock it at 113½ of the hardest miles
on the whole trip. The trail would be all theirs, or nearly, for much
of the Oregon and California emigration had already turned off on
Sublette's Cutoff on the western slope of South Pass, and the rest of

it would turn here, two miles beyond Fort Bridger, and go northwest until it met the cutoff road on the Bear River, short of Soda Springs. The road the Saints proposed to follow had been traveled by no wagontrains except the Harlan-Young and Donner-Reed parties of 1846, a total of fifty-seven wagons altogether. Unable to make much of Bridger's directions, the Twelve had to rely on Hastings' *Guide*, not yet discredited because none of them knew that the cannibal camp Brannan had seen in the Sierra Nevada was the direct product of Hastings' criminal irresponsibility. To most of them it seemed the product of Gentile quarrelsomeness and the vengeance of a just God. Hastings, then, and the suddenly fainter wagontracks. To prevent delay or mishap, and just possibly to get the insistent Brannan out of his hair, Brigham on July 9 sent him and Sergeant Tom Williams back with a copy of Hastings' map to meet the Sick Detachment.

The rest started out on Hastings' "road," up a steep hill and down a steeper one, around south of Bridger Butte and into camp on the Big Muddy. Next day a hard twenty miles over the Bear River Divide, which Pratt's barometer showed to be 7,700 feet, considerably higher than South Pass, and when they tipped down the western side they were in the Great Basin, at last inside the walls of that inward-looking sanctuary which, as Brigham had said in a letter to the main company, was still their destination "for the present, at least, to examine the country."

At Sulphur Creek the trail split inexplicably into two branches, one south, one west. Hastings' map showed no such fork. But a man they discovered in camp a couple of miles away with some States-bound Californians turned out to be, besides Jim Bridger, the only bona-fide settler of the region, the red-headed mountain man Miles Goodyear of whom they had first heard from Bordeaux at Fort Laramie. He told them to take the right-hand fork. He also said he had matured crops at his place in the Bear River Valley, and he gave an altogether better picture of the country's possibilities than either Harris or Bridger had. Thinking he had his eye on their trade and the usefulness to himself of any road they might build past his place, they were suspicious both of his road information and his recommendation of his valley; and within four months Henry Sherwood, following advice left by Brigham, would buy Goodyear out to prevent his place from becoming a haven for apostates and enemies. But they took his advice now and chose the north fork, thereby saving themselves some miles of pointless southing, for the two trails reunited at the head of Echo Canyon.

Two items of information they got from one of the Californians, John Craig, with whom Goodyear was camped. Craig had lost five horses on the dry drive across the desert on Hastings' Cutoff, a fact which might have reduced their confidence in Hastings as an authority. And he too had seen the gruesome Donner remains, and details of his story inflamed them into a new round of I-told-you-so's. Wilford Woodruff thought he remembered baptizing Mrs. Murphy; he thought the members of the party were mainly from the old anti-Mormon strongholds of Independence and Clay County, Missouri; and it seemed to him that the apostate Mrs. Murphy and her Gentile companions were "ripe for judgment," and that their fate was another piece of divine intervention. By no other kind of reasoning could Lansford Hastings have been construed as an instrument of Providence.

From their meeting on Sulphur Creek, Goodyear went on down the Bear to make contact with the emigration and sell it horses; Craig and his fellows went on east; the Saints, after admiring the novelty of a sulphur spring, a sweet-water spring, and an oil spring all in a row, and after greasing their hubs, shoes, and gunstocks from the latter, went on down the northern fork, a faint track that had been made by Lienhard and Jefferson of the Hastings party.

Their camp that night was at the head of Echo Canyon, near the cave that they named for Jackson Redding, who was the first into it. But the Lion of the Lord was not with them. At noon he had come down with a violent attack of mountain fever, and in doing so had demonstrated not only the virulence of the disease but the prerogatives of command. Any of the rest of them who had been stricken must jolt on over the boulders no matter how their joints and backs ached and no matter how they raved. When Brother Brigham was similarly taken they dared not risk for him what they accepted for themselves: his wagons and Heber Kimball's stopped and let the company go on. Next morning Kimball and Howard Egan rode ahead to suggest that an advance company be sent on into Weber Canyon to search out "Mr. Reid's route." So twenty-two wagons, mostly with ox teams, started on under the command of Orson Pratt. From that point on, thanks to sickness, uncertainty about the road, and difficult terrain, the pioneer company that had started out so stiffly organized from the Elkhorn straggled in two or three groups separated by a good many miles. Fortunately the grass was good, their water was from bright mountain streams or cold springs, the scenery was increasingly romantic and grand, and there was plenty of game. And they had no fear of Indians. Except for a few lodges of Sioux at Fort Laramie and a few of Shoshones at Fort Bridger, they had seen none since the end of May, back on the North Platte. For weeks now the night guard had consisted of only two or three men.

It is a kind of awkwardness in the strenuously encouraged Mormon myth that on the last leg of their long journey, just when they seemed about to break through the final barriers into the promised land, the Moses of this people—and not for any fault that had incurred the Lord's displeasure—should have been held back sick and raving in the rear. Wanting to be led into Canaan, the Saints had to lead themselves; wanting to focus upon the leader, the chroniclers have to shuffle unhappily between his rear-guard wagons and the advance party of Orson Pratt.

While the main company dawdled and waited for Brigham to improve, and amused itself shouting or shooting or tooting its band instruments against the cliffs, this advance group went down Echo Canyon to where it empties into the broad valley of the Weber, and down the Weber until it pinched in to become a narrow slot filled wall-to-wall by the river. The Harlan-Young wagons the year before had gone ten miles down that riverbed, floundering and crashing among the boulders in the swift water, and made it through;

the Donner party had turned aside and hunted another way through the mountains. It was the Donner trail, "Reed's Cutoff," that Pratt was searching for. On July 15 Port Rockwell found it, a dim trace that crossed the Weber and crawled south into the relatively welcoming gateway of what would some day be called Main Canyon, at the modern village of Henefer, Utah. Sending Rockwell back to report to Heber, Pratt put up a sign to mark the turnoff, and went on.

By the testimony of every diarist, the thirty-six last miles, from the Weber to the Salt Lake Valley, were worse than anything on the whole road. It was as if sanctuary withheld itself, as if safety could be had only by intensifying ordeal. The road had already been broken, if that was the word, by the Donner-Reed wagoners, but Orson Pratt's forty-two men, slaving with ax and shovel and pry-pole to make a few miles a day, fell into camp every night with a respect approaching awe for the quarrelsome Gentiles who had first taken wagons through those canyons. They had uphill, downhill, sidehill, boulders, creek-crossings, willows—above all willows, thick as a porcupine's quills and hardly less troublesome to get through. Growing, they screened rocks and holes and dropoffs that could break a wheel; chopped off, they left stumps sharp as spears, and ruinous to the feet of men and animals. When they had to travel, as they did much of the way, with one wheel in the creek and one blundering along a steep bank sown with these stubs, they could literally count their progress one wheel's turn at a time.

From the Weber there were five miles of stiff *up* over Hogsback Summit, then seven miles of equally stiff *down* along the sidehill into what is now called Dixie Hollow. On July 17 Pratt's company cut their way up what Pratt called Canyon Creek (now East Canyon Creek) for six exhausting miles. On the eighteenth, Sunday, they rested—for cause. That day, back near the mouth of Echo Canyon, the pioneers agreed to leave several wagons behind with Brother Brigham, who had rallied and joined them only to relapse again, while the rest followed Pratt as fast as possible, to hurry seeds into the ground. On Monday, July 19, Pratt's axmen attacked

the willows again, while the main company, making better time
because of the advance party's labors, but not such good time that
they failed to abominate the road, turned out of Weber Canyon
and made it over the Hogsback to Dixie Hollow. And out ahead
Orson Pratt, advance man for Zion and regent for Zion's Moses,
rode on with John Brown to reconnoiter the trail, which had finally
left the creek and started off to the right, up a ravine folded among
high, confusing ridges. Four miles up that difficult trace the two
tied their horses and climbed on foot to the crest.

They were on a very high place (7,245 feet) in the very midst
of wild mountains. Before them the land fell away, sagebrush-
covered on the southward-facing slopes, timbered with aspen and
spruce on the slopes that leaned north. Right, left, before, behind,
the mountains tossed up their granite and snow. Straight ahead, jut-
ting up like a front gunsight into the notch of the ravine that
began at their feet and deepened swiftly into a canyon aimed west,
was a dark isolated mountain, and many miles beyond that stretched
the towering, hazy crest of another range. They had no way of
identifying the far range, for it so far had no status in geography;
it would turn out to be the Oquirrhs, on the west side of the Salt
Lake Valley. But reaching to its feet, and visible on both sides past
the dark gunsight mountain, they could see a broad plain, treeless, shimmering pale gold and paler amethyst, and that they thought
they could identify.

Pratt and Brown hurried to their horses and rode down through
the dense brush of the ravine, expecting to come out of the baffling
mountains within a few miles. Instead, the apparently open canyon
closed in to become a slot as impassable as the lower canyon of the
Weber. They were on the spot that many years later would be the
site of the Mountain Dell reservoir, at the head of the canyon that
would be named Parley's for Orson Pratt's brother. In 1850 Parley
would open the Golden Pass road through the slot, and it would
ultimately become the route of the main highway into the valley,
U.S. 30S. But in 1847 it was no place to risk a wagon. The Donners
had so decided: their frustrated trail kinked back on itself and

climbed again, clear over the ridge to the north. Instead of following them further, Pratt and Brown rode back over the high pass of Big Mountain until they met the advance party, which by killing labor had cut another six and a half miles of willows and dug nine crossings of Canyon Creek during the day. According to Port Rockwell, who came up from the rear, the middle division was only nine miles back. Brigham was still sick in Weber Canyon.

The trail of July 20 up the side of Big Mountain impressed Levi Jackman, one of Pratt's road gang, as profoundly gloomy, "as thoug we were Shut up in a gulph," and it was so laborious that the company behind them temporarily abandoned there the cannon they had hauled 1,000 miles. Going down the other side was little if any easier, and the next day's hot switchback climb out of Mountain Dell and over Little Mountain into what Pratt called Last Creek (Emigration) Canyon, was as bad as anything yet. But from the Little Mountain ridge, before they started their wheel-locked slide down to the stream, they caught another glimpse: as Jackman said, "like Moses from Pisgay's top" they saw their "long antisipated home."

Whether indeed this valley was to be their long-anticipated home was not quite so plain to the leaders as to Jackman, but it was pretty sure to be their temporary stopping place. For now came Erastus Snow up from the main company with a letter from Willard Richards and George A. Smith containing the instructions of Brother Brigham, a leader who led even from the rear. He directed Pratt to steer away from Utah Valley, which had had the best billing from Bridger but which was inhabited in force by the Utes. "We had better keep further north towards the Salt Lake, which is more a warlike or neutral ground, and by so doing we should be less likely to be disturbed and also have a chance to form an acquaintance with the Utes, and having done our planting shall select a site for our location at our leisure."

Riding and tying one horse, Pratt and Snow went down Emigration Canyon to see what lay ahead. Four miles below the foot of the Little Mountain grade they found where the Donner-Reed party had pulled over an impossibly steep, narrow, dangerous hill to get out of the tree-and-boulder-choked V of the canyon. It has occurred to historians since that by that stage the Donner party would have climbed a vertical wall rather than cut any more willows. At Donner Hill the wall was as near vertical as wagons have ever managed. According to the diary of Virginia Reed Murphy, "almost every yoke in the train" of twenty-three wagons—which would have meant fifty or sixty animals—had to be hitched onto each one to get it over. That was where the Donner party took the heart out of their animals. If they had cut and dug instead of pulling Donner Hill, they might have saved the extra strength and the extra day or two of time that would have meant safety later.

Stephen Markham's road crew would dig around that hill in four hours the next day. For now, Pratt and Snow followed the gouges of the Donner wheels to the top. And abruptly there it was, the whole great valley shimmering in summer heat, one of the great views of the continent. From where they stood above the alluvial fan of Emigration Creek, the Wasatch ran in an abrupt wall southward, but on the north it swung an arm around to half enclose the valley. Beginning nearly straight west of them, perhaps twenty-five airline miles away, the high smooth crestline of the Oquirrhs also ran southward until it all but met the Wasatch at a low notch on the southern sky. And northward and westward from the northernmost foot of the Oquirrhs, fabulous, dark blue, floating its pale islands, lapping the world's rim, went the Great Salt Lake.

"We could not refrain from a shout of joy," Orson Pratt wrote. The developed legend says they swung their hats and cried three times, "Hosannah! Hosannah! Hosannah!" The twelve-mile circuit they made of the valley that day was amplified the day following by a more extensive tour taken by a larger group. They found hardly a whisker of timber, many rattlesnakes, many great black crickets; but the alluvial soil looked good, and the slopes were threaded by a half dozen good mountain streams. At the foot of the northwest corner of the mountains, below a hill that Brigham would shortly name Ensign Peak, were hot mineral springs.

Whether it was promised land or only temporary stopping place, they had no time to waste. On July 23, with the promptness and efficiency that had marked them as a community ever since Missouri, they moved their camp north onto City Creek and broke three acres of ground and several plows. By the day following they had completed a dam across City Creek and brought water in ditches to their fields. When Brigham was driven out of the mouth of Emigration Canyon on July 24, and Woodruff's carriage paused to let him take his first look at the valley, he looked down upon a camp that had already half committed itself by putting seeds and potatoes in the ground.

The spot where Woodruff's carriage paused is now marked by Mahonri Young's fine monument, erected in the centennial year; the highest achievement of Mormon art commemorates the high moment of the Mormon hegira. It is popularly called the "This Is the Place" monument, because Brother Brigham is supposed to have said, after remaining a moment lost in a vision, "It is enough. This is the right place, drive on." It is a great statement, one that gathers up in a phrase history and hope and fulfillment, and it is now an ineradicable part of the Mormon myth. But as Dale Morgan has pointed out, the phrase was not part of the original record. It does not seem to have been coined until the fiftieth anniversary of the Church, thirty-three years after the Mormon leader was brought to the brink of the valley. Woodruff's journal, written at the time of the arrival, reports that Brigham "expressed his full satisfaction in the appearance of the valley as a resting-place for the Saints, and was amply repaid for his journey"; and Brigham's own journal for that day says only that they had to cross Emigration Creek eighteen times before emerging from the canyon and joining the main camp at 2:00 P.M.

Nevertheless one is glad that Woodruff either resurrected or happily misremembered Brigham's words. If Brother Brigham didn't make that reverberating phrase, he should have; and once the decision had been made to stay there where the Donners' trail had led them, it could appropriately be put in his mouth.

The decision itself took several days, and was not quite so automatic as the myth and the sounding phrase suggest. Their uncertainties and their human prejudices persisted. When Willard Richards spoke to a prayerful meeting the day before Brigham's arrival, and exhorted them all to purify their minds and dedicate their efforts to the common good, Norton Jacob thought that "all seemed to partake of the unity of the spirit," but William Clayton angrily reported the sermon as one that offended many, and found that only censored obscenity could express his disgust: "A sermon of ———— from end to end." The visionaries and the realists among them looked differently upon every event in their new place. When, the first day of their plowing, they prayed for rain and got a shower, Wilford Woodruff (who was not yet there) reported it as a miraculous Sign. Orson Pratt said it barely laid the dust. The realists looked around and were concerned about the aridity of the climate, the lack of timber. The enthusiasts said that if this was not the right place God would not have led them to it.

On July 27, the evening of the day when Sam Brannan and Amasa Lyman rode out of the canyon to announce that the Sick Detachment was only two days away, the Saints sat down in meeting to talk things over. They had by then explored as far west as Skull Valley, beyond the Oquirrhs, and found everything in that direction pitilessly dry; they had reached Great Salt Lake and taken an unsinkable swim in its brine; some of them had discovered timber in Red Butte Canyon, within seven miles of their camp. Brigham, by that time recovering, put it to them outright. They had been searching for a home for the Saints. *Was* this the place, or should they look further?

One of the optimists moved to settle, Norton Jacob seconded, the motion was carried with one dissenting vote. Brigham told the lone dissenter, William Vance, that he was entitled to his opinion, but that he himself entertained no doubts. As Norton Jacob reported the meeting,

> The President then said, 'We shall have a committee to lay
> out the city, and also to apportion the inheritances, and who

shall it be?' It was unanimously resolved that the Twelve should be that committee. [No dissent likely there.] Says the President, 'We propose to have the temple lot contain 40 acres, to include the ground we are now on—what do you say to that? all right?—that the streets will be 88 feet wide, sidewalks 20 feet, the lots to contain 1 ¼ acre, eight lots in a block, the houses invariably set in the center of the lot, 20 feet back from the street, with no shops or other buildings in the corners of the street. Neither will they be filled with cattle, horses, and hogs, nor children for they will have yards and places appropriated for recreation, and we will have a city clean and in order...

So much for the City of Zion, half Garden City and half New Jerusalem. Brother Brigham, in his capacity as city planner, was once again only modifying ideas that had been originated by Joseph Smith, for this was a variant of the New Jerusalem paved with jasper and pearl that Joseph had projected at Far West. To match the physical order of the city, Brigham outlined an economic and moral order—things more closely allied in Mormonism than in most societies.

A man may live here with us and worship what God he pleases or none at all, but he must not blaspheme the God of Israel nor damn old Jo Smith or his religion, for we will salt him down in the lake. We do not intend to have any trade or commerce with the gentile world...The Kingdom of God cannot rise independent of the gentile nations until we produce, manufacture and make every article of use, convenience or necessity among our own people...I am determined to cut every thread of this kind and live free and independent, untrammeled by any of their detestable customs and practices.

And having gone that far in planning for a millennial self-sufficiency, Brigham felt to add a little sermon on duty, especially the duty of the sisters, whose function was to look after the house and children and not keep pestering their husbands. A man's duty, every day, was to ask, "Lord, what is Thy will?" A woman's was to ask, "Husband, what is thy will?" If a wife steadily resisted temptation and wilfulness, her offspring would be "larger, more strong and robust, the spirit mild and tractable, and in this way our race will become improved, until 'the age of man shall be as the age of a tree.' "

It was all there in one discourse—millennial city, hierarchical and patriarchal authority, isolationism, self-sufficiency, even that odd Mormon doctrine that justified polygamy much less in terms of personal liking or pleasure than by superimposing a theory of greater glory in heaven on the practical eugenics of a stock breeder.

This was what lay at the end of the Mormon Trail, the Kingdom that arrived there as Idea, ready to be built. One of the reasons for Brigham's laying it out, complete with word on the status and duties of women, was surely that when the main migration arrived, with its heavy disproportion of women, there must be no questioning of the authority of husbands or, what was essentially the same thing, of the priesthood. This was one revolution which was not going to be betrayed at the cookstove.

Just possibly, he may have been talking for the ears of the few women already there, especially those of his brother Lorenzo's wife Harriet. Though the trip had brought her some relief from her persistent "phthisis" and asthma, she had reached the end of the trail fatigued and far gone in pregnancy with the child who would be the third white child born in the valley. Looking out upon the new home from one of Brigham's rear-guard wagons on July 24, she did not like what she saw: "my feelings were such as I cannot describe everything looked gloomy and I felt heart sick." Her daughter Clara, who would spend that winter cheerfully enough living in a single room of the adobe fort with Eliza Snow, said her mother was heartbroken because there were no trees.

They were easterners, New Englanders and New Yorkers mainly. However well they might bear the hardness of the dry country as a route of passage, they expected something like home at the end, especially if the new place was labeled New Jerusalem. Instead they got gravelly dry ground, bunch grass, crickets, rattlesnakes, the unfamiliar high horizon of a mountain-rimmed valley, the flame of desert sunsets over a sterile lake. They had to adjust not only to discomfort, but to dislocation from all they knew. In building the Kingdom they had the problem of creating a whole new way of life, learning new arts of tillage, adapting to a new climate and unfamiliar weathers and lights and colors. A child born here would be forever different, responsive to another sort of beauty, to other habits, other customs.

But it was not totally strange. Foreign as it might be to their personal experience, it was close to the biblical echoes to which their faith was tuned. Eighteen miles west of them, in this desert that was as bleak as ever Palestine was, lay a Dead Sea as salt as that of the Bible. Into it flowed a stream, the effluent of Utah Lake to the south, that shortly in their consciousness of being of the tribe of Joseph they would name the Jordan.

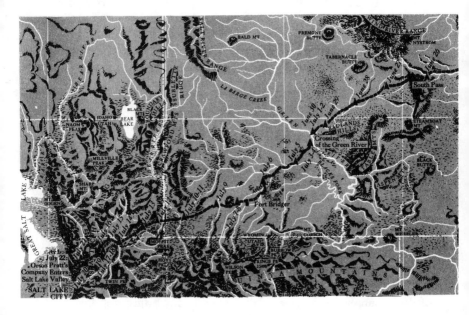

5

𝗒𝗒𝗒𝗒𝗒𝗒𝗒𝗒𝗒𝗒𝗒𝗒𝗒𝗒𝗒

"The Whole Route Having Been Carefully Measured..."

Though the valley to which the Lord had led them turned out to be the place where they voted to stay, there were many from the pioneer company who would stay only a few weeks. The pioneer company was just that. Having located the site, unloaded the equipment they carried, put seeds in the earth, begun lumbering operations and an adobe yard, and having started a fort and elected John Smith President of the Salt Lake Stake of Zion, the Twelve and a good many others, including many of the Battalion, put their outfits in repair and started back. They went in groups of every size, Ezra Taft Benson and Port Rockwell as messengers to the main emigration on August 2, Norton Jacob in charge of a group of hunters with a few wagons on August 11, William Clayton with eighteen ox teams and a new roadometer on August 17, Brigham and the Twelve and a considerable party of horse and mule teams on August 25. They made the trail populous through the late summer and fall, they had a series of cheering encounters with the Saints headed west, and they had their adventures, some of which we shall pick up in due time. But first there are the companies which followed the pioneers' wagontracks and road signs up the Platte.

In mid-June, while the pioneers were turning an honest dollar ferrying Missourians at Last Crossing, a great company was assembling at the Liberty Pole that had been set up on the bank of the Platte eleven miles from the Elkhorn ferry. In accordance with the word and will of the Lord, it organized itself into tens, fifties, and hundreds whose leaders were such stalwarts as Jedediah Grant, Charles Rich, Ira Eldredge, Orson Spencer, A. O. Smoot, Joseph Noble, Robert Pierce. Its ranking hierarchs were Brigham's brother John, designated president of this traveling Stake before the departure of the pioneers, and the two apostles who had remained behind, Parley Pratt and John Taylor. It included so many more women and children than men that many women had to act as teamsters. There seems no way of telling exactly how many they were; the usual guess is something over 2,000. Of wagons they had 566, of animals a multitude. Their draft animals alone, since every wagon was drawn by at least two and sometimes by as many as four yoke, would have totaled about 3,000, and William Clayton reports the total of their horses, mules, oxen, milk cows, heifers, calves, and sheep at 5,000. A host, the Host of Israel. In Mormon annals it is known as the First, or Big, Company.

We may follow them through the journals and reminiscences of some old acquaintances, including Eliza Snow, Ursulia Hascall and her daughter Irene Hascall Pomeroy, and Charles Coulson Rich and his six wives, three of whom were driving teams. Their experience on the trail is interesting only insofar as it differed from that of the pioneers, and it differed primarily because of their numbers, their high proportion of women, and the absence of Brigham's unifying authority.

Their journey began ominously when Jacob Weatherby and two others, driving back to Winter Quarters on an errand, were attacked by Omahas intent on robbing them. Weatherby, shot through the body, was brought back to the Liberty Pole camp and died there in Charles Rich's tent on June 21, the night before the last of the five great circles of wagons unraveled on the trail. But aside from stolen horses and mules, that was their last trouble with the Indians. In spite of the Weatherby episode, they seem to have paid far less attention to danger of that kind than had the pioneers, for where the pioneers had been repeatedly ordered to walk beside their wagons with loaded rifles in their hands or within reach, and never to stray alone from the train, these Saints, perhaps given confidence by their numbers, walked the road through Pawnee and Sioux country as if it had been a path across lots in town. Irene Pomeroy and some of the ladies not occupied as teamsters used to "go on ahead of the wagons, find some place of curiosity and wait for the teams to come up."

Despite the formal Mormon marching order, discipline was both slack and confused. This was a worm without a head, and consequently sightless. Before they had been out two days, a dispute about precedence on the trail involved Young, Pratt, and Taylor. In the midsummer dust and heat, with such heavy demands on grass and water and fuel, precedence was important. One guesses too that there must have been some jealousy about command, for certainly obedience was less than unanimous. A meeting on June 24 adjusted the first trouble "with good feeling," according to Eliza Snow, but through nearly the whole thousand miles of uncomfortable travel it kept breaking out again as bickering, road-hogging, and angry clashes of will.

Sister Snow herself, though she dutifully noted when one leader "demanded the road" of another, was at first too ecstatic to be much troubled. She and her friends had brought their glossalalia along into the wilderness, and almost every evening these first weeks they met in wagon or tent or grove and had a "refreshing from the Lord" as old-timers were revisited by the gift or younger ones caught it for the first time.

Their one real accident was, next to people's being run over by wagons, the commonest sort on the road. Corralling for the night in separate hundreds, they followed the usual practise of parking the wagons tongue out, with interlocked wheels, leaving only one narrow gate that could be closed by chains. The animals were all penned inside. On the morning of July 14 (the pioneers were then

stalled in Echo Canyon praying for Brigham to rouse from his delirium) Eliza's company saw the terrible power that panic could
inject into several hundred oxen. Something, a woman shaking out
a buffalo robe, some flash or report or flurry of fighting dogs,
stampeded the herd, which rushed against the chains, tipped over
the loaded wagons, mounted on the struggling bodies of their
downed fellows until oxen were as high as the wagonbows. Miraculously no man, woman, or child was hurt; they got off with a couple
of broken wheels, a dead milk cow, and the loss of some horns off
the oxen. But that experience, coupled with the general cumber-
someness of traveling in such large companies, led them thereafter
to corral by fifties and to drive only the loose stock inside. Over
the next twenty years, trail lore would be codified and regularized
until the procedures of a Mormon wagontrain achieved the precision of a skilled trade. Gentile trains, except for their guides, were
essentially amateur; but in all later Mormon trains there was a good
number of professionals who had been back and forth between
Salt Lake and the Missouri anywhere from five to forty times.

They had had no word from the pioneers since the trader Beaumont had brought the letters written at the head of Grand Island on
May 4. But on the evening of the stampede they found an inscribed
buffalo skull that read "All well—feed bad—only 300 miles from
W.Q.," and on July 17 some men came downriver bearing letters
that the pioneers had given them on South Pass. Those were the
returning Oregonians with whom Black Harris was camped when
Orson Pratt encountered him. Eliza Snow and her friends used the
good news of the pioneers' progress as excuse for another invigorat-
ing session of tongues.

Other sisters were having other sorts of experiences, not all ex-
hilarating. By now, the five different hundreds were scattered out
over twenty-five or thirty miles, the leading companies now and
then halting impatiently to let the slower ones catch up, and various captains periodically making a break to get out in front with
or without sanction. Inexperienced teamsters, especially the women,
suffered. Sarah Pea Rich and Emeline Rich, both driving ox teams,

were finding it a hard, tiresome trip, and after they reached the
buffalo country were often irritated that the men seemed more
eager to hunt than to get on with the journey. But Mary Phelps
Rich, also driving, had begun to take a different view. Like many
others, she found that hard physical exercise and the transition into
higher, drier air improved her health. Working like a man, yoking
up, outspanning, walking fifteen or twenty miles a day through
brush and sand beside the slow churn of the wheels, hunting up
strayed oxen on mornings when the sun stretched everything in-
credibly long up the Platte's long valley and meadowlarks whistled
sharp and pure, she began to feel whole again, began to feel that it
was "a pleasure to take hold and do something." She was one type,
a rather common type, of Mormon woman, capable, indefatigable,
unquestioning. She gives the myth of the Pioneer Wife footing in
reality.

Losing many oxen among the buffalo herds, but recovering most
of them, they passed through hundreds of hunting Sioux, thoroughly friendly, and saw a village go by with babies and household goods and dried meat loaded on the travois, and through a spyglass inspected painted lodges pitched across the Platte. Then the
brief excitement abated, the buffalo thinned and vanished; the quo-
tidian monotony of treeless valley, cheerless river, endless wagons,
lowing and bellowing and blatting herds, choking dust, went on.
Then on July 25, opposite Ash Hollow (the pioneers at that hour
were directing the water of City Creek onto their fields), Phineas
Young and nine other men came into camp. Young had left the
Green River with four companions twenty days before, and had
driven the Revenue Cutter wagon nearly five hundred miles while
the Big Company was making half that distance toward him. At
the Platte ferry, which had fulfilled part of its function by cleaning
up the later Oregon emigration and crossing the Sick Detachment
(charging the latter double the $1.50 per wagon rate, because Un-
cle Sam would be footing the bill) Young picked up five of the
ferrymen anxious to meet their families. One of these had to be
Francis Pomeroy. They expected to run into the Big Company

somewhere between the ferry and Fort Laramie, but not encountering it, were drawn on south and east down the valley emptied now of both wagontrains and buffalo. As their supplies shortened, they rode harder. Twelve exhausting days east of the ferry they spotted the first whitetops. For the last five of those days, Brother Phineas and his nine men had subsisted on the flesh of two prairie dogs and a skunk.

A couple of Young's party went on toward Winter Quarters; the rest, having found their families, turned back westward with the Big Company, which now, on Parley Pratt's suggestion, had begun not only to corral but to travel by fifties. The initial fragmentation had been their response to the difficulty of accommodating hundreds of people and animals to limited camping sites at a season when the feed was well eaten down. The second stage was a testimony to the strains that troubled every wagontrain, that more often than not split Gentile trains into constantly smaller and more wilful units, and in the absence of a strong leader could crack even the groupy cohesiveness of the Saints.

Other signs of breakup, and other news of the several groups of Mormons who had been scattered across the West, came to them down the great highway of the Platte. On July 31 James Davenport, one of the ferrymen, came through with some traders headed for the Missouri. He had quarreled with the other ferrymen over the distribution of blacksmithing fees, and was going home. On August 4 "many female faces were lighted with unusual joy," as Eliza Snow said, when Gen. Stephen Watts Kearney, taking John Charles Frémont back to the States to stand court-martial for mutiny, disobedience, and conduct prejudicial to military discipline, came down the trail escorted by fourteen members of the Mormon Battalion. In the fifteen months since their recruitment, these men had walked or ridden nearly the whole of a great circle from Council Bluffs to Fort Leavenworth, Fort Leavenworth to San Diego, San Diego to Sacramento, and Sacramento back across the mountains and deserts (burying some of the Donner party carrion as they passed) to Fort Laramie. Their brief and joyous meeting with the

Big Company came just as that company was burying its own first casualty, a Sister Ewing, wrapped in a quilt and without a coffin, about fifteen miles below Fort Laramie. The spot was nearly the same as that where Brigham had delivered his thunderous scolding at the end of May, when in the words of William Empey he called upon them "to repent of our sins and folleys wich we was giltey of before the Lord sutch as Dansing and Dice playing and card playing wich jumping Loud Lafter and all such habbits wich was a bomation in the sight of god and was a stink in his norstels."

If Brigham had been with the Big Company he might have found its behavior too a stink in the Lord's norstels, and the cause of another sermon. "All is well," wrote Eliza Snow on August 7, after they had forded the summer-shrunken North Platte and rolled past Fort Laramie without a pause; but she added at once, "may our union increase." The daily disputes over precedence were complicated by breakdowns on the rocky road along the Black Hills, and by delays occasioned by strayed or stolen stock. Men angrily demanded permission to leave their units because of clashes; hot letters went to Parley Pratt from Jedediah Grant, that zealot who a few years later would be the author of the fierce doctrine of blood atonement, and whose son Heber J. would much later become the president of the Mormon Church. They had no Missouri companies on the road with them to encourage their solidarity and direct their hostilities outward. On August 17, when Ezra Taft Benson and Porter Rockwell arrived with the word that the pioneers, the Sick Detachment, and the Mississippi Saints had all been gathered safely to the valley and were digging in to stay, Grant, John Young, and Joseph Noble got together to "rig themselves for herding" and bring in the animals, and Eliza Snow's heart "was made to rejoice at seeing our 3 head officers united in one thing—it surely is in accordance with the prayers of the sis." But two days later she burst out in the hope that "God will pour out His Spirit upon us—we seem to have the most difficulty when the most officers are with us."

God poured out His spirit impartially, blessing or testing. Sister Noble gave birth to a daughter in her wagon, Sister Love had a

wagon loaded with 1,600 pounds run across her breast, but within
a day was sitting up and combing her hair, and in another day or
two was getting around. Disputes kept flaring up. On August 21,
after another bitter altercation among the leaders about the rules
of moving, they held a meeting that ended by permitting any ten
to move out whenever it was ready, without regard to any prede-
termined order and without permission from "upper authorities."
So the trail had frayed out one more strand of their Saintly unanimity.

Nevertheless, when her wagon reached the Platte ferry on August 26, Eliza Snow felt to compose another of her camp songs, the
first for this western journey, and its motif was harmony.

> Beneath the cloud-top'd mountain
> Beside the craggy bluff
> Where ev'ry dint of nature
> Is rude and wild enough—
> Upon the verdant meadow—
> Upon the sunburnt plain,
> Upon the sandy hillock
> We waken music's strain.
>
> Beneath the sparkling concave
> When stars in millions come
> To cheer the pilgrim strangers
> And bid us be at home,
> Beneath the lovely moonlight
> Where Cynthia spreads her rays,
> In social groups we gather.
> We join in songs of praise.

As a poetess, Eliza had begun to look on the brighter side. As
a diarist, she reports troubles. On the night of August 25, half the
herd of her hundred went off up the trail and stalled them until
the companies ahead caught and sent the stock back. Within a day
or two their troubles were compounded by the poisonous water of
the alkali country. Carcasses were "strew'd all along the roadside"
as Eliza's company passed. A note left by Willard Snow at Independence Rock said that he had lost eleven oxen from his fifty.

By September 1 he had lost twenty-five, and was unable to move. In the end, that stretch of trail that for all the emigration was hardest on livestock, nerve, and spirits forced upon them a limited renewal of cooperativeness. "Capt. Snow ask'd assistance as a duty, saying he was not beholden to any man, &c., &c. Capt. G[rant] manifested a spirit of meekness & spoke with wisdom, &c. It was mentioned that the Capts. be authorized to act for the com, & yoke whatever in their judgment was proper to be put in service of cows, heifers, calves, &c. Some thought the motion oppressive & objected, but it was carried by the majority."

They were in that condition of unwilling cooperation when they began encountering, one after the other, groups of Saints returning from the Salt Lake Valley to Winter Quarters: on August 31 three Battalion men, apparently dissidents from Norton Jacob's party; on September 2 Jacob and his hunters; on September 3 William Clayton's thirty-three wagons drawn by ox teams and carrying seventy-one men; on September 4 Jesse Little, who had gone as far as Fort Hall with Brannan and Captain James Brown of the Battalion, and then turned eastward to return to the Eastern States Mission he had left in June, 1846; and on September 8 Brigham and the Twelve with the horse and mule teams.

There was a joyful reunion high up on the Sweetwater. The ladies prepared a feast to which 130 sat down and at which they got so interested in exchanging news that Indians stole forty head of their horses. But despite that serious loss, this was the end of their overt quarrelsomeness. Brigham lit on Parley Pratt, the handsome and eloquent mouth of Mormonism, for "neglecting to observe the order of organization," and gave him such a chastisement as he had given Erastus Snow for causing the loss of his spyglass. Pratt took the rebuke with meekness; it is a constant astonishment to an outsider how submissive even the apostles could be to this man who united with his own hard capacity for command the ultimate authority of the priesthood.

Submission and a renewed spirit galvanized them. From the Sweetwater on over South Pass, across the Green and past Fort Bridger and over the Bear River Divide, down Echo and Weber Canyons and up the excruciating road through the gulches of the Wasatch, these companies bickered less. When a company asked the company ahead to stop and wait, it stopped and waited. When they met for prayers and discussion, Eliza felt they talked things over in a "candid, intelligent, and brotherly manner." Though they had already experienced freezing nights and snow flurries, and felt the need of haste, "yet they did not like to transgress the principles of order and submission."

Before Brigham left them on September 10, Eliza had had a brief meeting with the man to whom she was sealed but who was probably, at least as yet, only her token husband. Who, she asked as he stopped to bless her in her carriage, would be her counselor for the year to come, before he returned with the next year's emigration? Eliza Snow, Brigham told her. "She is not capable," Eliza said in humility, to which Brigham replied, "I have appointed her president."

Like him or not—and many in his own time hated him at least as harshly as they hated the devil—he was an extraordinary leader. As he had done at Sugar Creek in the first days of their anguish, he made them one with his blessing and his voice, restored their courage, sent them on a renewed people. If they straggled now, they straggled less for reasons of contention than for convenience. They began arriving in the valley on September 24, and were all in by October 2. Their sufferings were not extraordinary—six or seven deaths, the loss of considerable livestock, the inescapable accidents and discomforts of the trail—and these they bore, each with his own kind and degree of fortitude.

Jedediah Grant's daughter had died on September 2 and been commemorated in one of Eliza's "mourn not" poems. On September 27 Grant went by Eliza's carriage in Echo Canyon, hurrying the body of his wife to the valley for burial. Those deaths, like the multiple losses of Hosea Stout, would only harden his already formidable zealotry; he took them as the Lord's testings. And so for others, such as Charles Coulson Rich, whose mother died two days after being brought into Zion. But others came more happily, and less harshly tested, to the promised mountain home. Rich's wife Mary, after a thousand miles of ox-driving, arrived healthy but so ragged she was not quite modest. "When we arrived in Emigration Canyon, the longest place on my dress was just a little below my knees. I had walked over the brush, driving my team, to keep them in the road, and could not stop to untangle my dress when it got fastened, but had to walk on, leaving part of my dress behind." And Irene Pomeroy, that sturdy defender of the faith, came in still clenched to the notion of shaming or persuading her New Salem relatives into the Gathering: "If we ever meet in the resurrection you cannot say I never told you ... I would die in one minute for this gospel if necessary or required of the Lord. Remember what I say to you, I expect Augustus before long." The long plains crossing had not worn Irene or her mother out, nor depressed their spirits as it had depressed those of Harriet Young. "The journey does not seem to us now as it did in Mass. Why we [would] not think any more of coming back than we used to of going to New York city."

Counting those of the pioneer party who stayed, the Mississippi Saints and the Sick Detachment who joined them on July 29, the Big Company, and the random Battalion members who came over the desert from California and did not continue on eastward, the valley population during the winter of 1847–48 was 2,200 to 2,300.* What they did, how they managed, how they made the first hard steps toward building the Kingdom, is not our story. Our story is the trail, and there are a few people still on it who must be accounted for.

Though Mormon historians make note of their journey, the myth-makers have rather naturally neglected the several parties which returned in the fall of 1847 to Winter Quarters. They are worth looking at, both for the hardships that some of them experienced and for their demonstration of what the trail and the frontier might have done to Mormon cohesion if Brigham Young and the power of the priesthood had not been an even stronger force. After all, the

* Brigham H. Roberts, in the *Comprehensive History*, says that 2,095 had arrived by October 10, 1847.

Mormons were of the same breed and blood as the Gentile emigrants, and were acted upon by the same wild border. Only their faith, the authority of the priesthood, and the peculiarly coherent social system that their faith encouraged made them different from the adventurous, independent, and violent men who made the trip under other auspices. Temporarily out from under the control of the hierarchy, they could have been expected to backslide, and furthermore they had left families and friends back on the Missouri, and had an incentive to hurry. The result was that the two principal groups who left the valley ahead of the Twelve—Norton Jacob's hunters and Clayton's ox teams—were close to mutiny and violence through a good part of their return journey, and arrived not as austerely disciplined companies but as a rabble of backbiting stragglers.

The instructions to Jacob's party, transmitted in writing from the High Council, were plain:

> As you are about to leave this place on your return homewards, we have thought best to select Norton Jacob to be your leader; which if you approve, we want you to agree that you will follow his counsel implicitly; and we desire that you will be agreed in all your operations, acting in concert and keeping together . . . Be prudent in all things and do not give way to a hurrying spirit, not letting your spirits run away to Winter Quarters before your bodies can arrive there. As soon as you arrive at a good hunting country, we wish you to stop and hunt, so as to supply the ox teams that will start from here in a few days; and then you will not be detained any longer hunting, but will be able to pursue your journey steadily to the buffalo country on the Platte. Be humble; be patient; be prayerful. Listen to the counsel given you, and obey it, and you shall be blest . . .

They were never humble, rarely patient, seldom prayerful, nor did they listen to counsel. Neither were they blest. Several of them were Battalion men who had not seen their families since July of the year before, several others were of that frontiersman breed that was least amenable to priestly or any other discipline. One of them was

Tom Brown. They had barely reached Echo Canyon before Henson Walker and Joseph Rooker, two Battalion men, cut out and headed east by themselves to meet the Big Company.* By the time they reached a branch of the Bear River, John Norton and Joseph Hancock were openly grumbling about Jacob's traveling too long. In camp that night Norton threatened to cowhide John Wheeler for being too lavish with the flour, though the flour was Wheeler's own. By the next day the "hurrying spirit," and perhaps a hankering after Jim Bridger's whiskey, led Tom Brown, James Oakley, and Madison Welsh to push on without any counsel to Fort Bridger; and on the next, Ezra Beckstead "manifested a rebellious spirit in leaving his place and starting his team ahead of the company." By August 21 John Norton was baiting Jacob and threatening to whip him, and on the twenty-second Jacob noted that "those soldiers were all full of cursing and swearing, except David M. Perkins. Thomas Brown was as profane as any of them, swearing they would leave the company and with their horses go ahead to Winter Quarters when we got to the Sweetwater."

Killing antelope, an occasional blacktail deer, now and then a lean buffalo bull, once a mountain goat, they went squabbling and scattering, re-forming only to scatter again, over South Pass. They met Ezra Benson bearing back to Brigham a census list of the Big Company, and on August 29, on the Sweetwater, they encountered Parley Pratt and the first of the westbound wagons. Periodically John Norton was still offering to whip Jacob, and now he gave to Parley's people so unfavorable an account of the valley that Jacob thought he disturbed their minds.

Below Independence Rock, where they found plenty of buffalo but poor feed, they stopped to dry meat, and here Joseph Hancock added to the division among them by expressing opinions chillingly close to blasphemy. He doubted that he would go back to the valley; maybe he would go back to Jackson County, Missouri, where Joseph had promised him his inheritance, and marry a Pottawattamie squaw

* These, presumably, were the ones Eliza Snow reported meeting on August 31, though she mentions three, not two.

and be ready on the spot when the inheritance was delivered. He did not believe in building temples just to sell them to the Gentiles. "Heber Kimball is as good a man as Brigham Young, and he does not receive revelations; and I do not believe that Brigham Young is a prophet or that he ever received any revelations but what he got from Joseph Smith, and they are all written down beforehand." Norton Jacob recorded his heretical tirade with horror. Who could wonder that such men, contemptuous of the authority of the Twelve, should be unruly and disobedient in other quarters? The Lord would recompense them. Troubled as much by the rebelliousness of his men as by the shortness of feed and of wood to dry his meat, he moved on through a rain that shortly became snow, and at noon on September 7 arrived at the Last Crossing, where on the following day Clayton's ox teams overtook him.

On August 10, a week before he started back for Winter Quarters, William Clayton had confided to his journal a secret gripe that put him, for the moment, almost on the side of Joseph Hancock.

> I have received from Elder Kimball a pair of buckskin pants, as a present I suppose, but as I have on similar occasions been branded with the idea of receiving a great many kindnesses without consideration, I will for this once state a little particular on the other side of the question. I acknowledge that I have had the privilege of riding in a wagon and sleeping in it, of having my victuals cooked and some meat and milk, and occasionally a little tea or coffee furnished. My flour I furnished myself. I have had no team to take care of. Howard Egan has done most of my washing until a month ago in consideration of the privilege of copying from my journal, using my desk, ink, etc. The balance of my washing I have hired. Now what have I done for Brother Kimball? Am I justly indebted on this journey? Answer: I have written in this journal 124 pages of close matter on an average of 600 words to a page, which if paid at the price of recording deeds in Illinois would amount to over $110.00. I have collected the matter myself, besides writing letters, etc. This has been for his special benefit. I have kept an account of the distance we have traveled for over 800

miles of the journey, attended to the measurement of the road, kept the distances from creek to creek and from one encampment to another; put up a guide board every ten miles from Fort John to this place with the assistance of Philo Johnson. I have mapped some for Dr. Richards and keeping my own journal forms the whole benefit to be derived by my family by this mission. I have yet considerable to write in Elder Kimball's journal before I return. I am expected to keep a table of distances of the whole route returning from here to Winter Quarters and make a map when I get through, and this for public benefit. Now how much am I considered to be in debt, and how often will it be said that I was furnished by others with victuals, clothing, etc., that I might enjoy this journey as a mission of pleasure.

Poor Clayton was doomed always to find his efforts unrewarded or unappreciated. Probably he should have reminded himself that at least he had been snatched from the vengeful presence of Hosea Stout. And at least his return journey as far as the Platte ferry was more restful than Norton Jacob's. The ox teams went in two divisions, with Tunis Rappleye and Shadrach Roundy as captains and with a mounted group whose duties were to hunt, drive loose cattle, and to scout the road and repair it where necessary. Better organized and more authoritatively led than Jacob's hunters, and with a new roadometer whittled by William King on the hub of one wagon (Appleton Harmon was still at the Platte ferry) they made good time and had no trouble as far as South Pass, though since they started with only eight pounds of flour, nine of meal, and a few beans each, they had to skimp on rations. Clayton, who had been told there would be twenty-five pounds of flour put in for his personal supply, characteristically found that it had been left out.

Encounters with the units of the Big Company raised their spirits and enlisted their cooperativeness, and Clayton spent a good deal of time drawing maps of the City of Zion for the curious. But the acids of the trail were eating on them. By September 7, as they were working through rain and snow down toward the Platte ferry, and

Clayton's ten had been held up by strayed cattle, John Pack requested the use of some of the loose animals to get their wagons in. Both captains "generously refused for some cause or other." And that was only the smallest opening symptom. Brotherliness was hard to sustain on that road, especially after Norton Jacob's hunters, relieved of their advance duties, joined their outfits and their disregard of counsel to the ox teams.

By Horseshoe Creek, where the roadometer broke down over the same rocks that had broken the other one coming out, and where they had begun to live on meat alone for lack of breadstuff, Clayton noted that "John Pack has got flour enough to last him through. We have all messed together until ours was eaten, and now John Pack proposes for each man to mess by himself. He has concealed his flour and beans together with tea, coffee, sugar, etc., and cooks after the rest of us have gone to bed. Such things seem worthy of remembrance for a time to come."

On September 14 they were joined by William Empey, Luke Johnson, and Appleton Harmon, who had come down to Fort Laramie after finishing their ferrying duties. Empey hooked on with Jacob's group, Luke Johnson went off with an interpreter to see if he could recover seventeen horses stolen from the Twelve back on the Sweetwater, and Harmon left them again to sign on as a blacksmith at Fort Laramie through the winter. Norton Jacob, self-righteously noting down every delinquency, observed that "Thos. Brown and the soldiers, except David M. Perkins, have been, ever since we came into the Green River Valley, bulling about going on ahead. This morning they, with Wm. Clayton and Jack Redden, made a break and away they went." Later Jacob's ten overtook the bolters camped on the spot where Brigham had blistered them all coming out, and Jacob was moved to wish to God "that a different spirit prevailed in this camp." His wish was not granted. Next day Tom Brown, Beckstead, Bird, Roberts, Welsh, and even the previously dependable David Perkins took out ahead again. With unaccustomed charity that might have reflected his own inclination to bolt, Clayton said they went on because they had no bread. After they had left, John Pack discovered his gray mare was missing. He instantly laid the theft on the men ahead—an opinion, said Jacob, "very much censured by Wm. Clayton, as though it was slandering the men who had just left us. But, on examining, the mare was tracked to their camp, 5 miles below."

Either as plaintiff or defendant, Pack was close to the center of their disputatiousness, and Clayton was their disputatious court reporter. On September 25, down on the North Platte, Joseph Hancock killed a fat buffalo cow and Pack "took the hind quarters and the best meat off the rest of the cow, together with all the tallow, then sent for Rapleyee to take what he had left and divide it amongst the company." Pack and Rappleye had high words. Bitterly censorious of such greed, Clayton felt that Pack had "disgraced himself in the estimation of many ... I do not think I can ever forget him for his treatment of me, but I cherish no malice nor feelings of revenge ..."

Their days were a round of petty squabbling. The second division had had better luck hunting, and had enough meat to see it home, but would not (said the first division) share it. Thomas Cloward "has manifested feelings and conduct worse than the general run of gentiles," Clayton wrote, and "for my part I shall remember John Pack, Thomas Cloward, Norton Jacobs and Joseph Hancock for some time to come." Sometimes Clayton's entries are cryptic, as is that of October 3, down on North Bluff Fork (Birdwood Creek): "Considerable anxiety and feeling has originated in the breasts of two or three brethren in consequence of a rumor being circulated which deeply concerns one individual but it is not known whom." Whatever it was, the rumor could have been started by Clayton himself.

In their counsels they were badly split between their desire to wait for the Twelve to catch up and their eagerness to reach their families, between the need to hunt and the need to press on to better grass. On October 6 they split again, eleven wagons going ahead with Redding, Empey, Hancock, Pack, Cloward, Jacob, Zebedee Coltrin, Clayton and others. Within forty-eight hours a threatening band of Pawnees had forced them to retreat upon the second division, which greeted them with jeers and laughter and "many hard speeches . . . such as "damned hypocrites,' 'damned liars,' 'mutineers,' etc.," and ordered all those who had started ahead to travel in the rear henceforth. "Young Babcock shook his fist in Zebedee Coltrin's face and damned him and said he could whip him. For my part," said Clayton, "I shall be glad when I get in more peaceable society." As was his habit, he felt that their quarreling would "leave feelings of revenge and hatred which will require some time to cover up." For a man filled with pious sentiments, Clayton spent a good deal of time reminding himself to remember injuries.

Fortunately for the future of their brotherly love, they were almost home. The day after their encounter with the Pawnees they met sixty United States soldiers hunting around Grand Island for the site for a fort (it would be built there next year, Fort Childs, later renamed Fort Kearney, one of the landmark posts on the Oregon Trail), and on October 14, just as they were fording the Loup Fork, men bearing a white flag hailed them from across the river and turned out to be Hosea Stout and a detachment of his Winter Quarters police, come anxiously out this far to meet the Twelve. Everybody rejoiced, presumably, except William Clayton, but even he had cause to rejoice a week later when he and eight others pushed on ahead and reached Winter Quarters a little before noon. Their journey had taken nine weeks and three days, the round trip a few days over six months. Clayton's family, though it had suffered some illness, was intact. Moreover, on the return trip Clayton had remeasured the whole length of the trail except for a few miles between Horseshoe Creek and the La Bonte, where the roadometer had broken down. "I find the whole distance to be 1,032 miles and am now prepared to make a complete traveler's guide from here to the Great Salt Lake, having been careful in taking the distance from creek to creek, over bluffs, mountains, etc. It has required much time and care and I have continually labored under disadvantages in consequence of the companies feeling no interest in it."

So Clayton had both his road information and a comforting sense of being unappreciated. The data he had gathered would be published in St. Louis, in time for the emigration of the next season, as THE LATTER-DAY SAINTS' EMIGRANTS' GUIDE, *Being a Table of Distances, Showing All the Springs, Creeks, Rivers, Hills, Mountains, Camping Places, and All Other Notable Places, from Council Bluffs to the Valley of the Great Salt Lake, also, the Latitudes, Longitudes, and Altitudes of the Prominent Points on the Route, together with Remarks on the Nature of the Land, Timber, Grass, &c. The Whole Route Having Been Carefully Measured by a Roadometer, and the Distance from Point to Point, in English Miles, Accurately Shown.* By W. Clayton.

It was the most complete and reliable guide available for any strand of the Overland Trail, including that section between Fort Laramie and the Dry Sandy where all the strands fused. Appreciated or not by Clayton's companions, it would be valued by thousands, both Mormon and Gentile, in the years to come—though actually more by Gentile than by Mormon, for the Saints, sheep guided by careful shepherds, had no need of a guidebook except to satisfy their curiosity about where they were. The copyright was in Clayton's name. There was no acknowledgment anywhere in the book of contributions by Willard Richards, or Appleton Harmon, or even Orson Pratt.

The return journey of the Twelve, though important because it brought the leaders back to those who had been left leaderless, and prepared the way for the mass emigration of 1848, has little to distinguish it as story. With Brigham among them, this company was in no danger of the dissension that had troubled the return of the earlier parties. Though they lost seventeen or eighteen horses in a snowstorm at Pacific Springs when a band of Sioux mistook them (they said) for horses of the Shoshones, they recovered most of them. And though they stopped for several days among the several groups of the Big Company, blessing and exhorting and instructing, they still made the return trip in nine weeks and four days. Like the Clayton company ahead of them, they came down the Platte through plentiful buffalo, and suffered no hardship except the late-season shortness of feed for their animals. But the last parties on the trail that season were less well equipped and less lucky.

At the end of their year of service, a few of the Mormon Battalion had re-enlisted. The majority, mustered out in the Pueblo de Nuestra Señora la Reina de Los Angeles, faced the problem of rejoining their families and people, wherever they might be. Plans to go overland toward the Great Salt Lake country by the Spanish Trail fell through. Instead, they made their way in several parties up the coast to Sutter's Fort—a good energizing six hundred-mile trip through the July heat of the Central Valley. Some found work in northern California, the majority made ready to go over the mountains. Though they had only a general idea of where the Saints might have settled, they were sure to. get information on the road. On July 24, the day when Brigham was brought to the mouth of Emigration Canyon, the Battalion boys ran into a man named Smith, who had been one of Sam Brannan's companions on his fruitless trip across the desert to intercept the pioneers and bring them to California, and Smith told them where they would have to go.

Knowing their destination now, the remnant of the Battalion rested a while and assembled outfits and then started across the Sierra, through the camps where their companions acting as General Kearney's escort had buried some of the Donner remains earlier that summer. A little east of Donner Lake they met Brannan himself, who had left Salt Lake City on August 9, and a day later Capt. James Brown, en route to California to get the discharges and back pay of the Sick Detachment. He had counsel for them from the Twelve, who advised that all without means of subsistence should work through the winter in California and bring their earnings on in the spring. About half of them turned back, some of them to work for Sutter and participate in the discovery of gold; the rest went on, arriving in the valley on October 16.

They arrived in tatters, so destitute that the destitute population of the valley had to take up a collection of old clothes to cover them. Some found their families in the valley, some were too worn

down to go any further, but thirty-two men under P. C. Merrill
and an unspecified number under Andrew Lytle determined to go
on, though the season was already so far advanced that they might
at any time find the passes closed by snow. After only a day or two
in Salt Lake City they set off, a day apart. Briefly they camped together at Fort Bridger, but thereafter did not see one another again
on the road.

They had cause to feel that the Lord was taking special care of
them. The returning pioneers had encountered snowstorms between South Pass and the Platte ferry as early as September 6, yet
these men, leaving the Salt Lake Valley on October 17 and 18, got
across all the passes without being stopped. It was very cold, the
North Platte so solidly frozen that they crossed on the ice, and
down along the North Platte between Fort Laramie and Scotts
Bluff they had to dig buffalo chips from under a foot of snow. On
one bitter night their mules' ears froze so badly that the tips later
fell off. As it turned out, they would have done well to clip the
frozen ears and save them for emergency rations, for just when they
decided to stop and dry some meat they found themselves utterly
out of the buffalo.

Traveling light, they had hoped to make it to the Missouri in
thirty days. In the event, it took them sixty. All down the treeless, buffalo-less, comfortless icy valley of the Platte they drove
themselves, famishing. Arrived at the Loup Fork, the Merrill party
found ice running in the swift current, and the quicksand bottom
so shifting and treacherous that they were eight days finding a
passable ford. Alpheus Haws, who had left California with five animals, lost his last one, with part of his outfit, in the Loup's icy water,
and lost his last pair of shoes in the quicksand. A skinny horse that
had mired and died standing up froze in solid during the night, and
in the morning they cut him out and made beef of him, but not
such beef as comforted the innards. Their plight as they struggled
on toward the Elkhorn affected even the Pawnees, who took them
in and gave them food. Living on an occasional deer or wild turkey,
eating even the feet and the entrails, they made it to the Liberty

Pole and across the Elkhorn on the ferry, left ready in the stream, and in one last thirty-mile effort reached Winter Quarters on December 11.

Lytle's company, a day or two behind, fared even worse. Expecting to buy flour at Fort Bridger, they found the supply exhausted by the Oregon emigration. All they picked up was a family named Thorne, desperate to return to the States. At Fort Laramie they were able to buy only a pound or two of crackers and a little dried buffalo meat, but below Laramie they found a fly-by-night trader who sold them a hundred pounds of flour for twenty-five dollars. That was about three pounds per man: they voted to use it only for thickening gravy, but it was an optimistic vote, for near Chimney Rock they too found themselves deserted by the buffalo, even the stragglers, and there was no gravy to thicken. And now it snowed on them, drifting in places to a depth of two feet.

By the time they neared the Loup Fork they were so ravenous that, finding the frozen heads of a donkey and a mule that the Merrill company had killed for food, they cracked them open and ate the brains. A day or two later they ate their rawhide saddlebags, no longer needed for carrying food. During a several-day storm they killed and ate a worn-out mule of Lytle's. The pet dog of the Thorne children, which they had been eyeing hungrily for a week, they finally traded to some Pawnees for a piece of dried buffalo meat.

Like the ox teams returning the previous autumn, they had split soon after passing Fort Laramie. Now their rear company came up just in time to keep the advance group from being robbed by the Pawnees—Pawnee charity was erratic, it seemed—and they traveled together for safety. The cornfields of the Pawnee town on Plum Creek had already been long harvested by the Indians and had been gleaned by several companies of travelers, so that all they found was a few rusty cobs. Mule meat, then, and without salt—ten days of it, and little enough of that. On December 17 they operated the Elkhorn ferry for the last time that season—its ready presence there was testimony that the Mormon Trail was already a road—and limped across the high prairie to Winter Quarters.

They were just in time for Brigham's resounding and confident Second General Epistle to the Saints throughout the Earth. On December 5, with a home for the Saints located a long way from Gentile interference, and with his personal authority consolidated among the Twelve, Brigham had seen himself chosen and sustained as President, Prophet, Seer and Revelator—what Joseph had been, what Sidney Rigdon had wanted to be, what Joseph Hancock did not think Brigham was, what Brigham himself was altogether too canny to ask to be until as President of the Twelve he should be pushed into it by the people's own desire. Now the Second General Epistle, besides acquainting the Saints throughout the world with what had happened since the expulsion from Nauvoo, came like the "great trumpet call to the hosts of Israel" that some Mormon historians have called it. It is an extraordinary document. Leader of a people scattered, harassed, impoverished, and disfranchised, Brigham did not speak like a leader on the defensive. He blew the attack, he cried the Gathering, just as Joseph Smith, newly escaped from Liberty jail and with a whole new city to build, had cried it in the early months of Nauvoo.

> Gather yourselves together speedily near to this place, on the east side of the Missouri river, and, if possible, be ready to start from hence by the 1st of May next, or as soon as grass is sufficiently grown, and go to the Great Salt Lake City, with bread sufficient to sustain you until you can raise grain the following season.
>
> Let the Saints who have been driven and scattered from Nauvoo, and all others in the western states, gather immediately to the east bank of the river, bringing with them all the young stock of various kinds they possibly can; and let all the Saints in the United States and Canada gather to the same place by the first spring navigation, or as soon as they can, bringing their money, goods, and effects with them; and so far as they can consistently, gather young stock by the way which is much needed here and will be ready sale; and when here let

all who can, go directly over the mountains, and those who cannot, let them go immediately to work at making improvements, raising grain and stock on the lands recently vacated by the Pottawattamie Indians and owned by the United States, and by industry they can gather sufficient means to prosecute their journey. In a year or two their young cattle will grow into teams; by interchange of labor they can raise their own grain and provisions, and build their own wagons, and by sale of their improvements to citizens who will gladly come and occupy, they can replenish their clothing and thus speedily and comfortably procure an outfit...

We have named the Pottawattamie lands as the best place for the brethren to assemble on the route, because the journey is so very long that they must have a stopping place, and this is the nearest point to their final destination which makes it not only desirable but necessary; and as it is a wilderness country it will not infringe on the rights and privileges of anyone...

There was outlined the evacuation of Winter Quarters, already under fire from the Bureau of Indian Affairs, and the establishment of Council Bluffs, which the Mormons would call Kanesville in honor of their most effective friend, as the outfitting point for the Mormon Trail. There was also reiterated the resilient and laborious spirit of Mormonism and its ant-like determination to build and re-build. There was forecast the continuing history of the trail, which would be the route of the Gathering until the transcontinental railroad, more than twenty years hence, would render it obsolete. And the railroad itself, a good part of the way, would follow the track of their laborious wheels.

6

_{ΥΥΥΥΥΥΥΥΥΥΥΥΥΥΥ}

The Gathering-up of Zion

THE HISTORY OF THE TRAIL is essentially the history of the Gathering, and the Gathering involved two principal groups of people: immediately, the Nauvoo refugees settled in and around Winter Quarters and on the Pottawattamie lands, and ultimately, the thousands of European converts, at first mainly English, later with a heavy Scandinavian infusion, eager to emigrate to Zion to get their inheritances and their anointings and their endowments. Both of these kinds were poor almost by definition, though the Saints in the western states were much more capable of taking care of themselves on the trail. For the next twenty years a substantial part of the Church's money and effort would be devoted to bringing the two groups in. Until 1852 that effort would be expended principally upon the American Saints; after that year, the Gathering would operate primarily out of Liverpool.

The migration of 1848 had as its nearly exclusive purpose the evacuation of Winter Quarters. Never sympathetic to Brigham's deal with Captain Allen, Superintendent Thomas H. Harvey of the Bureau of Indian Affairs had visited Brigham at the beginning of December, 1846, to protest his establishing a settlement west of the river on Indian Lands. Brigham retorted that the Battalion boys had left their teams and families in the road in order to enter the United

States service, and that the families would not be able to move until their men returned. It might possibly be two, three, four years before they would all be able to move out. Harvey was suspicious of their intention to move at all, and so reported to Washington. He estimated that there were 10,000 Mormons on the two sides of the Missouri, besides many down in the state of Missouri who pretended to be apostates but probably were not, and he thought they might be planning a chain of permanent settlements from the Missouri to the Pacific. Their improvements did not look like temporary improvements to him.

Before many years, the pressure of the overland emigration, both Mormon and Gentile, would force a change in the Indian treaties, and the Territory of Nebraska, running clear to the crest of the Rockies, would be carved out of the Indian Lands in 1854. But for now, the Bureau of Indian Affairs attempted to live up to its obligations and uproot the Mormon settlers west of the river. Inevitably, its efforts looked to the Saints like more persecution. William Huntington's son Oliver, arriving in Winter Quarters from his New York State mission in May, 1848, heard Brother Brigham in Sunday meeting curse the United States and its people with vigor. "He was never known to curse so much in his life as on that day. The nation, the land of Missouri, that sickness should not allow any but the righteous to live upon it, and old Colonel Miller an Indian agent for his meanness and abuse to the saints." Old Colonel Miller may have been acting out of Missouri prejudice, as they thought, but he was likewise acting on orders, and the orders said that the Mormons must clear out of Winter Quarters and Cutler's Park without delay.

Despite his belligerence, Brigham had already given in. He arranged the loan of sixty teams from the Pottawattamie Saints, in order to get as many families as possible from Winter Quarters to the valley. Those unable to buy or borrow an outfit he instructed to move across to Kanesville or one of the neighboring settlements. To judge from the journal of John Pulsipher, the reason given the Saints for the abandonment of Winter Quarters was that too few would remain there to be safe. By late May they were giving up—

for the third or fourth time, some of them—their houses and fields, and ferrying the Missouri back to the Iowa shore. Those with an outfit headed for the Elkhorn. Of these there were three great companies, the first two led off by Brigham and Heber on May 26, the third by Willard Richards and Amasa Lyman on June 30. Together, according to Little's compilation in *From Kirtland to Salt Lake City*, they totalled 923 wagons and something over 2,400 people.

We have acquaintances among these companies, Hosea Stout and Oliver B. Huntington for two, and Howard Egan, and Appleton Harmon, who had come in in March from his blacksmithing job at Fort Laramie to gather up his family. ("As soon as she saw me began to weep looked for the cause Could not see the little boy and on enquirey was told that he was dead.") There was also young John Pulsipher, who drove a wagon in the hundred commanded by his father Zera; and there was Ann Eliza Webb, a little girl of four, the camp darling. She danced to the hymns and the wagon songs in the evenings, and by day ran along the train gathering flowers and being petted even by Brother Brigham, who twenty-one years later would make her his twenty-ninth wife and find that he had married a Tartar.*

These and others have left accounts of the 1848 emigration, but it would be worse than tedious to follow in detail a trip that differed little, in its route or its experiences, from those we have already accompanied. Some of the details do astonish us—Hosea Stout's note that one hot day an ox "melted and died," for instance, or Oliver Huntington's report of the death of Sister Taylor: "She took the measles on the steamboat coming, and after them the canker set in and carried her off. She said all the time that she should die, she was mortified before death." But most of their hazards and accidents were run-of-the-road—people run over by wagons, cattle strayed or stolen or killed by poison water, skunks under the wagon that even Hosea Stout had to "deal mildly with," sheep that suffered and

* As with Joseph's wives, there is some uncertainty about the exact number. Irving Wallace calls Ann Eliza No. 27; the book issued by the Young family shortly after Brigham's death, and signed by Brigham Young Jr., and by eight surviving wives, gives the total as 26.

sometimes died from the arrow-grass of the Platte valley. Like other companies, they had their grumblers and their jokers. On a night after Brother Gates' wagon tipped over and he blamed his women, a horsey guard went around crying, "Eleven o'clock and all's well, and Gates is quarreling with his wife like hell." Like other companies, they nursed a sense of continued persecution: they thought the soldiers building the fort at the head of Grand Island were somehow aimed at the Saints, not the Sioux. Like other companies, they divided on the trail for easier traveling, Heber's company and one ten of Brigham's even crossing to the south side of the Platte at Ash Hollow, rejoining the rest of the company at Fort Laramie.

Nothing special—a summer's journey with hardly an incident to mark it except the wounding of Howard Egan, William Kimball, and Thomas Ricks in a fracas with some Omahas back on the Elkhorn. Once in a while a journal gives us an intimate peep into the Mormon mind. Here, for example, is the poem that young John Pulsipher composed on his twenty-first birthday, out on the plains:

> This is the day that gave me birth
> In eighteen twenty seven
> From distant worlds I came to Earth
> Far from my native heaven
>
> Twenty & one long years have past
> To grief and sorrow given
> And now to crown my woes at last
> We're to the mountians driven
>
> 'Tis not for crimes that we have done
> That by our foes we're driven
> But to the world we are unknown
> And our reward's in heaven
>
> What troubled scenes may yet ensue
> To strew our paths with sorrow
> 'tis not for us to know its true
> For we know not of tomorrow

> One thing is sure, this life at best
> Is like the troubled ocean
> We almost wish ourselves at rest
> From all its dire commotion
>
> But let it's troubled bosom heave
> Its surges beat around me
> To truth, eternal truth I'll cleave
> It's waves can never drown me.

His jingle is a compendium of Mormon self-righteousness and long-suffering expressed in ladies' magazine clichés. Somewhat different is the utterance that boiled out of Appleton Harmon out along the North Platte, while he was in charge of the hunters for Isaac Higbee's hundred of Heber Kimball's company:

> Meney a sportive day we had and Meney a long tramp after the Buffalo and Antelope until our legs would git wearied looking for game or tracking them on the Sandy plains, wounding them, then in the chace, until the Sun would Sink behind the Rockey mountain range and we to our waggons repair, the night Creap on. the wolves howl and we by the range of Some promentory glittering in the pale Moons rays, gide the weary hunter to his home, with his venson.

It makes you wonder what Appleton Harmon had been reading, marooned the winter before at Fort Laramie, and it demonstrates what the wild country could do to a mind prepared by inspiriting literature. It pops out of this blacksmith's ordinarily prosaic narrative like a djinn out of a bottle. Dangerous stuff, illustrative of the fact that this people's religious and literary susceptibilities were not unrelated, that both were part of the romantic movement, and that both throve best when given thoroughly conventional channels and flues of escape. Most of the profound Mormon attitudes—for instance that one about the desert blossoming as the rose—are expressible in cliché. The profile of a pious Mormon's religious or literary effusion is likely to be as predictable as Old Faithful's—

which does not in the least lessen its force. The Byronic, mortuary, or accusingly long-suffering tone of much Mormon literature, including diaries, provided the only adequate substitute for a full belly and a comfortable life. "We have suffered & endured such a continuation of persecution & cruel treatment from those who boast of Civilization," said Pulsipher on his birthday, "that we now choose to make our home in the Desert among Savages rather than try to live in the garden of the world surrounded by Christian Neighbors. The Lord Almighty is preparing a scourage for this nation. The blood of the Saints is crying from the ground for vengence on that wicked nation...We are glad the mountain valies are so far off as they are..."

Gleanings such as these are the principal reward of a search through the 1848 journals—these and certain details of the trail itself. Oliver Huntington especially is illuminating on the practical aspects of wagontrain life. He described the Elkhorn ferry, for instance, one of the first and most substantial of the trail's improvements:

> A raft of logs very strongly pinned and fastened together with hewed slabs 3 inches thick, fastened across the raft at the right distances to receive the wheels of a wagon, and butmants for a landing on either side of the river, then lastly of all to consider, was that it was situated on a very short bend of the river at the extremity and a chain was hitched from the raft to the shore, in a direction straight up from the center of the river at the extreme bend, so that when the raft was loaded (which took but one wagon) by letting loose the fastenings it swung within a few feet of the opposite butmant, but had to be drawn back by a rope, and there was always men a plenty for that, and a wagon was crossed in five minutes the day through.

Huntington also described in detail the difficulty of the Loup Fork ford, and the way "the wheels would rise up on the sand, the sand break and let the wagon fall, striking hard and the same constantly repeated rapidly, gave the sensation of riding over a stony road." And he summarized as well as any the routine camp tasks:

As soon as we had struck our wagon in the corral, unyoke the cattle, gather wood, or buffalo chips for cooking, and usually to save fuel, dig a hole in the ground about 3 feet long, one wide, and 6 inches deep. This prevented the wind from blowing the heat away ... The next thing was to get the cows (they were drove all together clean behind all the company) and milk, then drive stakes to tie the cattle to an about this time the drove would come in and then get the cattle and tie them.

These were regular and sometimes as many more, according to camping ground, sometimes have to go a mile and a half for water and sometimes had to dig wells. Each ten herded their cattle and every man and boy able to do it took their regular turn according to the number of the ten. In the ten I was in there was an increase until the number of wagons amounted to 24 and 25 persons to herd, and it came each ones turn once in 5 days taking 5 to each days company.

The guarding of the camp fell on each man proportionally once in 7 and sometimes 6 nights, and then half the night, only. The herding and guarding together with my daily tasks kept me beat down and wore out all the time. The women were as well drove beat down as the men.

Sundays were scarcely a day of rest nor could it be if we travelled Monday.

Beat down and wore out, but otherwise healthy, they made it to the Sweetwater, where they unyoked the sixty teams borrowed from the Pottawattamie Saints and sent them back. After a few days of waiting, replacement teams came up from the valley, and they went on, not hurrying. In Weber Canyon they camped to rest and fish, and to let Brother Brigham come up from the rear. Thus properly led by the President and the Twelve, the first companies of the 1848 emigration made a more fitting entrance than had the pioneers the year before. The Richards-Lyman company, following without incident, was all in by October 19. Together, the 1848 emigrants doubled the valley's population, and changed Great Salt Lake City from a desert outpost into the effective center of the Church of Jesus Christ of Latter-day Saints. Behind them, at the other end of the trail, Winter Quarters was a ghost town, and

Kanesville was being converted into the staging point for the emigration.

The principal agent of that conversion was Orson Hyde, the President of the Quorum of the Twelve Apostles, and the only one of the Twelve who had not yet been to the valley. He was assisted by George A. Smith and Ezra Taft Benson. Their principal instrument of information was the *Frontier Guardian*, which Hyde began publishing in Kanesville on February 7, 1849. In one of its earliest articles, the *Guardian* issued instructions to Saints planning to emigrate during the 1849 season. Companies would go whenever fifty wagons, appropriately armed and equipped and supplied, were assembled. If they were not adequately supplied and armed, they would not be allowed to go. Because of the shooting-up of Egan, Kimball, and Ricks the previous spring the Omahas and Otoes were less trusted, and organization therefore would from the beginning be strictly military. Also, since the winter along the Missouri had been unusually severe, Hyde had to assume, in the absence of word from the valley, that it had been severe there too, and that breadstuff well beyond that needed for the trip would not be out of order.

Hyde's guess about the severity of the winter in Salt Lake was sound. The season had been so severe, in fact, and the hardships of the valley population so great, that when the long-awaited General Epistle finally arrived in Kanesville it poured cold water on the enthusiasm of the Saints eager to gather.

> For the future, it is not wisdom for the Saints to leave the states or California, for this place, unless they have teams and means sufficient to come through without any assistance from the valley, and that they should bring breadstuffs sufficient to last them a few months after their arrival, for the harvest will not be gathered nor the grain ready for grinding. The inhabitants of the valley will be altogether dependent on the crop of this season for their support, and will have no time to leave their tillage with their teams to bring in emigrating camps as they have hitherto done.

In the circumstances, that was minimal caution. Self-sufficiency in the desert did not come easily, and there was no surplus for new-comers. Through the winter and spring most of the valley Mormons had been living on half rations or less, digging thistle roots and camas bulbs, eating crows and coyotes, begging, borrowing, making do, doing without, sometimes selfishly hoarding, sometimes nobly sharing or giving away, and they had barely made it through. So instead of the come-all-ye enthusiasm of the 1848 General Epistle, this one was cautious and selective. The emigrant it encouraged was the one who could bring at least three hundred pounds of bread-stuff—one hundred for the trip, two hundred for the six months following—besides milk cows, livestock, "and as many little necessaries and comforts as he can procure and haul."

As usual, there is some discrepancy among the estimates of the 1849 numbers. Howard Egan took the first company of twenty-two wagons (something had already happened to the fifty-wagon minimum) out the south side of the Platte, apparently about the middle of May. (Kate B. Carter's census of the emigration, notably unreliable, dates the departure April 19.) Mrs. Carter lists an Orson Spencer company of a hundred wagons that left on June 6, an Allen Taylor company of the same size on July 12, and a Silas Richards company, unspecified as to size, that left July 10. It is certain that George A. Smith and Ezra Taft Benson led out the last company of the season on July 14. Altogether, the year's emigration was guessed in the October General Epistle to have been between five and six hundred wagons, which should have meant at least fifteen hundred people.

For adventures they had stampedes, until they learned to tie the oxen outside, and corral only the loose stock inside the wagon circle; for anxieties they had cholera. Egan, traveling the south side in the midst of the first great surge of the California gold rush, met company after company hurrying as if trying to outrace the taint of horror and death they carried in their wagons, and a lieutenant at Fort Kearney told him that between Independence and Grand Island there had already been sixty cholera deaths. But among the Mormon companies who traveled the north bank, only four cholera deaths were reported, and the big company under Smith and Benson had no deaths whatever, from any cause.

The cholera even eased their way, for the Indians had fled from the deadly vicinity of the trail; and confirmed their self-righteousness, for they saw many Gentile graves rifled by the wolves, but not a single Mormon grave that had been touched.

> Among the graves of those whose bones lie around bleaching in the sun, their flesh consumed by the ravenous wolves, we recognize the names of several noted mobocrats from the states of Missouri and Illinois . . . Among others we noticed at the South Pass of the Rocky Mountains, the grave of E. Dodd, of Gallatin, Missouri . . . The wolves had completely disinterred him. The clothes in which he had been buried lay strewed around. His under jaw bone lay in the grave with the teeth complete, the only remains that were discernible of him. It is believed he was the same Dodd who was a prominent mobocrat and who took an active part in the murder of the Saints at Haun's Mill, Missouri. If so, it is a righteous retribution. Our God will surely inflict punishment upon the heads of our oppressors in His own due time and way.

Thus the *post hoc ergo propter hoc* of their tribal sense of wrong. These signs shall follow them that believe.

More significant than anything that happened to the Mormon companies on the road in 1849 was the news that came back from the valley with Almon Babbitt early in September. The Gentile trains boiling toward the gold fields had not only suffered severely from cholera and measles, especially during the first half of their journey, but they had been reckless of their animals and equipment all the way, and they suffered the consequences after they left the easy Platte valley and came into the mountains. Babbitt reported that the gold seekers, convinced that warnings against the saleratus water beyond Last Crossing were a "Mormon humbug," had suffered crippling losses of animals, and that the stretch between Last Crossing and Independence Rock was all but impossible to travel through because of the stench from the 2,000 dead oxen along it. And there was more than ox carcasses along the road. Furniture, clothing, food, tools, wagons, had to be thrown away or abandoned as the animals gave out and men converted in desperation to packhorse or shank's mare. The profitable pastime of scavenging the trail, sometimes as far east as Fort Laramie, got its start among the Saints during this year. But they hardly had to scavenge the trail, for hundreds of California pilgrims limped into the Salt Lake Valley in a state of collapse, and most of them either sold off belongings to lighten their loads across the desert, or converted wagon outfits into packtrains for the last leg, or bought food and livestock to replace what they had lost. The Saints so enjoyed the experience of skinning the Gentiles that they were in danger of trading away too much of their hard-won grain crop and bringing another lean winter on themselves. Apart from that danger, the whole summer was a great profitable picnic. A man might get three or four good heavy wagons for one light one, six or eight worn oxen or mules for a single team of fresh ones, and after three or four weeks in the valley pastures the worn-out ones would be freshened up for another profitable trade. Cloth, clothing, tools, everything that great expectation had loaded up for California fell into Mormon hands at half its wholesale cost in the States, and in a single season corrected the condition of painful shortage in which the Saints had been living.

The good grain crop and the windfall from the Gentiles changed the valley's economic situation sharply for the better, and the tone of the October General Epistle reflected that change. Now there were no more warnings or cautions. The confidence and exultation of the 1848 Epistle were renewed.

> We have great occasion for thanksgiving to Him who giveth the increase, that He has blest our labors so that, with prudence, we shall have a comfortable supply for ourselves and our brethren on the way who may be in need, until another harvest; but we feel the need of more laborers, for more efficient help, and multiplied means of farming and building at

this place. We want men; brethren come from the States, from the nations, come! and help us build and grow, until we can say enough; the valleys of Ephraim are full.

The same Epistle contained official notice of the means that the Twelve had devised for bringing in the poor unable to pay their own way. It was called the Perpetual Emigrating Fund, it was to be raised and increased by voluntary contributions, and its agent, Bishop Edward Hunter, would be coming east with the next mail.

> As soon as Bishop Hunter shall return with . . . his freight of Saints to this place, the cattle and teams will be disposed of to the best advantage, and the avails with all we can add to it, will be sent forth immediately on another mission and we want you all prepared to meet it, and add to it, and so would we continue to increase it from year to year until when 'a nation is born in a day' they can be removed the next if the Lord will. Therefore ye poor and meek of the earth, lift up your hearts and rejoice in the Holy One of Israel, for your redemption draweth nigh: but in your rejoicings be patient, for though your turn to emigrate may not be the first year, or even the second, it will come.

Another trumpet blast, and like the Epistle of 1847, heard around the world. Bishop Hunter, who left the valley with a group of missionaries on October 19, arrived in Kanesville on December 11, 1849. In his saddlebags he had the first $5,000 contributed to the P.E. Fund, and he had specific instructions to make his funds stretch as far as they would. He was to buy young stock that could later be sold to advantage in the valley; he was to buy no wagons, which were now plentiful in Utah, but to encourage people to make their own cheap wagons with little expensive iron in them; he was to issue a minimum of supplies. "The poor can live without the luxuries of life on the road and in the valley as well as in Pottawattamie." In those instructions was established the pattern of hard frugality that would mark the Mormon emigration for many years to come. Frugality had the double effect of permitting the gathering of more Saints per dollar, and of simultaneously testing and trying them and making them strong in the faith.

In the minds of the Twelve, the gathering of the Pottawattamie Saints took precedence over emigration from abroad. They had hopes of doubling the population of the valley every year, and of using the augmented manpower of each year to raise grain to support a doubled population the next. To that end, they held back for the time being the elders who might have been sent on missions abroad, and dedicated them to the raising of crops. Later, the word was, they would go out "by the thousands." Until they did, the most easily gathered, and the most capable of becoming immediately productive frontier farmers, were the Mormons stranded on the former Pottawattamie lands. But moving them did not turn out to be a job for a season, as clearing Winter Quarters had been. Not only was the P.E. Fund too small to help all who needed help, but there was a considerable reluctance among the Mormons in Iowa to uproot themselves once again just when their squatter farms began to produce. It took three more years before all of them who had not drifted away from the Church could be removed to Utah. In addition to the 500–600 wagons of 1849, about 700 went out in 1850, at least 500 in 1851, and 1,300–1,400, carrying perhaps as many as 10,000 people, in 1852.*

All of those years were bad cholera years, but the Saints, sticking generally to their north bank trail and thus avoiding contact with people who had brought the disease by riverboat from New Orleans, kept comparatively free of infection. Orson Hyde, writing from the Last Crossing of the North Platte at the end of July, 1850, reported five hundred new graves on the south bank and only three on the north. In 1852 at least two Mormon trains besides a train carrying sugar-making machinery to Salt Lake City traveled the south bank, and lost a good many of their members to the disease, which by the estimate of Abraham Smoot had filled 1,000 graves between the Missouri and South Pass before July 4. But on the whole the Saints, aloof, well-organized, with better camp rules, a larger proportion

* Again the figures are uncertain. The *Deseret News* list, admittedly incomplete, contains about 6,000 names. Gustive Larson accepts James A. Little's figure of 10,000.

of women, and a probable advantage in cleanliness, suffered far less than the Gentiles. Mormon missionaries moving eastward against the tide of the emigration reported with horror and pity the miseries of companies in which the disease had broken out, and noted with some complacency that cholera seemed to like Missouri and Illinois trains better than others.

In a similar mood, Orson Hyde looked back from a comfortable camp on the Sweetwater in August, 1850 and commented on the hundreds of dead horses and cattle along the fifty miles that the Saints called "the valley and the shadow of death." "And oh! the sacrifice of wagons, clothing, firearms, beds, bedding, buffalo skins, trunks, chests, wretchedness and woe, and yet thousands and tens of thousands follow on the way with the hope of securing the wealth of the world."

Nothing could have expressed the difference between Mormon and Gentile so eloquently as the differing motivations that drove them across plains and mountains. Gold was no temptation to any Saint who was truly strong in the faith and who really hearkened to counsel. Gold, as Brigham Young remarked, was for paving streets. Well-led by experienced plainsmen, the Saints passed safely across the country that killed or demoralized so many gold seekers, and found their sanctuary in the mountains with a minimum of hardship. But even with the assistance of the P.E. Fund, and even with re-peated trumpet-calls crying the Gathering, the seasons of 1850 and 1851 by no means cleared the Pottawattamie lands of Mormon set-tlers. So in the winter of 1851–52 Jedediah Grant and Ezra Taft Benson were sent to Kanesville with orders to complete its evacua-tion, and with enough P.E. Fund money to do it.

It took some extraordinary organizational and logistical work, but they succeeded. In March, having done its job, the *Frontier Guard-ian* ceased publication. During May, June, and July, twenty-three separate companies, averaging sixty wagons each, departed from Kanesville. One of these, Captain Foote's company of 105 wagons, which traveled the south side, had serious trouble and suffered at least twenty-two deaths, mostly from cholera. If others had com-

parable losses they do not seem to have been recorded. And losses
or no losses, fear of cholera or no fear of cholera, there was no
resisting the urgent shooing of Benson and Grant. Apostle John
Taylor, who passed through Kanesville in midsummer, found empty
houses, empty barns, stripped grocery stores, deserted streets, "as
though they were swept out with a besom."

With that energetically pushed exodus, the first phase of the
Gathering was over, the Nauvoo refugees finally gathered in. And
as early as September 3, 1850, as if to prefigure the future, there had
arrived in the valley a train composed of thirty-one wagons of English converts led by Abraham Smoot. They brought Captain Pitt's
Brass Band to the mouth of Emigration Canyon for that one, and
fired off the artillery, and held a feast and a dance. For these were
European paupers, the so-called "Poor Company," the first of the
English poor to be brought to Zion under the protection of the
Perpetual Emigrating Fund. Not many like them would follow until the Pottawattamie lands were cleared, but after 1852 most of the
companies that traveled the Mormon Trail would not be American
frontier farmers with pioneering skills in their hands and muscles,
but English millhands and miners, Corn Law paupers, incipient
Chartists, Scandinavian farmers, German servant girls—the indus-
trially dispossessed, the chronically unemployed, the widowed, the
orphaned, those for whom Zion in the tops of the mountains was a
far golden word, a pillar of fire or cloud, a star shining in the West.
More than ever, because of their weakness and inexperience, they
had to be brought across an ocean and a continent not by their own
spontaneous efforts, but by the systematic effort of experts.

One further matter. At a meeting of 107 missionaries about to go
abroad in August, 1852, Brigham Young decided to announce publicly the doctrine of spiritual wives, and the announcement, together
with the doctrinal justifications by Orson Pratt, was published in
the *Deseret News.* Not even after this would missionaries discuss
polygamy freely; they were instructed to say as little about it as
possible, and it is likely that many a convert arrived in Salt Lake
City in the later 1850's still persuaded that it was an ugly rumor

perpetuated by the enemies of the Church. Nevertheless the admission was public, and could be corroborated in the newspapers, and it must have had something to do with the decline in number of conversions and the large number of apostasies during the '50's. And yet not so many apostasies and not such a decline in conversions as one might have expected. Between 1840 and the end of 1854, 15,642 British Saints, plus 1,003 Scandinavians and fifty Germans, had been shipped from Liverpool by Church agents. Nevertheless the London *Times* estimated that there remained in Great Britain alone between 30,000 and 40,000 Mormons, a good proportion of whom were bent upon gathering. This was the deep and constantly renewed well that after 1852 scores of missionaries would pump with the aid of the Perpetual Emigrating Fund.

7

TTTTTTTTTTTT

Artist in Transit

On February 5, 1853, Frederick Hawkins Piercy, a young artist from Portsmouth, set sail from Liverpool in the ship *Jersey*. His destination was the valley of the Great Salt Lake, by way of New Orleans, St. Louis, Kanesville, and the Mormon Trail. His purpose was to sketch "the principal and most interesting places on the Route," as well as characteristic Salt Lake City views and portraits of Mormon leaders, these to be published later by the Liverpool agents of the Church along with "suitable descriptions and statistics." Piercy, though only twenty-three, was a competent artist and a sharp observer. Not a Mormon himself, he had relatives who were, and he could view Mormon affairs with both sympathy and detachment. The journal that he kept reports the characteristic journey from Liverpool to the valley with more objectivity than most Mormon diarists were able to muster, and the sketches that he made along the way are all of them valuable, some of them unique. Since their publication in Piercy's *Route from Liverpool to Great Salt Lake Valley*, in 1855, they have been reproduced as illustrations in two dozen histories, and they remain to this day the best pictorial record of the trail during the height of its use, as well as of certain early monuments and personages of Mormonism.

The *Jersey* carried three hundred Mormon steerage passengers,

about half English and half Welsh, who were organized according
to Mormon practise into wards—Piercy calls them "districts"—
with a president and two counselors over each. These leaders en-
forced the most scrupulous cleanness, with regular morning
scourings and frequent fumigations and sprinklings with lime. They
established rules of moral conduct and set hours of prayer and
instruction and tried to regulate the bedlam of the galley and to
persuade the pilgrims of the danger of uncovered lights. Despite
their warnings, they had a deck fire, and despite their sanitary efforts they had one death, but their behavior by and large was ex-
emplary and, after the first seasickness, their health good. In every
way it was a representative Mormon emigrant ship, a floating village. It is not clear from Piercy's account how many were P.E.
Fund charges, but a good many of them probably were—plain
godly people who behaved themselves and hearkened to counsel
and took pleasure from the adventure of their voyage, who flocked
on deck to watch sunrise and sunset and were awed by the vastness
of ocean, who were edified by the instruction of the elders and faithful in their prayers. After six weeks they got up one morning to
see the water around them muddy gray-green instead of blue, and
later a great Mississippi River steamboat helped them over the bar,
and another of the same kind hooked on and towed them for four
days upriver to New Orleans. There their presidents and counselors
fought off the thieves and confidence men who swarmed on the
docks, and handed the converts over to James Brown, once a captain
in the Mormon Battalion and now the Church agent charged with
shipping the emigrants from New Orleans to St. Louis.

Brown and his assistants gave them more warnings: beware of
swindlers and people who offered treats of ardent spirits, beware
of eating too heartily of fresh meat and vegetables after their six
weeks on salt pork, sea biscuit, and rice. Brown arranged their passage on the steamer *John Simonds*—the fare to St. Louis $2.25 for
adults, half that for children between three and fourteen, children
under three free—but Piercy took a more leisurely trip, sketching
the river towns and setting down in his diary the overflowing life

of the Mississippi as it was in 1853. His precise, idealized drawings represent New Orleans, Baton Rouge, Natchez under and Natchez above the hill, Vicksburg, Memphis, St. Louis; and his diary is filled with Negroes, Irish Americans, riverboatmen, the geography and commerce and navigation of the great waterway on which three years later young Sam Clemens would become a cub pilot. A couple of weeks after parting from them in New Orleans, Piercy caught up with the converts in a camp on the bluffs above Keokuk. Perhaps because of their sanitary precautions, perhaps because they were a little ahead of the sickly season, they were in good health as they prepared under the tutelage of Ira Eldredge, Isaac Haight, and Cyrus Wheelock to make their way over the old Nauvoo-Council Bluffs road to the Missouri. (Old? Seven years—but it seemed something that had been there a lifetime.)

Piercy's sketch of the Keokuk camp is disappointing, merely a cluster of tents and a rutted road in the open woods atop a bluff, and the sketch he made of Nauvoo from across the river at Montrose was taken from such a distance that it shows little more than a far-off town on a hill. But in Nauvoo itself Piercy sketched the single standing wall of the great temple, and that drawing is of historical importance, for it shows architectural details, including the moon-faced capitals said to have been modeled on a face Joseph saw in a vision, that were later destroyed. The temple had been set afire by an arsonist in November, 1848, and further damaged by a tornado in May, 1850, so that the French Icarians who had finally bought the property pulled most of it down for safety's sake. But what Piercy saw, that single wall towering in ruin, impresses us as no other picture does with the opulence of the imagination that conceived the building and the ant-like Mormon industry that could erect it on a raw frontier.

The Mansion House, Joseph's old dwelling, was being run as a hotel by Joseph's first wife, Emma. Piercy stayed with her, but for some reason did not take her portrait, nor did he report in his journal what was surely the burden of her conversation—her bitter denial, against all the evidence, that Joseph had ever advocated or practised polygamy. But he did draw Joseph's two sons, Joseph Jr. and David, and he produced a quite remarkable portrait of Joseph's mother, Lucy Mack Smith. Later he visited Carthage and drew the bleak stone jail squatting inside its rail fence, the bullet-pocked room where Joseph and Hyrum had been sitting with Willard Richards and John Taylor when the mob stormed the stairs, and the well-head against which militiamen had propped Joseph's body to fill it with bullets after he fell from the window. Piercy was right in believing that those sketches "would possess undying interest for tens of thousands."

Because Piercy did not cross Iowa with the emigrants, he left no sketches of Garden Grove or Mt. Pisgah or any of the other way stations along that once-woeful road. But as soon as he had taken the steamboat to St. Joseph and made his way overland to Kanesville (since its evacuation by the Mormons called Council Bluffs City) he took up once again his recording of salient points on the emigration route. His "Entrance to Kanesville" is perhaps the earliest picture of that town. (The next one, so far as I know, was a pencil sketch made by the folk artist George Simons in 1858.) His "View of the Missouri River and Council Bluffs, from an Elevation," is an accurate representation of the cottonwood-lined bottoms as seen from across the river, near Winter Quarters. And his romantic "Council Bluffs Ferry," much reproduced since, is the Missouri frontier idealized into an eighteenth-century English landscape.

Council Bluffs, already filled up with Gentiles, could stand a little idealizing. Piercy found it dirty, expensive, and full of sharpers. His journal advised travelers who needed a milk cow to see her milked before they bought, travelers stocking up on bacon or biscuit to taste before laying down their money, travelers purchasing a wagon to examine the axles for shakes and flaws, travelers buying teams to test them in the yoke before closing the deal. In the same practical vein, he recommended fustian trousers, red Guernsey shirts, high-top boots, goggles, and beards for the men, and for the ladies short skirts, India rubber galoshes, and very large sunbonnets. (Somehow Hollywood has not accustomed us to think of pioneers in goggles and galoshes, but there they are.) Observing how emigrants very shortly had to throw away their heavy trunks and boxes, and repack in sacks, Piercy suggested as the best plains container a wicker basket lined with zinc, which would be light and waterproof and which would have a usefulness as metal on arrival. He speculated some on the possibility of gutta-percha overshoes for oxen. Then, having exhausted the possibilities of Council Bluffs and the practicalities of preparation, he crossed to visit Winter Quarters and found that someone had just set fire to the last house remaining there. His view of the river, with the burning cabin in its lower right-hand corner and two wagons pulling out upper left, thus commemorates symbolically the end of one chapter of the Mormon story.

One gathers that Frederick Piercy enjoyed his journey across the plains. He adapted himself handily to camp routines, learned to gee and haw an ox team, set the broken leg of a wagonmate; and he acquired an enormous respect for Brothers Miller and Cooley, the two elders who led the company and who had to cope, constantly and patiently, with accidents, weather, strayed stock, incompetent drivers, and all the personal problems of the ignorant and innocent sheep under their charge. He reports no dissension or lack of discipline: by 1853 Mormon Trail leaders had got their daily patterns down to a science, and when they were both competent and agreeable, as Miller and Cooley evidently were, the sheep went trustingly as they were taught to go.

The sketches that Piercy took back to be engraved in steel and wood made visual for thousands of European Saints the journey they longed to make, the city they longed to enter, the leaders they longed to know. After arriving in the valley, he sketched Brigham, Heber, Jedediah Grant, and John Smith, and on the way he drew the landmarks with the romantic names—Elkhorn ferry, Loup Fork ferry, camp ground at Wood River, Chimney Rock, Scott's Bluffs, Fort Laramie, Laramie Peak, Independence Rock, Devil's Gate, Fort Bridger, the Witches Rocks in Echo Canyon, the City of the Saints itself bowled in its great valley. Arriving ahead of his company as part of an express to ask relief supplies, Piercy took a bath in Emigration Creek, changed his clothes, and set down the accomplished journey in neatly tabular form.

Liverpool to New Orleans	5,000
New Orleans to St. Louis	1,173
St. Louis to Kanesville	620
Kanesville to Winter Quarters	12
Winter Quarters to G.S.L.C.	1,035
	7,840

Seeing it put so succinctly, English converts could learn to think of the journey to Zion as easy. Seen in Piercy's pictures, too, the road looked altogether softer than it was, for Piercy was no uncompromising realist. The Kanesville of his drawing shows none of its dirt, disorder, dust, mud, and ruffianly population, the Council Bluffs ferry is dominated by cottonwoods that look astonishingly as if they had been painted by Gainsborough or Constable, the Missouri which serenely reflects the loaded ferryboat looks like the Severn on a windless day, instead of Old Muddy full of snags and eddies and ropy currents. The forlorn shanties roofed with buffalo hides at the Elkhorn and Loup Fork ferries look more picturesque than depressing, and the litter of barrels and old wagon tires around them is artfully arranged instead of random and ugly. The camp at Wood River is a dream—a velvety meadow hard by a copse. One thing Piercy never learned to do was to represent realistically the stark western earth, bare or stony or prickly with weeds and bunch grass. His eye nearly always showed him turf even where the buffalo grass had run out and there could be no turf. On rocks he was better. His Chimney Rock and Scott's Bluff show the light-touched erosional pleats that they show a modern traveler, his Independence Rock is really exfoliating granite, his Devil's Gate has its authentic grain, his Witches Rocks could be nothing but erosional forms carved out of level sedimentary beds. It is no small achievement, for the West demanded a new eye of its artists, a new comprehension of structural geology, a new palette, a new way of painting light. Piercy's trick of accenting with Chinese white was by no means an ineffective one. Despite his idealizations, which were the inevitable marks of his time and tradition, he realized the trail vividly for thousands of his contemporaries, and he realizes it for us.

Piercy's diary and drawings represent well the route and the experiences of Mormon emigrants who sailed from Liverpool between 1848 and 1854. The elaborate notes compiled by his editor, James Linforth, include a history of the Perpetual Emigrating Fund and of the emigration through 1854—by all odds the most dependable data on the English emigration. Linforth assembled statistical charts of sailings, the numbers of emigrants by ship and year, and elaborate lists of the trades and occupations represented. These last are in themselves instructive on the question of how the Mormons were able so swiftly to create a thriving commonwealth in the desert. Though these English Saints might be incompetent on the trail, they had their own skills; they were bookbinders, bleachers, bakers, butchers, and bobbin reelers, dollmakers and diesinkers, file hardeners and fustian dressers, hackle-and-gillpin scourers and horse-nail forgers, ropemakers and riggers, swordmakers and stone cutters and saddlers, tinners and throstle tenters and table-knife hafters, warpers and wheelwrights and whitesmiths. In the valley there was use for all but the most specialized; nearly all skill could be put to use. (Thus the tabernacle organ would be built by an Australian whittler, and when the Mormons moved to develop their own basic industries such as iron smelting and the manufacture of beet sugar, they could look among their own numbers for the men who knew how.)

So long as Nauvoo had been the place of gathering, New Orleans was the port at which they landed, and the Mississippi the route of their journey inland. Essentially the same route was re-established in 1848, with the addition that emigrants either went overland on the Mormon Road from near Keokuk to Council Bluffs or, like Piercy, took a Missouri River steamboat from St. Louis to the frontier. But in 1854 Brigham Young wrote to Franklin Richards, in charge of the English mission, instructing him to abandon the Mississippi River route because of the cholera and malaria on the river, and ship his passengers to Philadelphia, Boston, or New York, from which Church agents would send them by train to Pittsburgh, by Ohio River steamboat to St. Louis, and by Missouri River boat to some staging point. Because of this change, Kanesville fell into disuse as the jumping-off place. During 1854, Westport (essentially Kansas City) was the assembly point for the plains journey; in 1855 Mormon Grove, just outside of Atchison, Kansas, about midway between Westport and St. Joseph; from 1856 through 1858, either Iowa City, the first capital of Iowa, or Florence, Nebraska, which had grown up on the ashes of Winter Quarters. After 1858 all Mormon trains staged at Florence until the extension of the Union Pacific westward from the Missouri allowed a longer and longer train ride into the plains. In 1864, 1865, and 1866 emigrants rode the cars as far as Wyoming, Nebraska, in 1867 they could ride as far as North Platte, in 1868 to the city of Laramie and later to Benton, Wyoming, along a route that diverged from the old Mormon Trail at the forks of the Platte and crossed the mountains considerably to the south of South Pass.

By the time those developments had occurred, the systematic Church emigrations had taken new forms. First there was the handcart experiment, beginning in 1856, and after 1860 there was an almost complete change to the system of Church trains, which left the valley early, picked up freight and passengers at the railhead, and returned at once to the valley. During these years travel would be interrupted by the outbreak of the Sioux in 1854, then by the abortive Utah War, when the United States sent an armed expedition against the Mormons in 1857, and later by the Indian troubles coincident with the Civil War. All would affect the Mormon movement of people, but none would stop it more than briefly. Since our topic is the trail, not the political troubles of the Mormon commonwealth, we had better keep our attention focused on the Gathering and its practical means. First, the handcart experiment.

8

Ordeal by Handcart

In all its history, the American West never saw a more unlikely band of pioneers than the four hundred-odd who were camped on the bank of the Iowa River at Iowa City in early June, 1856. They were not colorful—only improbable. Looking for the brown and resolute and weather-seasoned among them, you would have seen instead starved cheeks, pale skins, bad teeth, thin chests, all the stigmata of unhealthy work and inadequate diet. There were more women than men, more children under fifteen than either. One in every ten was past fifty, the oldest a woman of seventy-eight; there were widows and widowers with six or seven children. They looked more like the population of the poor farm on a picnic than like pioneers about to cross the plains.

Most of them, until they were herded from their crowded immigrant ship and loaded into the cars and rushed to the end of the Rock Island Line and dumped here at the brink of the West, had never pitched a tent, slept on the ground, cooked outdoors, built a campfire. They had not even the rudimentary skills that make frontiersmen. But as it turned out, they had some of the stuff that makes heroes.

Mainly Englishmen from the depressed collieries and mill towns, with some Scots and a handful from the Cape of Good Hope and the East Indian Mission, they were the casualties of the industrial revolution, life's discards, to whom Mormonism had brought its irresistible double promise of a new start on earth and a guaranteed Hereafter. They did not differ in any essential, unless perhaps in their greater poverty, from hundreds and thousands who had started for Zion before them. But their intention was more brash—was so impudent it was almost sublime. Propertyless, ill-equipped, untried and untrained, they were not only going to Zion, they were going to walk there, nearly fourteen hundred miles, hauling their belongings on handcarts.

The marathon walk of the handcart companies, though it involved only a few thousand of the total number of Mormon emigrants, was the true climax of the Gathering, and the harshest testing of both people and organization. In urging the method upon Europe's poor, Brigham and the priesthood would over-reach themselves; in shepherding them from Liverpool to the valley, the ordinarily reliable missionary and emigration organization would break down at several critical points; in accepting the assurances of their leaders and the wishful importunities of their own hope, the emigrants would commit themselves to greater sacrifices than even the Nauvoo refugees; and in rallying from compound fatal error to bring the survivors in, the priesthood and the people of Mormonism would show themselves at their compassionate and efficient best. The story of the 1856 emigration is a story of hardship and horror crowned with heroism. The batch of tenderfeet on the bank of the Iowa River in early June would experience mainly the hardship; the horror and the heroism would come later.

Brigham Young, pondering ways of quickly peopling his empire and making it strong against the inevitable renewed clash with the Gentile world, had thought up the handcart scheme himself, and very soon after the settlement of the Salt Lake Valley. As early as the General Epistle of October, 1851, he had suggested that if gold seekers could walk to California with their belongings on their backs or in a wheelbarrow, then Saints seeking a higher god than gold ought to be able to do as well. "Yes, start from the Missouri River with Cows, handcarts, wheelbarrows, with little flour and no unnecessaries and come to this place quicker, and with less fatigue, than by following the heavy trains with their cumbrous herds which they are often obliged to drive miles to feed." In the spring of 1852 a handcart plan was projected, but came to nothing. That was the year the Church decided to give all its energies to the final clearing of the Pottawattamie lands, most of whose settlers had teams and wagons and hence were not likely to test Brigham's theory.

For three years after the Great Migration of 1852, Church agents in Liverpool labored to make the P.E. Fund stretch to cover all those anxious to cross to Zion. In 1855 alone they sent 4,225 converts over. But despite the heavy flow, there was still a great backlog of poor Saints, many of whom had been saving shillings and pence for the trip for several years. The longer they had to wait, the higher became the costs. A plan whereby the agents contracted to deliver a man from Liverpool to Salt Lake City, all expenses paid, for £10, turned out to be uneconomic. Then in 1855 a grasshopper plague sharply reduced the crops in Utah, and was followed by a very hard winter that killed many cattle and horses. Supplies, draft animals, and contributions to the P.E. Fund were all short. The suspended handcart scheme was revived.

Some converts, especially those able to pay their own ship fare, had made a practise of settling temporarily in the eastern or midwestern states, wherever they could find jobs that would help them assemble an outfit to bring their families in some comfort to the valley. Plenty of the poor would have jumped at the same chance, if the Church would have brought them across the Atlantic. But all Church experience indicated that among those who stopped short of Zion there was a high apostasy rate. In his letters of instruction, Brigham warned against those who would use the P.E. Fund's help simply as a means of getting to America and escaping their economic trap. It was desirable that all emigrants sent under P.E. Fund auspices be sent all the way at once. That meant a greater expenditure per person; and the effort to reduce that expenditure meant, inevitably, the proposal to bring them across the plains with their small belongings in handcarts.

"Let all things be done in order," said the Thirteenth General Epistle of October 29, 1855, "and let all the Saints who can, gather up for Zion and come while the way is open before them; let the poor also come, whether they receive aid or not from the Fund, let them come on foot, with handcarts or wheelbarrows; let them gird up their loins and walk through, and nothing shall hinder or stay them."

Coming from one who had three times traveled the Mormon Trail, who had seen hundreds of the trailworn emerge from the mouth of Emigration Canyon, who was in constant touch with the missionaries and captains bringing in converts, and who had himself served in the British mission and knew the physical specimens that the missionary nets dredged up there, the Epistle was recklessly optimistic. It was the statement of a man who wanted something to be possible, not of one who knew it to be. It was more hortatory than sound. It minimized difficulties, especially those related to illness and infirmity; it failed to sound adequate warnings; it persisted in the statistical view of an earlier letter Brigham had sent to Franklin Richards: "Fifteen miles a day will bring them through in 70 days, and after they get accustomed to it they will travel 20, 25, and even 30 with all ease . . . the little ones and sick, if there are any, can be carried on the carts, but there will be none sick in a little time after they get started."

Those have been described by anti-Mormon writers as the words of a man willing to break eggs to make an omelet. It is perhaps fairer to say that in this instance Brigham was letting his impatience for growth and strength cloud his usually sound judgment, or was perhaps depending too incautiously on the caution of his agents. But he was surely not averse, either, to the principle of trying and testing his people, nor were they unwilling to be tested. Because he was the Prophet of the Lord, what he said was totally accepted, and used by both missionaries and converts to justify an adventure which common sense undazzled by prophecy might have annulled, or at least limited. Brother Brigham urged it, his missionaries and agents urged it, Piercy's *Route from Liverpool* showed them idealized scenes of a road along which he and a company of people like themselves had passed without incident, their friends and relatives in Zion wrote urgent letters, saying "Come."

Franklin Richards, ardent and devout and worshipful of Brigham, was immediately under strong pressure from converts frantic to be taken. He did not dissuade them or try to quench their enthusiasm, but called upon them to walk through with their families like ancient Israel, and promised them miracles of manna and quail. His editorials in the *Millennial Star* were fervid, and his circular of February 23, 1856 assured the English Saints that "the gathering poor, if they are faithful, have a right to feel that the favor of God, angels, and holy men is enlisted in their behalf. The present plan is peculiarly the Lord's . . ."

They believed. From letters, from the talk of missionaries, from a reading of Piercy's book, they thought they knew something of the trail. Already it had for them some of the quality of myth—they would recognize the country as they passed through, in the way they would have recognized the wilderness between Elim and Sinai. LeRoy and Ann Hafen, who have made the most extended study of the handcart companies, assemble plenty of evidence that the European Saints not only accepted the handcart proposal, but clamored to be included in it. "Do you like this way of traveling?" the tentative Epistle of 1851 had asked. "Do you think Salvation costs too much? If so, it is not worth having." Now from every branch of the European mission the answer was the same. "All feel Zionward . . . Tobacco smokers have resolved to quit, and put their savings thereby in the P.E. Fund, and those who have quit tea-drinking will also put their savings in the same." "The fire of emigration blazes throughout the Pastorate to such an extent that the folks are willing to part with all their effects, and toddle off with a few things in a pocket handkerchief." "Respecting emigration, I beg to assure you that I would not wish to see a greater desire for that than is evidently pervading every class, in every locality. 'Do help *me* to get to Zion,' 'When shall I go home?' 'Oh, do try to help me off this time,' are so often reiterated in my hearing . . . that they tingle in my ears."

The *Millennial Star* of January 12 had outlined the plan in detail, the February 23 circular repeated it. All P.E. Fund emigrants would sign a bond agreeing that once they reached the valley they would repay, with interest if required, the money advanced for their passage. Some converts would be able to pay in advance the full fare of £9 (half that for infants under one year), while some would be able to make a down payment and some would be total charges of the Fund. Handcart pilgrims would ship from Liverpool to New York City, from which place they would take the train to the end of the Rock Island Railroad at Iowa City. There Daniel Spencer and other Church agents would have handcarts and a few supply wagons waiting. There would "of course be means provided for the conveyance of the aged, infirm, and those unable from any cause to walk." Missionaries returning from Europe would escort the emigrants all the way from Liverpool to the valley. To these missionaries, perhaps because a few cautious ones had voiced doubts, Franklin Richards issued the closest thing to a warning in all the preliminary discussion.

> To toil along with handcarts through a journey of 1,000 miles [he characteristically softened it; it was nearly 1,400 miles] over the 'desert plain' and rugged mountains, through streams and kanyons, will be no easy task even for those who are accustomed to the fatigues and hardships of mountain life . . . None of the emigrating Saints have ever crossed the plains who have had greater demands on the shepherds of their flock, than those who will travel in the handcart companies the coming season . . . It is our constant desire not to mislead the Saints concerning the difficulties of the journey to Utah. We wish them calmly to make up their minds that it is not an easy task, and to start with faith, trusting in Israel's God.

Warning, but such a warning as, given the temper of the pilgrims, would only harden their resolution. Make up your mind it will not be easy, and then *start*.

Between the end of November, 1855, and the first of June, 1856, eight chartered ships carried 4,395 Mormon converts to America. Of these, about 2,000 planned to settle temporarily in the States and about 2,400 expected to go straight through. Of these 2,400, some had paid their own fares and some had had them paid by relatives in Utah, but 2,012 were P.E. Fund charges, paupers essentially, fully committed to the handcarts. Directing the emigration were Franklin Richards in England and John Taylor in New York. In Iowa City, charged with purchasing wagons, draft stock, and milk cows, and with supervising the construction of the carts, was a succession of agents including at one time or another Daniel Spencer, W. H. Kimball, George D. Grant, James Hart, and Chauncey Webb— this last a skilled wagonwright and the father of little Ann Eliza, now twelve, who would become Brother Brigham's twenty-ninth wife and Mormonism's most spectacular apostate. Attending each shipload of emigrants was a group of returning missionaries. Of these, Edmund Ellsworth, Daniel McArthur, Edward Bunker, James Willie, and Edward Martin would each captain a handcart company across the plains.

The handcart people were carried over in four ships; because stormy weather delayed shipping and made chartering slow, even the earliest did not sail until March 23. This was the *Enoch Train*, carrying 534 passengers. The *S. Curling*, laden with 707 Welsh, departed on April 19; the *Thornton* with 764, mainly English with a few Scandinavians, on May 4; and the *Horizon*, a monster that accommodated 856 passengers, on May 25. Thus in early June, when all of them should have been setting out from the Missouri, they were anywhere from 300 to 6,000 miles short of that frontier. The passengers from the *Enoch Train* had been stalled in Iowa City since May 12 because something had gone wrong and their carts were not ready for them. The *S. Curling's* Welshmen were about to land in New York, and would arrive in Iowa City before the *Enoch Train* people got away. The *Thornton* was on the high seas, the *Horizon* had barely left Liverpool.

Nothing was wrong with their shipping arrangements except

the lateness of their start. The ships, in fact, were an experience that most Mormons quite enjoyed. For a Mormon charter ship differed as sharply from the usual emigrant vessel as a Mormon village on wheels differed from the usual Missouri wagontrain. It was organized to the smallest corner and to the ultimate quarter-hour. Hardly had the pilgrims been delivered to their ship than the Mormon agent, usually the president of the European mission or his representative, came aboard and appointed a president and two counselors from among the returning missionaries. As soon as these had been "sustained" by the company, they divided the ship into wards and created bishops to head them. The elders worked out a sequence of duties, to be signaled by bugle or ship's bell: rising, cleaning quarters, disposing of refuse over the side, prayer; then breakfast in orderly groups, each group using the galley for a half to three-quarters of an hour and turning it over, clean, to the next. Throughout the day, instructive talks by the elders, prayer meetings, fairly often a wedding, sometimes a baptism, occasionally a burial; then another orderly assault on the galley and another spell of cleaning; in the evening, music or a dance or group singing; at eight or nine, by bugle or bell, prayers.

Their quarters were cramped, families often could not be accommodated together, the men as often as not slept on deck while the women and children took the cabins. But the scale of provisions fixed by the English and American Passenger Acts had improved upon the old emigrant rations, and sometimes at the end of a prosperous voyage friendly captains would let the emigrants keep the unused supplies. More than once, shipfuls of clean, pious, and well-behaved Mormons so worked on crews and officers that they converted them wholesale. From the very beginning of the operation, Mormon charter ships were show windows open to the world, effective advertising for the faith. Skeptics came to jeer and stayed to praise; and during the 1850's and 1860's all sorts of people, from Charles Dickens to Parliamentary commissions, were led to express public admiration for the efficiency and good order of these ships.

As surely as the Mormon wagontrains, they were villages in

transit. Made up in the first place of families who were often related or at least acquainted, they improved their social organization and frequently their morale during the month or two of the voyage. Each such ship was a sort of boot camp for the volunteers of Zion, and each had its top sergeants. Bewildered the pilgrims might be as they shuffled their little luggage through Ellis Island and gathered for roll call and were picked up by couriers at the dockside and escorted to the trains with hardly a pause—bewildered, but never afraid and never undisciplined. With good reason, they had complete faith in the efficient organization that had brought them this far. If nothing went wrong, they might arrive in the valley without having to confront a single difficulty of the kind that often desolated ordinary immigrants. As a general thing, converts came down the Mormon channels as smoothly as boxcars follow an engine down a track.

Unless things went wrong somewhere, as this time they did. In Iowa City Daniel Spencer had found prices high, labor scarce, seasoned lumber difficult to get. So the sisters who had improved the long sea voyage by sewing into tents and cart covers the heavy drilling issued them in Liverpool found immediate use for the tents, but none for the cart covers. They camped there four full weeks while the skilled men among them pitched in to make the carts.

They were utterly green. So far, they had caught only straining glimpses of America from harbor or wharf or station platform, or through smeared train windows. Now they encountered things that hope had not allowed for and piety alone could not deal with. The Iowa heat was steamy. Reared in England's gray cities, the pale novices sweltered, crowded three or four families to a tent. Children whined with prickly heat, the Iowa natives were often surly. In the long grass of riverbottom and woods, unseen insects bit English ankles and left red, swollen, itching patches. In Liverpool nobody had mentioned chiggers. And when the heat wave finally broke, the rain came with such a rush of thunder, lightning, and wind that it trampled their tent town as if stampeding elephants had run over it. Archer Walters, a carpenter from Sheffield who had worked all day building carts, was up most of that night of tempest tending his wife and daughter, both sick with some barbarous frontier ailment they called the American fever.

Archer Walters was more skilled than many of his companions— a fact which meant primarily that he had to work twice as hard— but his experience was otherwise representative. Four nights after the thunderstorm blew their camp about their ears, a woman in the Walters tent bore a baby—of course at one-thirty in the morning, to the maximum disruption of sleep. Five days later Walters made his first coffin, a small one. Two days later he made another, also small. The sickly, stick-legged children had small resistance to the "American fever" and the "cholera morbus." The words "hardship" and "sacrifice," at first abstractions hazed by zeal and piety, began to take on a concrete meaning.

During their long wait they would have examined curiously the growing line of carts in the wagon yard: flimsy boxes on wheels set to the usual five-foot track of a wagon. Some were no more than open frames covered with ticking, and with the side pieces extended into shafts that were joined at the front by a crossbar against which a man could set his hands or chest. Others were the heavier and solider "family carts" with hooped covers. These sometimes had iron axles, or iron skeins on a hickory axle tree, and some had thin iron tires; but the rims of many were merely wrapped with rawhide, and some had both axles and rims of unprotected wood.

Ideally the lumber should have satisfied a wagonmaker's specifications: hickory for axles, elm for hubs, white oak for spokes and rims, ash for shafts and box, and all of it well seasoned. In practise, and especially later in the summer as time and supplies both ran short, the carts were made of whatever could be found, most of it oak and hickory and a lot of it green. Here, as in other aspects of the handcart experiment, an original over-optimism was complicated by unforeseen difficulties of organization and supply. Economy or no economy, those carts should never have been designed without iron axles and iron tires, and should never under any circumstances have been built with green lumber. The shrinking aridity beyond the 98th meridian, the sand of the Platte valley, the rocky Black Hills, were all so familiar to the authors of the scheme that they should have known. And no matter what they were made of, it was a fatal miscalculation that the carts were not ready when the first converts arrived. The delay, merely awkward for the Saints from the *Enoch Train* and the *S. Curling*, was progressive; it became disastrous for the emigrants from the *Thornton* and the *Horizon*.

At last the earliest ones were ready. At the end of the first week of June they organized into two companies, 274 under Ellsworth and 221, of whom nearly half were Welshmen from the newly arrived *S. Curling* company, under Daniel McArthur. Together they were just under five hundred people, with one hundred handcarts, five wagons, twenty-four oxen, four mules, twenty-five tents. Though they carried only enough provisions to last them to Florence, they were all pulling their maximum load of 400–500 pounds, for few of the pilgrims at first would obey the rule of seventeen pounds of luggage for adults, ten for children. After Florence the carts would carry more flour, fewer clocks and dishes.

The Ellsworth company strung out across the Iowa prairie on June 9, the McArthur company two days later, and nobody's heart was heavy to be moving. They made it a celebration, with jokes and songs, and some young sisters stepped out ahead of everybody. Even those so sick they must ride in wagons or carts—and for those the accommodations were less ample than they had expected, and the extra weight of a woman or child on a cart was hard on those who pulled—were exhilarated at the start. At night they danced to the Birmingham Band that had come over on the *Enoch Train*. On Sundays there was morning and evening meeting, with prayers and exhortations for all and scoldings for the slack or frivolous.

But from the beginning some families stood anxiously around pallets where the sick grinned up with the enameled lips of fever, or walked soberly beside handcarts on which children babbled in delirium under a propped blanket or the hot hooped drilling. The elders prayed, laid on hands, anointed with consecrated oil, sometimes rebaptized for health, as they had done in every Mormon company; but every so often the camp gathered at a grave to testify to God's inscrutable power.

It was for children that Archer Walters went on making coffins. On June 15, one for John Lee's son and another for Sister Prator's [Preater's] child. On June 17, one for Job Welling's son. James Bowers, aged forty-four, interrupted the series of children's deaths on June 22, and Walters made his first full-sized coffin, but on June 26 he was back to the small ones—one for Sister Sheen's [Shinn's] child, and on July 2 one for Brother Card's daughter. All across Iowa's hot green miles, along the road that would one day be essentially the route of U.S. 6, through Newton and Fort Des Moines, they marked their way with wooden headboards, and on mornings when one of those graves must be left behind there were men and women who went numbly, head down, pushing like sleepwalkers at the crossbars and feeling the heaviness of the cart drag like the total weight of what they there gave up. But when Iowa Gentiles came to their gates to watch them pass, and they heard jeers, or the indignant murmur that it was a disgrace and a sin to make people pull loads like cattle, the Saints closed ranks, stepped out, made it clear that what the Gentiles thought an outrage they thought a privilege and a joy.

They bowed to God's will, and they trusted His promises. Somewhere up or down the line someone would break out in a foolish marching song, and it would spread until it took them all raggedly in, out of time like the music of a long parade:

> For some must push and some must pull
> As we go marching up the hill,
> As merrily on the way we go
> Until we reach the Valley, oh.

It was as much their personal song as Clayton's "Come, Come Ye Saints" had been the song of the Nauvoo refugees. They were singing it as they ferried the dirty Missouri and came into Florence. Despite the deaths they were in good shape, and so were the members of McArthur's company who came in behind them. Both companies had suffered a few dropouts, both had had a good number of faintings and heat prostrations. But they had pulled and pushed their carts nearly three hundred miles in less than a month, the sun had burned them brown, camp life and hard walking had toughened their muscles. As Brigham had prophesied, there were fewer sick. The children who marched barefooted into Florence to the tooting of the Birmingham Band had already hardened into health, and from here on would stand the trail much better than their elders. After a rest while they repaired their carts and laid in supplies, they took off again cheerfully to walk the last thousand miles.

Signs of God's power on the exposed plains were awesome to them. On July 26 ". . . we had not got far and it began to lightning and soon the thunder roared and about the middle of the train of handcarts the lightning struck a brother and he fell to rise no more in that body. By the name of Henry Walker, of Carlisle Conference, aged fifty-eight years. Left a wife and children . . . I put the body, with the help of others, on the handcart and pulled him to camp and buried him without a coffin for there were no boards to be had."

Thus Archer Walters. The lack of boards relieved him of the coffin-making that had sometimes kept him up half the night after an exhausting day, but there was no relief from the deaths. As the road lengthened up the interminable Platte valley and the sand ground on their unprotected axles and the carts warped and the spokes loosened in the dry air, as rations shortened and fatigue grew, the older and weaker members began to droop. Brother Missel Rossin (the official census shows no one by that name, but Walters mentions him) was found dead beside the trail. A couple of weeks later, still along the Platte, Brother Stoddard, aged fifty-four, gave out. Two days later Brother Sanderson [Sanders in the official census] lay down and did not get up.

Still, the two companies, traveling only a couple of days apart, constituted a fair-sized village, and the scattered deaths were not more frequent than they might have been in the average wagon-train, especially in a cholera year. Some, including Archer Walters' wife Harriet, even improved in health as they went on, though Walters, who had had to pull her a good deal of the time in the handcart, weakened as she grew stronger, and he told his diary privately that his wife was "very ill-tempered at times."

Strain, yes, fatigue, yes. Nevertheless their story is only the story of a walk. They slogged on under the searing sun, took shelter as they could from the wild plains weather, suffered the incomprehensible Welsh, with whom, as Walters said, their spirits were not always united. They greased their sand-weakened axles with tar or bacon rind or anything they had; they saw Indians, saw buffalo, had some fresh meat but rarely enough because they had no horses for hunting. And they watched the landmarks of the mythic trail fall behind them: the forks of the Platte, Ash Hollow, Chimney Rock, Scott's Bluff. Something in the nature of things seems to have demanded a spiritual purging near the halfway point, for at almost the same spot where Brigham had administered his monumental scolding, Captain Ellsworth in meeting complimented the first company for having grown less quarrelsome, but promised the low-down sneak thieves who had stolen food from the wagons that "unless they repent their flesh would rot from their bones and go to Hell."

On their part, the pilgrims muttered a little, but more privately, at Brother Ellsworth. He was too fond of walking ahead of the column with several young sisters. And how did it happen that if a sick person wanted to ride, the captain was always disgusted, but if one of the young sisters blistered her heel, there was always room for her in a wagon? (They were not far off in their appraisal of Ellsworth. Shortly after their arrival he would marry two of the young sisters, Mary Ann Bates and Mary Ann Jones. Something profound may be indicated about him by the fact that he already had a wife named Mary Ann Dudley. At least, with his system of always marrying girls of the same name, he saved himself awkward slips of the tongue.)

Actually, their morale problems were minor, and if anyone did snitch food from the wagons he stole from pure hunger, for their rations by now were lean. At Fort Laramie Walters swapped a "dagger" for some meal and bacon, and was so powerfully taken with the bacon's odor that he and his son Henry ate some raw.

It is not clear whether or not the Ellsworth company met any supply wagons from the valley, though it seems they must have, since Twiss Bermingham of the McArthur company reported that his company met such relief wagons at Deer Creek. Even with some relief supplies, they were certain to run short, for the Ellsworth and McArthur companies together, at the usual ration of a pound of flour per day per person, would have consumed a ton of flour every four or five days, and they had only five supply wagons. By Fort Laramie they were on short rations, and if they picked up flour they could not have picked up much. "Very poorly, faint and hungry," they crossed the Platte for the last time and labored up Avenue Hill toward the Sweetwater. The harder the way and the leaner the rations, the harder Ellsworth drove them. The day before they passed Devil's Gate they walked twenty-six miles. (That day Brother Nipras [Neapris] died and was laid in an alkali grave.) The day they crossed South Pass to Pacific Springs, they walked twenty-eight miles, nearly all uphill, and there was muttering at Ellsworth for walking so fast, nearly four miles an hour. Brother Ellsworth could have been walking that fast because he was worried, or because as leader of the first experimental handcart train he wanted to set a record, or because he was in a hurry to get home and marry two more Mary Anns, or because he thought it good for the Saints' souls that their bodies be tested. Whatever his reasons, he almost surely killed some of them with the pace he set.

The last entry in Archer Walter's journal records, appropriately, a death—Sister Mayer's. There the journal stops because Walters had no more strength for journals. Weakened by overwork and exposure and a diet of a few ounces of flour a day, he managed to drag his cart across Green River and the Bear River Divide and through the Wasatch to the valley. We may assume that he joined in the cheering when the Ellsworth company met on the road Thomas Bullock, Parley Pratt, and a party of missionaries bound for England to "thrust in the sickle" and harvest others like themselves. Probably he felt a thrill when they came out of Emigration Canyon on September 26 and he saw the great valley and the holy city of his hope, with the entire population drawn up to welcome them, crying hosannah and offering a feast of cool melons. Seeing in the flesh Brother Brigham and the other leaders waiting there with Captain Pitt's Brass Band would have been like meeting Gabriel and his angels and all the heavenly choir.

Footsoldiers of Zion, they did hornpipes for joy, or burst into unexpected tears, remembering the graves in the wilderness. But when the valley Saints asked why they had sent no early express of their coming, the pilgrims pulled from their pockets letters they had written in Florence, a thousand miles ago. There had been no one to hand them to. The scrawny paupers from England's mean streets, the ragged cavalcade of old men, women, and children, could brag that they had beaten everything on the road.* The McArthur company, which had that day walked all the way from the east side of Big Mountain—a hard three-day haul for the pioneers—came in while the greetings were still going on, and doubled the rejoicing.

Captain Ellsworth reported the handcart experience to the assembled Saints in the outdoor auditorium they called the Bowery. Personally, he regretted that they had had a single wagon with them. Not only had they been delayed many times by strayed oxen, but the presence of the commissary wagons had weakened the faith of the brothers and sisters: every time they had felt a little peaked they had wanted to ride. "I am persuaded," said Captain Ellsworth, "that if there had been no wagons for such people, there would have been none sick, or weak, but that their faith would have been strong in the name of the Lord."

Maybe so. To Harriet Walters, who had been weak and sick for two-thirds of the journey, and had watched her patient husband

---

* Though there were undoubtedly Gentile companies on the road with whom the handcart pioneers might have exchanged letters, there was only one Mormon train with which they could have had contact. This was the John Banks company, the third Mormon train of that season, which left Florence on June 15 carrying 300 people in 60 wagons. It thus left Florence four days after the McArthur company left Iowa City, and it arrived in Salt Lake City on October 1, five days after the McArthur and Ellsworth handcarts. So far as I know, no journal mentions the handcarts' passing the wagontrain on the road, though they clearly did, and though such an event should have produced a considerable lift to the handcart morale.

nearly kill himself pulling her or their sick daughter Sarah, walking all day at Ellsworth's fanatical pace and mending carts or burying the dead at night, that must have seemed hard doctrine. It must have seemed harder when two weeks later Archer Walters died of his walk to Zion. But in his way, Ellsworth was right. The more the Lord or the Lord's top sergeants demanded of His people, the more they would give. The first two companies, who between them suffered twenty-one deaths, thought they had given a good deal. The third company would be asked to give about the same, the fourth and fifth much more.

The third company, made up entirely of Welsh from the *S. Curling*, left Iowa City with sixty-four handcarts and a few supply wagons on June 28. Their leader was Edward Bunker, as mighty a walker as Ellsworth (he had been with the Battalion, and had already walked a good many thousand miles of the West) but quite evidently more tender of his charges. Few of his company could speak English, and their experience with oxen was such a blank that at first they could not even recognize their own teams in the morning, much less yoke up. Crippled with rheumatism brought on by a drenching, Bunker nursed them along the trail, and "nursed" is the correct word: in one tent of them were two blind persons, a one-armed man, a one-legged man, and a widow with five small children. One of the blind men, Thomas Giles, lost his wife and baby en route, and was himself so ill that Bunker had to leave him behind, with a couple of companions to bury him when he died. He did not die, but survived to become the Blind Harpist of Zion, presumably because Parley Pratt, coming past with the eastbound missionaries, pronounced a potent blessing on his emaciated head.

Others of the Bunker company did die on the road, and all were nearly always at the point of exhaustion, and all suffered from short rations despite supply wagons from the valley. But they did have eighteen milk cows and a reserve of beef cattle, and they did have a humane leader. Their journey from the Missouri River took them sixty-five days, an average of sixteen miles a day for over two months. Bunker's assistant David Grant, who had three times traveled the trail with horse and ox teams, wrote from the Platte valley that he had never made such fast time, and predicted that with one or two fixed supply points established out in the plains, the Saints would be crossing with handcarts for years to come. Like other enthusiasts, he chose to dwell on the seventy-three-year-old woman who had walked every step of the way, rather than on the lame, the halt, and the blind who found the trail a Sisyphean torment. And there was no gainsaying that the Welsh company had made remarkable time; it pulled into the valley only a week behind Ellsworth and McArthur.

But for the last two companies it was a different story.

The Church agents in Iowa City, having outfitted Bunker's company, had a right to feel that because of the lateness of the season there would be no more. Instead, they were inundated on June 26 by the *Thornton's* 764 passengers, and while they were frantically trying to get them equipped and on the road they were totally swamped by the great company from the *Horizon*, who arrived on July 8. In both groups there were some who had paid in advance for wagon outfits that weren't ready either, but the great majority were P.E. Fund poor. Thus late and with failing supplies of lumber and labor, the agents must somehow get together more than 250 handcarts and nearly a hundred wagons and teams, plus basic supplies for nearly fifteen hundred people for two to three months.

Hafen, who is generally protective of the hierarchy, suggests that things were so unprepared because the Iowa City agents had little warning of the arrivals, that labor and materials were very hard to assemble, and that possibly there was an intention of saving money by waiting until the emigrants arrived and then having them build their own carts. But if there was no adequate notice, why was there not? Was notice slow in coming because, as the Gentiles later charged, John Taylor in New York was not on good terms with Franklin Richards in Liverpool, and dragged his heels? And if there was really the intention of saving money by letting the emigrants build their own carts, it is hard to call such economy, considering the lateness of the season, anything less than criminally careless.

To the P.E. Fund pauper and the emigrant who had paid in advance to have a wagon ready for him, the reasons for the delay were less important than the fact itself. They waited a long, irritable, wearisome time before Captain Willie finally got away on July 15 with five hundred people hauling carts hastily thrown together out of green lumber. The fifth company of 576 under Captain Martin did not leave until July 26. Bringing up the rear were two ox trains, one of thirty-three wagons under W. B. Hodgett, the other of fifty wagons under John A. Hunt. These in themselves were not small: between them they carried 385 emigrants.

As far as the Missouri they made reasonably good time and had no serious difficulties, Willie's company arriving in Florence on August 11. There in a mass meeting they discussed the question raised by some of the more cautious of the elders: whether to push on through or go only so far as some good camping site along the Platte, perhaps Wood River just beyond Grand Island, and there hole up until spring. Taking part in the debate were several of the Iowa City agents, including W. H. Kimball and G. D. Grant, who had hurried on to the Missouri as soon as Iowa City was cleaned out. Like many others present, they knew the trail and the uncertain fall weather of the mountains; like many others, they were intoxicated with zeal to prove the handcart plan sound. They joined, and to some extent probably strengthened, the eagerness of the tenderfeet to go on. These told themselves that they had not come this far only to winter in a dugout out along the Platte. They had come to join the Saints in Zion, and they had come by God's own plan.

One voice, that of Levi Savage, was raised strongly on the other side. He said that such a mixed company would surely suffer greatly if it tried to cross the plains and mountains so late. With the best of luck it would be nearly the end of October before they could arrive, and the trailwise knew it could snow in the mountains a good two months before that. He would not risk it. But when they took a vote, he voted alone. The Lord, the others thought, would temper the wind to His lambs. Savage's response did him honor both as a Saint and as a man. He said, "Brethren and sisters, what I have said I know to be true; but seeing you are to go forward, I will go with you, will help you all I can, will work with you, will rest with you, will suffer with you, and if necessary I will die with you." It would not prove necessary that Savage die with them, not quite. But some of them would owe him their lives before they reached the valley, for he was one of the hardy and experienced ones who kept them going.

Willie's company set out from Florence on August 18. On August 21 Franklin Richards and a group of high-ranking elders arrived from Liverpool, in time to give assistance and encouragement to the Martin company and the two wagontrains as they regrouped in the Florence campground. Richards found them all in good spirits, and one of his party, Cyrus Wheelock, who had helped organize Frederick Piercy's companions for their march across Iowa in 1853, reported that "hundreds bear record of the truth of the words of President Young, wherein he promised them increasing strength by the way." After only three hundred miles, with summer still gilding the Missouri bluffs, they could talk that way. It was still the Lord's plan.

Martin's company left Florence on August 25, and both wagon companies were moving by September 2. Richards, getting ready to make his own dash homeward, was moved by the fervor of men who wrung his hand and thanked him personally for the chance to come this year. On September 3 he was of the opinion that except for the lateness of the season all was propitious. Significantly, he noted that the costs would be at least as low as they had hoped. He thought they should have a prosperous journey, for his intentions had been the best and he had worked very hard. "From the beginning we have done all in our power to hasten matters concerning the emigration, therefore we confidently look for the blessing of God to crown our humble efforts with success, and for the safe arrival of our brethren the poor Saints in Utah, though they may experience some cold." If he had been God's worst Enemy, instead of the essentially good man that he was, God could not have denied his expectations more harshly. One wonders if Franklin Richards had felt a similar confidence when he left his two pregnant young wives and his sickly child at Sugar Creek in the summer of 1846.

It was not that they did not have omens and premonitions, and not that all of the missionaries were blind to them, as Richards seemed to be. The night after the Martin company left Cutler's Park, seven miles out of Florence, some of the missionaries in camp saw a nightlong glow on the sky in that direction, and in the morning Joseph A. Young, a son of Brigham's, rode out to investigate. He found the Loader family, composed of father, mother, son, five daughters, son-in-law, and two grandchildren, stranded and left behind by the company. Zilpha, the married daughter, had borne a child the night before; another daughter was too sick to move. Captain Martin, applied to, had given permission for the two sick ones to ride the wagon, but he would permit no one to go along and take care of them, and rather than leave them untended, the family had stayed in camp. The glow on the sky had been their fires, kept going to scare away the wolves.

Joseph A. Young does not seem to have done anything for the Loaders, beyond suggesting jocularly that Zilpha name her new boy Handcart. But another young missionary, William Cluff, rode a good distance out the trail the day following, and was so troubled to see the frail father and the women pulling the two sick ones and two small children that he hitched on with his lariat and gave each of the two handcarts a long boost along the road before he had to ride back. Twenty-two miles from Cutler's Park, at two in the morning, after being threatened by five Indians and frightened by coarse squatters and by the wolves that howled all that moonlit night, this family of the ill and the incompetent caught up with the rest of the company, went to bed on a supper of water gruel, and rose after two or three hours of sleep to tug their carts through another day of Platte valley sand. Two of the family—the father and the older grandchild—would die on the trail, the rest, as we follow them in Patience Loader's diary, will come to seem unkillable. But the word he got about them at the very beginning was not such word as should have persuaded Franklin Richards that their trip looked propitious.

One precaution both handcart captains had taken, as insurance against trouble. On each cart they had laid an extra hundred pound sack of flour in addition to what could be hauled in the commissary wagons. The human draft animals pulled this overload, and the carts bore it, until they crossed the invisible line into the arid West, beyond the Loup Fork. Then their green carts began to disintegrate and need constant repair. Long before, *métis* pemmican hunters in the Red River country had learned not to grease their wooden-axled carts, submitting instead to a devilish amount of shrieking and grating, because any grease collected dust and sand that acted like emery paper on the spindles. The Mormon handcart companies had not learned that trick, and when their axles began to wear and their wheels to wobble, they sacrificed their bacon and their soap, their bootlegs or their cooking tins, to grease or sheathe the hickory. Still the axles wore, and often broke, as they hurried at their terrific laboring crawl up the Platte.

At Wood River the Willie company suffered the piece of bad luck that meant they would have no chance to make it through unassisted. The valley was swarming with buffalo, which one night stampeded directly through and over their camp, far less of a barrier than a solid wagontrain would have been. When the walkers crawled out from under their carts and wagons they found no one hurt, but thirty head of cattle gone, dispersed in a wild herd of tens of thousands. Almost horseless, they had no luck finding them, but must start on without their insurance beef and with their draft animals very short. When they yoked up, they hadn't enough to pull the heavy supply wagons.

They had been using up the flour carried on the carts, relieving the weaker people first. Now, when they had hitched even their milk cows to the wagons without being able to move, they put back on the decrepit carts another hundred pound sack apiece, and men who had just straightened their backs from the excessive loads bent them again, and pulled.

At North Bluff Fork (Birdwood Creek) the Willie company was overhauled by a fast-traveling group of carriages. John Chislett, one of the captains of hundreds, whose recollections provide one of the two or three most graphic accounts of the handcart disaster, described the meeting:

> Each vehicle was drawn by four horses or mules, and all the appointments seemed to be first rate. The occupants we soon found to be apostle F. D. Richards, elders W. H. Kimball, G. D. Grant, Joseph A. Young, C. G. Webb, N. H. Felt, W. C. Dunbar, and others who were returning to Utah from missions abroad. They camped with us for the night, and in the morning a general meeting was called. Apostle Richards addressed us. He had been advised of the opposition brother Savage had made, and he rebuked him very severely in open meeting for his lack of faith in God. Richards gave us plenty of counsel to be faithful, prayerful, obedient to our leaders, etc., and wound up by prophesying in the name of Israel's God that 'though it might storm on our right hand and on our left, the Lord would keep open the way before us and we should get to Zion in safety.'

Chislett also says that the missionaries expressed a need for fresh meat, and that Captain Willie killed for them the handcart company's fattest calf. "I am ashamed for humanity's sake to say they took it."

Chislett's recollections were written after he had apostatized, and his bitterness is probably not fully representative. But after Richards had advised the handcart company to ford the Platte and proceed up the south bank to Fort Laramie, and after his own fast carriages had rolled across the sandy ford and disappeared westward, there must have been others besides Chislett among the footsore paupers who watched with complicated feelings. Richards himself must have understood by then—the Willie company, leading this belated emigration, was still more than seven hundred miles from the valley—that his prophecy was mainly tactical encouragement;

for as he passed up the Hunt and Hodgett wagontrains, and then the Martin company, and then the Willie company, he promised all the captains that he would send relief supplies back from the valley with all speed, and when he passed through Fort Laramie, and again at Last Crossing, he bought buffalo robes to be distributed among the handcart companies when they should arrive. In his own words, they might "experience some cold."

Chislett says that the Willie company reached Fort Laramie on September 1, which has to be a misprint for October 1. But there was no misprint in his statement that Fort Laramie had no flour to sell, only a barrel or two of crackers. Counting heads and estimating marches, Captain Willie cut the flour ration from a pound a day to three-quarters. Like other companies, but in more desperate measure, they found that their rations grew smaller and their strength less as the road grew harder and the weather colder. In order to be able to move the carts that dragged like millstones at their heels, many threw away belongings, even heavy clothing and bedding.

John Richard, the same Frenchman who had guided the Mississippi Saints from Fort Laramie to Pueblo in the summer of 1846, had built a bridge across the North Platte at Deer Creek in 1851. This, and the more substantial one that replaced it in 1853, had put the Mormon ferry twenty-seven miles above out of business, so that there was no longer any permanent or semi-permanent Mormon station on that stretch of trail. There is no evidence that the Willie company used the bridge—presumably, traveling as they were on an economy tour and coming at a season when the river was low, they would not have. And in October, Indian summer, wading was no especial inconvenience; that would be reserved for the companies behind. But every day after they crossed and started uphill toward the Sweetwater brought them into higher and colder altitudes. Nights that had been chilly on the Platte were cold, and then freezing, on the Sweetwater. At Independence Rock, having found a letter from Richards advising him that no supplies could possibly reach them short of South Pass, Captain Willie had cut the flour ration again, to an average of ten ounces a day—twelve to working men, nine to women and old men, four to eight to children.

The Sweetwater, Chislett said, "was beautiful to the eye, as it rolled over its rocky bed as clear as crystal; but when we waded it time after time at each ford to get the carts, the women, and the children over, the beautiful stream, with its romantic surroundings ... lost to us its beauty, and the chill which it sent through our systems drove out from our minds all holy and devout aspirations, and left a void, a sadness, and—in some cases—doubts as to the justice of an overruling Providence."

Fatigue, malnutrition, cold, failure of faith, wore them down, and now those who wore out were as often as not their strongest, the men who had labored all the way to protect their families and the weaker members. These days, they stumbled into camp with their faces drawn and set, and sometimes if they rested a few minutes before putting up the tents they lay down and died without ever knowing how completely exhausted they were. "Life went out," Chislett wrote, "as smoothly as a lamp ceases to burn when the oil is gone. At first the deaths occurred slowly and irregularly, but in a few days at more frequent intervals, until we soon thought it unusual to leave a campground without burying one or more persons ... Many a father pulled his cart with his little children on it, until the day preceding his death." And as the strong died, the weak were left weaker. "Every death weakened our forces. In my hundred I could not raise enough men to pitch a tent when we camped ... I wonder I did not die, as many did who were stronger than I was. When we pitched our camp in the evening of each day, I had to lift the sick from the wagon and carry them to the fire, and in the morning carry them again on my back to the wagon. When any in my hundred died, I had to inter them, often helping to dig the grave myself ... We traveled on in misery and sorrow ..."

Hopelessness ate like a slow acid at their spirits. There was a gray October morning when the people plodding in a ragged column along the Sweetwater felt something brush their faces, and looked up. Snow. They did not pause; they dared not, for they had sixteen miles to pull their carts before their designated camping place. But at noon, as they were resting briefly, they heard fast hooves and the grate of wheels, and a light buggy rocked and jolted in from the west. When it drew up and they gathered eagerly around it they recognized Joseph A. Young, one of Brigham's sons, and Stephen Taylor. Joseph A. had been with Apostle Richards' party of missionaries when it passed them weeks ago, back on the Platte. He told them to take heart, that relief was coming behind him, and then he whipped his horses on to carry the message of hope to the Martin company, wherever that might be.

Renewed hope, then; they did take heart. But their hope was chillingly mingled with fear, for that morning Captain Willie had issued the last ration of flour, and the valley was still nearly three hundred appalling miles away.

For the Martin company, which in flurries of sleet and snow was just fording the Platte at Last Crossing, it was closer to four hundred miles away. Two days earlier, at Deer Creek, they had had to make an impossible choice. Faced with more than a month's struggle through the wintry mountains, and with their strength daily growing less, they had thrown away not only all those small cherished possessions that they had carried this far, but much of their "excess" bedding and clothing as well, including most of the heavy buffalo robes that Franklin Richards had hoped would protect them against the cold. Their baggage allowance from Deer Creek on—and few had murmured at the reduction of the loads—was ten pounds per adult, five pounds per child.

For some reason, presumably to save toll charges, they had not crossed the North Platte on the bridge, but had walked up the south side to Last Crossing. The river faced them, shallow but many rods wide, and floating mats of slush ice. Captain Martin said they must cross it that afternoon and go on several more miles. Having no choice, they caught their breath and plunged.

Even before the river crossing they were in a deplorable state. A Brother Stone had dropped behind that day, and when some of his friends went back to look for him they found him half eaten by wolves. Their deaths had been frequent and agonizing, their strength was drained. Inexorably the Captain drove them on, for he too had long since lost any possibility of choice. The fortunate ones caught rides with wagons from the Hodgett wagontrain, which they found camped there. A few, among them Patience Loader's mother, were given lifts behind the riders of mules or horses. The rest, like Patience, hiked their skirts and started to wade.

> ... the water was deep and very cold and we was drifted out of the regular crossing and we came near beign drounded the water came up to our arm pits poor Mother was standing on the bank screaming as we got near the bank I heard Mother say for God Sake some of you men help My poor girls ... Several of the breathren came down the bank of the river and pulled our cart up for us and we got up the best we could Mother was there to meet us her clothing was dry but ours was wett and cold and verey soon frozen Mother took of one of her under skirts and put on one of us and her apron for another to Keep the wett cloth from us for we had to travle several miles before we could camp ... when we was in the midle of the river I saw a poor brother carreying his child on his back he fell down in the water I never Knew if he was drowned or not I fealt sorrey that we could not help him but we had all we could do to save ourselvs from drownding that night we had no dry cloth to put on after we got out of the water we had to travle in our wett cloths untill we got to camp and our clothing was frozen on us and when we got to camp we had but very little dry clothing to put on we had to make the best of our poor circumstances and put our trust in God our father that we may take no harm from our wett cloths it was to late to go for wood and water the wood was to far away that night the ground was frozen to hard we was unable to drive any tent pins in as the tent was wett when we took it down in the morning it was somewhat frozen So we stretched it open the best we could and got in under it ...

In that numb camp few had clothing adequate to warm them. Aaron Jackson, who had collapsed in mid-river and been rescued by his wife's sister and one of the elders on a horse, was hauled into camp on an empty cart by Josiah Rogerson, and put to bed and covered with everything he owned. When Rogerson was called at midnight to go out and stand guard, he stumbled over Jackson's legs, so suspiciously stiff that he stooped and put his hand on Jackson's face. "I found that he was dead with his exhausted wife and little ones by his side all sound asleep . . . I did not wake his wife." Mrs. Jackson, awaking later and not hearing her husband's breathing, also reached to touch him. She cried out, and even as she did so realized that there was no help anyone could give. Until morning she lay beside the stiff corpse, and in the morning helped wrap it in a blanket for burial in the snow—and the giving up of that blanket was a concession that only love would have made. The ground was frozen too hard for the digging of a grave, and she wanted him to have *some* covering.

Twelve others went into the snowdrift beside Aaron Jackson that morning, one of them a girl whom Margaret Dalglish had seen die the night before in the act of raising a cracker to her mouth. When the burial squad was done, the Martin company, because there was still no alternative, broke loose the ice-locked wheels of its handcarts and struggled on. It was still snowing.

9

TTTTTTTTTTTTTTT

Victims, Heroes, and Scapegoats

Franklin Richards and the other missionaries had reached Salt Lake City on October 4, on the eve of the fall Conference of the Church. His trip from Florence had taken only thirty days—a tribute at least as much to his outfit as to his concern, for he did not seem even yet to have fully comprehended the enormity of what was happening on the trail behind him. On October 5, addressing the Conference, he could still speak of the handcart pilgrims' faith that it would be an open fall, and that God would "overrule the storms that may come in the season thereof, and turn them away, that their path may be freed from suffering more than they can bear." He was inclined to feel that "such confidence and joyful performance of so arduous labors to accomplish their gathering, will bring the choice blessings of God upon them."

Brigham Young, now that the facts were before him, suffered from no such delusions. From the moment Richards arrived with the word that more than a thousand walkers and nearly four hundred wagon emigrants were still on the road, he had a coldly accurate view of how much the Lord was likely to be able to do for such inexperienced travelers in the mountains in October. At once he announced the theme of the Conference as the rescue of the Saints caught out on the trail. He said he wanted sixty or sixty-five mule or horse teams, twelve or fifteen wagons, forty young hardy teamsters, twelve tons of flour, and contributions of "hoods, winter bonnets, stockings, skirts, garments, and almost any description of clothing." "You may rise up now," he told them, "and give your names."

They rose up and gave their names, and more than their names. Though they had no information on exactly how bad the condition of the companies might be, they had enough experience to guess. With the unanimity of effort which had always been their greatest strength, they oversubscribed Brigham's first request, and when new requests were made, they met those too. By October 7, three days after Richards' arrival, the first contingent of the rescue party was heading eastward into the mountains under the leadership of George D. Grant and William H. Kimball. The presence of those two, like that of Brigham's son Joseph A. Young, Cyrus Wheelock, and others, was significant. These were the missionaries who had converted a good many of the handcart emigrants in the first place. They had worked in Iowa City and in Florence to get them outfitted. They had contributed to possible disaster by encouraging the tenderfeet to set out so late from Winter Quarters. They may have felt partially responsible, or have felt the Church to be responsible, for the delays at Iowa City. Whatever may be said of their excessive zeal in the first place, they were neither indifferent nor cowardly once they knew the handcart companies might be in distress. Separated from their families for two years or more, restored to the valley no more than forty-eight hours, they turned unhesitatingly around and drove out again with the rescue wagons.

Six days after their start they were in Fort Bridger, where they cached some of their flour and picked up some beef. No sign or word of any emigrants, no travelers carrying information down the snow-blocked trail. They pushed on three days farther, to the Green River. Still no sign. Sending Joseph A. Young, Abel Garr, Cyrus Wheelock, and Stephen Taylor on ahead as scouts, they went on over South Pass, which they crossed in a snowstorm that finally grew too fierce to travel in, and stopped them on Willow Creek, on the upper Sweetwater, on October 19. On the evening of October 20 it was still snowing hard when two skinny mules appeared out of the smother and Capt. Joseph Willie and Joseph Elder fell stiffly off to tell them that the Willie company was out of food and perishing, a day's hard march down the Sweetwater. If rescue did not reach them immediately there was no point in its reaching them at all.

Storm or no storm, the rescue party broke camp before daylight and made it in one day through deep snow to the Willie company camp, twenty-five miles downstream at what later was called St. Mary's Station. There the emigrants had lived for two days on a few crackers and the beef of two oxen so lean that they grew hungry chewing it. Almost the whole camp had dysentery, many had frozen feet or hands. The night before, nine had died. To that lamentable camp the hearty young men from the valley were angels of mercy, giants of strength. Their axes bit down trees at a stroke, their great legs churned up the snow dragging up wood for fires. In their wagons they had beef and flour, potatoes and onions, quilts and blankets and buffalo robes. "That evening for the first time in quite a period," Chislett says, "the songs of Zion were to be heard in the camp, and peals of laughter ... The change seemed almost miraculous, so sudden was it from grave to gay, from sorrow to gladness."

But a few robust young men and twenty-odd wagonloads of food and clothing were only the delusive shape of safety, not its true substance, and even these could not all remain. In the morning, leaving William Kimball with half the teams to help the Willie company along, George Grant took the rest of them on down the Sweetwater through foot-deep snow. It took them five days to make Devil's Gate, where they found their four express messengers holed up in some abandoned traders' cabins awaiting further orders. They had seen nothing and heard nothing of either the Martin company or the wagontrains.

From Devil's Gate, where the feed was good, Grant was unwilling to risk his own party without further information, and so on October 27 he sent Joseph A. Young, Abel Garr, and Dan Jones down across the miserable, snow-swept, wolf-haunted sagebrush country eastward. A day later, a little beyond Red Buttes, no more than one day's journey past Last Crossing, where the Martin company and the Hodgett wagontrain had been snowed in together for days, a sister happened to look westward. She leaped to her feet, screaming, "I see them coming! I see them coming! Surely they are angels from heaven!" As others strained to see what her sharper eyes had caught, she began to wave her shawl, crying, "We are saved!"

But the Martin and Hodgett companies, which had suffered fifty-six deaths since wading the North Platte, were even less surely saved than the Willie company. All the three angels from heaven had with them was one pack mule of supplies. The best they could do was to distribute their pitiful hundred pounds of aid and urge the camp to start moving again—something which in its weakness and apathy it had not been able to do for days—while they themselves galloped on to see how things went with the Hunt wagontrain, fifteen miles farther down.

Coming back two days later after getting the Hunt party started, Jones and Garr overtook the Martin company struggling up Avenue Hill. Jones says, "A condition of distress here met my eyes that I never saw before or since. There were old men pulling and tugging their carts, sometimes loaded with a sick wife or children—women pulling along sick husbands—little children six to eight years old struggling through the mud and snow. As night came on the mud would freeze on their clothes and feet. There were two of us and hundreds needing help. What could we do? We gathered on to some of the most helpless with our riatas tied to the carts, and helped as many as we could into camp."

That afternoon as Patience Loader was resting in the brief warmth of the winter sun, a strange man appeared to her. He came and looked into her face earnestly and said, "Are you Patience?" She said, "Yes." He said, "I thought it was you. Travel on, there

is help for you. You will come to a good place; there is plenty."
"With this he was gone he dissapeared I looked but never saw whare
he went this seemed very strange to me. I took this as some one sent
to encourage us and give us strength. We traveld on."

Several more of the Martin company died that night. But in the
morning, when Joseph A. Young had come up from the Platte
bridge, the three express riders hurried back to Grant's half of the
relief party at Devil's Gate, and by the day following Grant and
most of the wagons had moved on down and met the handcarts at
Greasewood Creek. By November 2 they had the whole tail end
of the migration, Martin's company and the two wagontrains, en-
camped around the traders' cabins at Devil's Gate. On November
3 Joseph A. Young, who was doing a good deal of traveling these
days, was on his way back to Salt Lake City with Abel Garr to enlist more help. He would find that Brigham and Heber Kimball
did not need his news to guess the extent of the emergency. Before
he ever left Devil's Gate they had 250 rescue wagons spaced out
along the trail.

Exhaustion and death are not rendered impossible because a few
friends arrive with a few tons of food and a great load of hope. The
Willie company, being herded anxiously over the trail by William
Kimball, shortly began meeting new wagons with new supplies, but
even so Chislett buried fifteen in the camp at Willow Creek, fourteen miles east of South Pass, and every day thereafter two or three
more. Once over the pass they found warmer weather, and at Fort
Bridger they met many more relief wagons so that most of the
sick and weak could ride. Along the wintry way to Salt Lake City
the constant passage of wagons kept the road packed for them, and
at particularly snowy places such as Big Mountain, details of men
drove up and down on the trail to keep it open.

East of South Pass, blizzards lashed the high country. Men who
had been many times over the road had never seen so much snow
along the Sweetwater. Some later groups of rescuers, concentrated
between Fort Bridger and South Pass, found the waiting so uncom-

fortable that some persuaded themselves the Martin company could not possibly be alive, and turned their wagons around and went back. A few hung on. Eph Hanks, one who like Port Rockwell, Howard Egan, and John D. Lee had demonstrated his capacity as a frontiersman (he would soon be carrying the mail for the Y.X. Express across these mountains) rode eastward from the pass to see what he could find out. He had the luck to shoot a buffalo on the way, and packed his mule with meat. When he encountered the Martin company they had all but used up the rescuers' supplies, so that Hanks's providential mule-load found famished takers. Hanks also found need for his rough frontier surgery, for dozens in the company had frozen feet or hands. "Many such I washed with water and castile soap, until the frozen parts would fall off, after which I would sever the shreds of flesh from the remaining portions of the limbs with my scissors. Some of the emigrants lost toes, others fingers, and again others whole hands and feet."

And worst than frost, sometimes. At Willow Springs a young girl sleeping beside her family in the tent they shared with a pair of brothers named Whitaker or Whittacar awoke screaming with pain in the night to find Brother William Whitaker eating her fingers. Dragged away, he began to eat his own. In the morning he was dead.

Thanks to Eph Hanks's ride down from the pass, four wagon-loads of food now came east to meet Grant's company of cripples, and a little later ten more, and later more still. Among the last group was William Kimball, who had got the Willie company to the valley and turned straight around and come back out for the rest.

Patience Loader adds a note. Coming to one of the crossings of the Sweetwater where the cattle and wagons had broken the ice, she and her family found

> three brave Men there in the water packing the women and children over on there backs Names William Kimble Ephrem Hanks ans I think the other was James Furgeson those poor breathren was in the water nearly all day we wanted to thank them but thay would not listen to My dear Mother felt in her

heart to bless them for there Kindnes she said God bless you for taking me over this water and in such an awful rough way oh D——m that I don't want any of that you are welcome we have come to help you Mother turned to me saying what do you think of that man he is arough fellow I told her that is Brother William Kimble I am told they are all good men but I daresay that they are all rather rought in there Manners but we found that thay all had kind good hearts this poor Br Kimble Staid so long in the water that he had to be taken and packed to camp and he was along time before he recoverd as he was child through and in after life he was allways afflicted with rhumetism . . .

A hundred years away in time, and from a position of soft contemporary ease, it is hard to imagine that road and the emotions of rescue, the dazed joy of being snatched from the very edge of a snowdrift grave, and then the agony of being forced to put out more effort when the whole spirit cries to give up and be taken care of. It is hard to feel how hope that has been crushed little by little, day by day, can come back like feeling returning to a numbed limb. It is hard even to imagine the hardship that rescue entailed—the jolting, racking, freezing, grief-numbed, drained and exhausted three hundred miles through the snow to sanctuary. In Echo Canyon, between the battlements of red sand rock where in another year some of these same young Mormons who were rescuing their fellows would be lying behind crude barricades of stones waiting for the advance of the United States Army, a child was born in a wagon to a sister named Squires. How the mother survived long enough to bring her to birth, and how she survived the birth itself, will never be understood by any twentieth-century woman. The infant was wrapped in the garments, the holy underwear, of a rescuer, and named, with a haunting appropriateness, Echo.

The first of the Willie company had been brought into the valley on November 9. Until the last of November others were straggling in, most riding in wagons, a few still grimly hauling their battered carts, still defiantly on their own legs. Margaret Dalglish of the Martin company, a gaunt image of Scottish fortitude, dragged her handful of belongings to the very rim of the valley, but when she looked down and saw the end of it she did something extraordinary. She tugged the cart to the edge of the road and gave it a push and watched it roll and crash and burst apart, scattering into Emigration Canyon the last things she owned on earth. Then she went on into Salt Lake to start the new life with nothing but her gaunt bones, her empty hands, her stout heart.

Something more than two hundred of the Willie and Martin companies lay dead between Florence and the valley, sixty-two from the Willie company * and between 135 and 150 from Martin's, besides an unestimated number from the Hodgett and Hunt wagontrains, which understandably suffered far less. A good many of the survivors had endured surgery like that of Eph Hanks, and had lost fingers, toes, feet, a few of them both legs to the knee. "We want you to receive them as your own children," Brigham told the valley Saints on November 30 when he heard the last detachment of the Martin company was being brought in. "I would give more for a dish of pudding and milk, or a baked potato and salt, were I in the situation of those persons who have just come in, than I would for all your prayers, though you were to stay here all afternoon and pray." Unlike Apostle Richards, Brigham was likely to value faith supported by practical strenuousness somewhat more than pure faith alone.

But he was not all fatherliness and compassion. On November 2, in the heat of his anger over the setback to the handcart scheme, the loss of property and time that rescue involved, and the murmurs that reached his ears blaming the First Presidency for what had happened, he had erupted and poured the lava of his wrath over everybody involved in the emigration, and especially over Franklin D. Richards. His tabernacle speech of November 2 was raging, harsh, boastful, and without mercy toward those he had selected as scapegoats.

"You know my life," he thundered at them. "There is not a per-

* Hafen's estimate. Chislett says sixty-seven.

son in this church and kingdom but what must acknowledge that gold and silver, houses and lands, etc., do multiply in my hands. There is not an individual but what must acknowledge that I am as good a financier as they ever knew . . . therefore there is no ground or room for their suspecting that my mismanagement caused the present sufferings on the plains." Forgetting his Epistle of 1851, which had said that seventy days were ample time for a handcart passage of the plains, he said that no such company should ever have been permitted to start from Florence later than June, so that three months could have been allowed for a comfortable journey, with time at the end for the emigrants to help with the harvest and the fall planting.

> But the Elders abroad say, by their conduct all the time, that we here in the mountains do not understand what is wanted in the East, as well as they do . . . Their actions assert that they know more than we do, but I say they do not. If they had sent our immigration in the season that they should have done, you and I could have kept our teams at home . . . This people are this day deprived of thousands of acres of wheat that would have been sowed by this time, had it not been for the misconduct of our immigration affairs this year, and we would have had an early harvest, but now we may have to live on roots and weeds again before we get the wheat. I look upon this matter as plainly as I do upon your faces . . .

In exculpating himself and the First Presidency, Brigham let neither good intentions nor past faithfulness shield the man who sat in the meeting wincing at every blow.

> Here is br. Franklin D. Richards who has but little knowledge of business, except what he has learned in the church . . . and here is br. Daniel Spencer . . . a man of age and experience, and I do not know that I will attach blame to either of them. But if, while at the Missouri river, they had received a hint from any person on this earth, or if even a bird had chirped it in the ears of brs. Richards and Spencer, they would have known better than to rush men, women, and children on to the prairie in the autumn months, on the 3rd of September, to travel over a thousand miles . . . If any man, or woman, com-

plains of me or of my Counselors, in regard to the lateness of
some of this season's immigration, let the curse of God be on
them and blast their substance with mildew and destruction,
until their names are forgotten from the earth.

Fulminating, furious, he returned again and again to worry the
rag-like remains of his apostle and devotee. He destroyed him, buried
him, sowed his grave with salt. "You cannot hear George D. Grant,
Daniel Spencer and others of the lately returned missionaries speak
without eulogizing Franklin D. Richards. They are full of eulogizing Franklin D. Richards, but they need to be careful or they will
have the 'big head' and become as dead and devoid of the Spirit as
old pumpkins."

This was what happened to a man who crossed Brother Brigham,
or failed to perform as Brigham thought he should, or by his actions
brought criticism on Brigham's head, or (is there some jealousy of
Richards' popularity in this tirade?) was too much admired by too
many. Like Erastus Snow taking an insulting scolding for causing
the loss of Brigham's spyglass, like Parley Pratt being flayed for not
being leader enough to hold the 1847 emigration together, Richards
bowed before the thunder meekly. Some Gentiles and apostates
whose sympathy for Richards was enhanced by their antagonism
to Brigham said it was years before Richards was ever again of
much consequence in the councils of the Church, though he retained his position as a member of the Quorum of the Twelve.

But the handcart scheme that might have been discredited for
good by the disaster of 1856 was not suspended. Brigham did not
want it suspended, he wanted it justified. By November 16, in the
very midst of the rescue, with the suffering handcart emigrants visible all through the community and their story in every mouth, Brigham was telling the tabernacle congregation that the sufferings of
the Willie company were no worse than those of many a company
that contracted cholera crossing the plains, their deaths no more
frequent and less agonizing. God send us all such good fortune as
to die while eating, with bread in our hands and with never a groan
or a struggle. He strongly implied that if all the Willie company

had been faithful, it was perfectly within the power of the Lord to have sent fat buffalo to lie down within twenty yards of their camps. "My faith is, when we have done all we can, then the Lord is under obligation and will not disappoint the faithful." To a Gentile, that looked remarkably like Franklin Richards' faith.

"We are not in the least discouraged about the hand-cart method of traveling," he told them. He said he was ready to entertain a motion that all missionaries leaving the valley should travel with hand-carts or with knapsacks on their backs. With the casualties still streaming in, he insisted that "as old as I am I can take a hand cart and draw it across those plains quicker than you can go with animals and with loaded wagons, and be healthier when I get to the Missouri river."

If he didn't starve, or freeze, or fall ill, perhaps he could. He was entitled to some confidence in his own abilities. But from now on he would be more careful to control the zeal of those whom his confidence fired. On November 2 he had told them that he would "lay an injunction and place a penalty, to be suffered by any Elder or Elders who will start the immigration across the plains after a given time; and the penalty shall be that they shall be severed from the Church."

In 1856, when trouble with the United States was brewing and when the fanaticism known as the Reformation was working men up even to the Blood Atonement doctrine that would pollute 1857 with the Mountain Meadows Massacre and the sacrifice of an unknown number of other "guilty" ones, that threat was a heavy one to the pious. They bent their necks and resolved to do better, and to avoid Brigham's curse.

There would be more handcart companies in 1857, 1859, and 1860, but there would be no more disasters. And with Brigham's example roaring in their ears, all the Saints could concentrate their reproaches on the head of poor Franklin Richards. The scapegoat was as authentic a part of their Old Testament society as the patriarch or the high priest.

10

︴︴︴︴︴︴︴︴︴︴︴

The Man That Ate the Pack Saddle

THE STORY OF THE MORMON TRAIL is as pat with crises as a horse opera; especially in 1856, ordeal along that thoroughfare was not climactic but serial. And so the rescuers of the Martin company had hardly pulled away up the Sweetwater with a clinking of harness metal and a crunch of broad tires in snow-crust and a great fume of breath in the cold air before another ordeal began at Devil's Gate. If the theme of the handcart episode was the suffering of the innocent, the theme of this one was the steadfastness of the strong. Its hero, except for his Mormonism, could step into the boots of any western hero who has been endangered, tested, suspected, and finally vindicated.

His name was Daniel W. Jones—not to be confused, though some historians do so confuse him, with the Dan Jones who looked as if he might convert all of Wales to Mormonism in the 1840's and early 1850's, and who in 1856 had come on with Franklin Richards' missionaries as far as the Platte bridge, where he stopped to find out about a cached threshing engine, and so missed the rescue. This Dan Jones was an ex-Missouri Puke, an orphan, a harder Huckleberry Finn who from the age of eleven had made his tough way on a tough frontier. "Probably as willful a boy as ever lived," he said he had never been controlled except through kindness, "and

this I did not often meet with." Like Huckleberry, rather than submit to being civilized, he had lit out for the territories: the Mexican
War led him into the Southwest as a member of the Missouri Volunteers, and for some years afterward he lived among hair-trigger
borderers in Texas and New Mexico.

But whether he knew it or not, he had the seed of civilization in
him. Fighting, Taos Lightning, and Indian women did not fully
satisfy. Helping to drive a band of sheep from Taos to California
along the old Spanish Trail, he shot himself accidentally in the groin,
and convalesced under the care of a Mormon family at the mouth
of Spanish Fork Canyon, in Utah Valley. The kindness with which
he was treated smote his orphan heart; he found himself hankering
after the security of the Mormon confidence in the Lord. Before
long he joined the Church, married a Mormon girl, and settled
down. It was proper that when Brigham Young stood up in the
tabernacle at October Conference in 1856 and said that men were
needed to rescue handcart emigrants caught by snowstorms somewhere on the other side of South Pass, Dan Jones should volunteer.
Kindness for kindness. He was a man who honored his obligations.

Two or three weeks later, 327 miles of snowy mountains to the
eastward, he volunteered again, more recklessly. When there seemed
no way of getting the weakest emigrants in without unloading the
freight from all the Hunt and Hodgett wagons, Jones said he would
be one to stay behind and guard the cached freight. With two valley
boys and seventeen of the strongest teamsters from the wagon companies, he organized a little Stake of Zion in the cabins of the trader
fort just above Devil's Gate, and prepared for six months of snow,
cold, and isolation. They were fifty miles from Last Crossing, where
some mountaineers wintered, and 215 from Fort Bridger. And they
weren't exactly prepared to stay: for supplies they had a few crackers and perhaps seventy-five head of skin-and-bones cattle too
broken-down to go farther. Even these they were not supposed to
eat if they could help it.

Around Devil's Gate at least two hundred cattle had died of bad
water or in the early storms; the trail to the east was strewn with

their carcasses. The scent of death blew east toward the Platte and west toward South Pass and north and south along the Laramie Range, and wolves from miles of wild country gathered to the barbecue. Trying to fatten their scrawny herd by driving it away from the fort to better feed, Jones's outfit found themselves facing packs that even in daylight looked dangerous. Wolves cut down cattle at high noon, under the rifles of the herders; and at night the corralled herd was sure to erupt at least once in a flurry of attack and a snarl of shadows and a panicked bawling, and when the guards arrived swinging firebrands they would find another steer down, and the snowy darkness ringed with the green flare of eyes. Within a week the wolves took twenty-five head.

The winterers did what they must—killed the remaining forty or fifty cattle before the wolves could beat them to it. A teamster who had once been a London butcher dressed and hung their beef in classy style, putting aside the worst of it, along with the offal, to be used as wolf bait in case they somehow managed to get hold of some traps. In the best Mormon cooperative work-party fashion they fell upon the cabins and rechinked them, laid floors of ox yokes in some and stored the freight in them, fixed a stable for their four saddle horses, and added to their stores (keeping careful account of what they borrowed) some coffee, sugar, dried fruit, and candles that they found while making their inventory.

Their pastimes were hunting for buffalo, which was generally unproductive, and shooting at wolves, which netted them greater results. Shortly their crackers and fruit gave out and they were down to beef alone; their salt gave out and they ate their leathery beef unsalted. A day or two before Christmas two Mormons, Eph Hanks and Feramorz Little, a nephew of Brigham Young's, came eastward with the valley mail and a letter of advice from Brother Brigham. He said among other things that they had better ration their flour (they had never had any) to make it last until spring, and he gave them permission to kill an occasional ox rather than run large risks hunting in Crow country. But Feramorz Little had a piece of more practical advice. Looking around just before he and Hanks took off for the Platte bridge, he suggested they ought to take good care of the hides of the slaughtered cattle. They might come in handy.

A few days later the Missouri mail came in from the east, switched from coach to packmules at Devil's Gate, went on until it ran into a massive blizzard on South Pass, barely made it back to Devil's Gate again, and finally dribbled back to the Platte bridge to winter at a lower altitude, leaving a passenger, Joseph Heywood, behind them. Heywood ten years ago had been one of the trustees left behind in abandoned Nauvoo, later he had been Salt Lake City's first postmaster, now he was going out as United States Marshal for Utah. He saw no reason to go back to the Platte bridge, for Dan Jones had recently beaten his way back there only to find the mountain men flourless and living on game alone. All Jones had got was some wolf traps.

They baited none of those traps. Twenty-one men eating nothing but meat can chew their way through forty skinny carcasses in a very short time. All the beef they had thought edible was shortly used up, and now they began on the wolf bait, so stringy that it satisfied their hunger not at all and nourished them little more. Then that too was gone, and after an unwilling interval they boiled a hide. It provided a gagging, gluey broth and strips of sheet rubber, both of which made them sick. While they redoubled their efforts to find game, they lived on coffee, but after a while coffee lost its power to satisfy, and one man threw a fit from drinking too much of it. East and west, the empty miles of the trail were snowed over without a track. It was still only early January.

One kind of script, at this point, calls for them to draw straws to see which should first be killed and eaten, but the Mormons, whatever their other capabilities, never showed any talent for cannibalism. Instead they did something totally unacceptable in a horse opera. They knelt in meeting and prayed for the Lord to direct them. He directed them back to the hides.

These lay stacked outside the cabins, half snowed-over, frozen as stiff as crumpled sheet metal. Reluctantly they scalded and scraped

the hair off another one and cut it up and boiled it until it was soft
enough to be chewed. It still had a lot of unpleasant glue in it, but
they got it down this time; it stuck to them, Dan Jones said, somewhat longer than they desired. So Jones asked the Lord for further
directions, and the Lord passed on His favorite recipe for boiled
hide. Scalding seemed to give hide a bad taste. Scorch and scrape
it, therefore, to get the hair off. Then parboil for one hour in plenty
of water, throwing away the water and glue. Then wash and scrape
again, rinsing often in cold water. Then boil to a jelly and allow
to cool. Serve with a sprinkling of sugar.

It was a lot of trouble, but then they had plenty of time, and their
interest in experiment had been aroused by three days of fasting.
They asked the Lord to bless their stomachs and adapt them to this
food, and then they fell upon the hide and devoured it. For six
weeks they ate virtually nothing else. No one, Jones reported, got
the gout.

But then came a day toward the middle of February—the
monthly fast day, appropriately enough, for they still kept fast days
—when it became clear that something ugly had begun to come
among them. Some were secretly cutting meat off the unclean carcasses of cattle that had died months before and that had lain too
close to the fort for the wolves to get. Some were casting looks at
the offal in the butchershop, and at the frozen wolf carcasses, nearly
a hundred of them, stacked in the yard. In such a winter, only the
wolves were fat; they could see yellow slabs of fat among the mus-
cle. But Dan Jones did not favor using unclean flesh. Eat those
wolves, and what next? Man-meat, Mormon-meat. He allowed that
they were on the Lord's business and that the Lord would provide
clean food if they would purify their hearts. In their re-united and
refreshed state of mind, and as a climax to a fast day that had no
foreseeable morning, they hauled all the cattle guts and the old
frozen cattle carcasses and all the skinned wolves down to the Sweetwater, cut a hole in the ice and dumped them in. Then they went
back and washed out their storehouse and "presented it before the
Lord, clean but empty." Lord's move.

That afternoon a visitor dropped in; for a moment it looked as if he might be bringing the clean supper they aspired to. But he turned out to be an Indian as empty-handed and hungry as they, and instead of getting anything from him they had to offer him their last piece of boiled rawhide. He took it gratefully, indicating by signs that he'd eaten it plenty of times before. Nobody was able to talk to him except in signs. Jones tried him on Spanish and Ute, and concluded he was a Snake. He did not offhand appear to be a messenger of Providence.

Then they heard a noise outside, and hushed. Human voices. "Here comes our supper!" yelled Joseph Heywood, and led the rush to the door. The McGraw mail coach, making a second try to get through, was stuck in the snow. The noise they had heard was a French Canadian swearing at the mules, a music that needed no interpreter. Jesse Jones, the mail carrier, was glad to see them, for down at the Platte bridge they had concluded that the whole Devil's Gate crowd must by now be dead. But he was astonished at how happy they seemed to see *him*, and inquired the cause of their excessive friendliness. Because you are bringing us our supper according to the Lord's promise, they told him, and would not take no for an answer. Almost his entire stock of provisions, calculated to last to Fort Bridger, went into the pot, and the twenty-six of them left just enough for a skimpy breakfast.

Nothing in such a basic western plot as this is wasted. The French driver knew Shoshone, and could talk to the Indian, who said that his band was camped a day upriver, out of meat and hungry, but that he thought he could find game if some of them would come along to protect him from the Crows. The mail outfit, now without provisions to go on, had no choice but to lie over to see if the Indian could prove his brag. He did. He took ten men out and brought them back after dark with their mules laden with buffalo meat.

When they left, the mail carriers took Heywood along. That left only twenty men at Devil's Gate, but twenty were adequate to clean the cupboard. By March 4 it was bare again, and really bare this time. They had eaten up all the stray scraps of hide, all the worn-out moccasins, all the rawhide tires off abandoned hand-carts and rawhide wrappings off wagon tongues, even a chunk of buffalo hide that had been used for months as a door mat. Now they took inventory and found nothing edible in the whole place except a set of harness (dubious) and a rawhide pack saddle (sporting).

In the snow, which was from eighteen inches to three feet deep, hunting on foot was an exhausting grind, for they wallowed, were easily spotted by the game, and as often as not missed out of sheer nervousness or exhaustion when they did get a shot at something. The wolves had killed three of their four saddle ponies. Jones judged that none of the men, unless possibly himself, was strong enough to make a desperation dash to the Platte bridge to see if there might be help there. He was just about to try what would have been a very desperate chance indeed when the Lord intervened again. This time His messengers were the Danite Bill Hickman, later notorious as a strong-arm man and self-confessed murderer second only to Porter Rockwell, and several companions. They were bringing through the first installment of mail for Brigham Young's new Y.X. Express, which had obtained a contract to carry the mail between Salt Lake City and Independence. The Devil's Gate boys had just put the pack saddle on to simmer, but seeing meat on the express men's pack mules, they took it out of the pot and consented to drink buffalo broth instead. Hickman and the other express men were a long time getting over that dinner they saw on the fire. For years they called Dan Jones the man that ate the pack saddle. He always denied it, but admitted that if they hadn't arrived just when they did he might have been talked into taking a wing or a leg.

None of their windfalls lasted them long. Having eaten their way clean through the rawhide, they had to live from day to day, but as the winter wore away and the trail began to open, windfalls became more frequent. Some of the mountain men from the Platte bridge made their way through with some beef to sell, and took their pay in calico from one of the freight boxes. Their hunting went better, too, because Hickman had left them two mules. Moreover, the Snakes and the Bannocks came down in small hunting parties from the Wind River country, and with the help of a word-book he got from the French Canadian mail driver, Jones was able to make deals with them for meat. Their first uneasiness about the Indians, at least about the Shoshones, disappeared. In fact, from then until the end of his life Dan Jones liked and valued Indians, the only people other than Mormons who had shown him kindness. These Ishmaels were full of the helpfulness of mutual starvation. It was probably they who passed the word down to the Platte bridge that the Devil's Gate boys were hungry, and so brought the mountain men with their load of beef. Indians and Mormons drank a lot of coffee and thin belly-filling soup and ate a lot of thistle roots together, and as March thawed off into April and the snowline crept up the hills and the game began working into higher country, the Indians brought in meat that they offered not so much in the spirit of trade as in the spirit of brotherhood. To Jones, old Chief Toquatah seemed to feel toward the Mormon boys "something like a mother with a lot of hungry children."

Travel loosened along the trail as the weather warmed. The second installment of the Y.X. Express passed eastward, leaving them a little flour, salt, and bacon. The first biscuits they had eaten in months choked them. Then a yoke of good oxen, one wearing a big bell that had probably kept the wolves off, wandered into the fort from somewhere and were promptly corralled as beef insurance. Just as promptly, they got loose and wandered off again, taking security with them. Jones and Ben Hampton pursued them on mules, but at sunset, after thirty hard miles, had not caught up. After dark they went on, feeling out the tracks in the snow, until they were stopped by a gulch full of snow that, only half frozen, would not support the weight of the mules.

They were deep in Crow country, the stars were glitters of ice, the night set in to freeze hard. Even if there had been sagebrush for a fire, they would not have dared light one, and they had not come prepared with robes for a night out. Lying on the frozen ground, they chattered and shuddered and hugged one another like lovers until, after some hours, they judged that the snow-bridge had frozen hard enough to let them cross. Then, trying to get up, they barely could. Their jaws were locked, their hands were tongs, their legs were sticks. They bumped into one another, fell down, couldn't hang onto the saddles to saddle up. It was so ridiculous that they had to laugh, and laughing, began bumping one another around, and bumping, stirred up enough life to get the saddles screwed down and go on. Forty-five miles from home they caught up with the runaway oxen, still so fresh that they took the back-trail at a trot.

Along in the afternoon, Ben Hampton's mule gave out so that thereafter they had to take turns walking, whipping along the cripple and the unspeakable and inexhaustible oxen. Long before they reached it, they could see Independence Rock, and off beyond it Castle Gate and the Rattlesnake Range, all of it somber elephant-color streaked with crevices of snow. Just past sundown, the distances would have been blue and cold. Even when the belly is full, the heart is low enough at that time of a winter's day. But Jones and Hampton had not eaten since breakfast the day before, had ridden and walked a good eighty-five miles since then, had slept, if you could call it that, without covering on the frozen ground. Their hearts would have been low indeed. And then, beatitude. Smoke above the traders' cabins at the foot of Independence Rock, and as they pulled up bleary-eyed and groggy, the smell of roasting meat. Their stomachs rose up in them and grinned like wolves. Supper here, an hour or two of rest, and the remaining six miles to Devil's Gate might be faced.

Supper was offered them, even urged upon them. By all the free-masonry of the mountains they were welcome. But these were Mormon frontiersmen, and the scripts are often wrong for them. They discovered that the four men they found at Independence Rock were stragglers harder up than themselves. They had come famishing into Devil's Gate the night before, one of their number with his feet frozen so badly he might lose them: he lay gritting his teeth now from a blanket on the floor. The meat the men were cooking had been given them by the Mormons at Devil's Gate; it was all they had to get them to the Platte bridge. They had forty-four miles to go, and they had been all day making the six miles from Devil's Gate.

Maybe Jones, being who he was, would have refused to take the meat out of their mouths even if he had not been a Mormon. But it is legitimate to believe that his faith in the Lord, Who had already rescued them several times that winter, gave him the strength to say, Oh no thank you, they weren't hungry, they'd just warm up a little and be getting on back home. They clamped their teeth to keep from howling, and swallowed the juices surging up into their mouths, and turned out into the icy blue dark again. On the way the worn-out mule, for some reason that only the Lord could have answered, chose to run away, and had to be chased nearly a mile.

At Devil's Gate the worried brethren had been keeping a kettle full of meat and dumplings hot all day. Long after dark Jones and Hampton came in, sat down on a pile of wolf skins by the fire, accepted the plates that were handed them, and began to eat. They ate unhurriedly until nearly daylight, when the pot, which had contained rations for seven hearty eaters, was finally empty. Then they belched and rolled over and slept, to awake next day without a stiffness or a pain. But one thing they attended to immediately: rather than risk having to chase those independent and wandering oxen again, they made them into sudden beef, thus assuring themselves of meat to take them through to good hunting weather.

A little later, when a bunch of cornfed Valley Mormons came through setting up and stocking stations for the Y.X. Express, and said too loudly that they thought the Devil's Gate boys had been badly used and brought to a pitiable state, Dan Jones proposed an Indian wrestle of rawhide versus corn, and pulled the stakes of the strongest of them, just to teach them not to waste their pity.

One fact not normally stressed by the official histories of Mormonism is that the City of Zion, however millennial it might look from Wales or the black counties of England, was sometimes disappointing to converts who had torn up their lives by the roots to go there. Instead of the City of Enoch, paved with jasper and pearl and stones of fair colors, it was a ten-year-old adobe town in a desert valley; and to eyes made unhappy by that realization, even Brigham Young might look sometimes less like a prophet of God and more like a local tyrant consolidating his power over a gullible people and growing personally rich by their labors. The Profit, the Gentiles called him behind closed doors, and with the growing rumors of blood atonement and holy murder and the growing crisis with the United States territorial officials, the names they called him, and he them, grew brisker than that. Great expectations and gentle piety, brought to the valley, could crash against a reality that was often bleak and hard; the more the Church consolidated its power in the valley, the more that power came into conflict both with the temptations of California gold and with the external control that the United States, through territorial appointees who were sometimes the sweepings of the political caucus rooms, attempted to impose. It was inevitable that there should be numerous apostasies, that some who had barely made it to Utah should take the first opportunity to get out, either on to California or back over the trail to the States.

Some of these apostates were tough—it took nerve to defy Brother Brigham in the 1850's. For the purposes of our horse opera, which is seen through the eyes of Dan Jones, they may be designated the Bad Guys, though in the eye of impartial history they were often men of honor and some of them ended up as victims, rubbed out by Port Rockwell, Bill Hickman, Hosea Stout, or other fanatical Danites. But now, for this purpose, Bad Guys, to be treated with stiff-legged suspicion by any good Saint.

So around the first of May twenty well-armed Mormons came in from Salt Lake to reinforce Devil's Gate, saying that forty or fifty apostates under Tom Williams were on the trail, and would shortly be demanding a lot of the freight cached there, though many had refused to pay the Church freighting company on the grounds that their goods had never been brought through. These men shortly appeared, and camped on the Sweetwater above the fort. To some who presented receipts and orders, Jones released freight from the storehouse; others who had no orders or whose orders looked forged he turned down. His refusal brought on a big dramatic scene, with Tom Williams and his apostates riding up in force and the forty Mormons taking cover behind cabins and posting themselves at portholes.

This whole scene goes like pure horse opera, and just possibly is. The apostate bully shouts his demand at the cabin, the camera pans first over his hard-faced henchmen and then over the faces of the defenders sweating behind their barricades. Then the door opens and the hero walks out alone into the open yard, in as ortho- dox a walk-down as ever Gary Cooper made. Williams demands, Jones refuses. Williams asks his men if they elect to take their stuff by force, the sound camera brings us their short, sharp, raw-meat growl. There is the moment of quiet while the mouth tastes metal and the held breath may let go any minute to the sound of gunfire. At the breaking end of that silence the hero says he wants to say one thing. His voice, not loud, carries even to the rear rank of horsemen, but his words are addressed to Tom Williams. In the pauses of his speech we can hear the tender rattle of young cottonwood leaves and the soft roar of the Sweetwater pouring its spring flood through Devil's Gate.

"We have been here all winter eating poor beef and raw hide to take care of these goods," Jones says. "We have had but little fun, and would just as soon have some now as not; in fact would like a little row. If you think you can take the fort, just try it. But I don't think you can take me to commence with; and the first one that offers any violence to me is a dead man. Now I dare you to go past me towards the fort."

Tom Williams was an uncle by marriage of Dan Jones's wife, and he knew what he was up against. After a minute he said, "For your family's sake I will spare you, for I think you d——d fool enough to die before you would give up the goods." And turned away, buffaloed.

That is how Dan Jones reports the episode. A man as steady, dependable, and brave as anyone between the Missouri and the Great Salt Lake sounds here as if he were quoting a dime novel. Nevertheless we should not let the falsity of the tone lead us to doubt the essential probability of the story. Whatever the expansions in Dan Jones's rhetoric, and whatever the justice of his cause as against that of the men wanting their freight, he may very well have walked out alone before fifty armed men and backed Tom Williams down. He was man enough.

Jones's heroics took care of the Bad Guys, but the Honest Citizens, unable to tell a Lone Ranger from a rustler, began giving Dan trouble as soon as he got back to Salt Lake City in the early summer. People whose goods had got lost on the desperate trail, people who may even have thrown their own goods away to lighten the wagon, now began to say that Jones had probably stolen them. They were full of the self-righteousness of the Reformation, which put neighbor to spying on neighbor and made everybody's sins everybody else's business; they had a normal Mormon suspicion of a man who had joined the Church only recently, and who came from Missouri at that; and they were truly Mormon in having a stern sense of property. They made so much talk that Jones went to Brigham Young and got from him the sort of security clearance called a "recommend." But even that did not suffice. Eventually his accusers brought Dan up before the High Council for theft.

They should have known better. Dan was good at these walk-downs and face-downs, and unjust accusations could not unravel his sense of humor. Among the charges brought against him was one which said that he *must* have doctored the accounts he turned in to Brigham, in which he had charged up the keep of twenty men all winter at seventy-five cents a week. He was obviously a liar in presenting so ridiculously small a bill, and therefore must be a liar in his account of what had happened to the freight. So Dan itemized the winter's expenses for them: forty head of cattle already dying, on whose meat and hides they lived for two months—no charge because they should have been paid for eating them; game on occasion—no charge; two weeks of thistle roots—no charge; one week of wild garlic bulbs—no charge; three days of minnows caught in a dip net, fish too small to clean and rather bitter to taste—no charge; several meals of roasted prickly pear lobes—no charge; quite a few days of nothing but water—no charge. What brought the costs to seventy-five cents a week per person was some meat bought from the Indians and eaten without salt, some beef bought from the mountain men from the Platte bridge and paid for in calico; and some soap, candles, and coffee taken from the stored freight.

Like the Bad Guys, the Honest Citizens backed down. Brother Brigham lit into them and was about to pronounce one of his more vigorous anathemas when Jones interrupted. He said he could bear the accusations better than they or anyone else could bear Brigham's curse. So instead he received Brigham's blessing and the assurance that if he had set fire to the whole caboodle at Devil's Gate, and ridden off by the light of it, Brigham would not have found fault. Brigham's recommend said the same thing. It ended, "The men who find fault with the labors of Brother Jones the past winter, we wish their names sent to this office, and when the Lord presents an opportunity we will try them and see if they will do any better."

But Brigham did not, as he had intended, send Jones back to manage the Y.X. Express station now established at Devil's Gate. He said he guessed Dan had had about enough of Devil's Gate for any one man. And anyway, by that time it was midsummer, and by midsummer all of the stations ambitiously projected to give the Saints substantial control of the trail from the Missouri to the mountains would have seemed precarious. A few, particularly those at Fort Bridger, at Deer Creek, and at Genoa, a Mormon colony deliberately planted on the Loup Fork as a permanent way station on the model of Garden Grove and Mt. Pisgah, were already well established, along with others of a more tentative kind. But all would have been rendered dubious by the word that Porter Rockwell and some other riders brought to the anniversary picnic in Big Cottonwood Canyon on July 24. The word was that Utah's long festering quarrel with the United States had finally provoked President Buchanan to order an army of 2,500 men to march on Salt Lake City and bring the rebellious Mormons to obedience.

11

ŢŢŢŢŢŢŢŢŢŢŢŢŢŢ

War and Peace

A BOOK ABOUT THE MORMON TRAIL had better not concern itself with the Utah War, but it cannot avoid mentioning it. Buchanan's *posse comitatus* was brought on by more than simple outrage at polygamy (which after all was perfectly constitutional) or anger at Brigham Young's refusal to cooperate with the territorial officials, though anger surely had some weight in the decision. Somewhere behind the determination to impose the federal will on the stiff-necked Mormons and to weaken Brigham Young's absolute control of church and state there lay reasons of political opportunism. From one point of view the Utah War was a diversion created by Secretary of War Floyd to: 1) deflect public attention from slavery, 2) weaken the power available to the Union in the event of trouble, by sending an expedition into the West, and 3) fill his own pockets. From another point of view, it was an attempt by Buchanan to discourage secessionism in the southern states by a show of firmness in suppressing secession in the territories. From the Mormon point of view it was more Gentile persecution. This was a war that began as political maneuver, turned into a military fiasco, was resolved by compromise without any shooting, and ended by becoming a good business proposition for the people it was supposed to discipline.

All of this is history readily available. Just as available, but in-

finitely more confused, is the history of the religious fanaticism
that swept Zion during and immediately after the years of conflict.
In part this was a direct response to outside threat, as Mormon
hearts purified themselves the better to resist God's enemies. But it
had begun well before Buchanan announced his decision to send
a force—had begun in the summer and fall of 1856 when the doctrine of blood atonement was preached from the highest pulpits
and when the frenzy of revivalism inflamed Saint against Gentile
and apostate and even set Saint against Saint in a darkness of guilt
and terror and Old Testament vengefulness.

Eight years of suspicion, blood, and drivings, plus ten on the
frontier, had not softened the Mormon grain. The rescuers of the
handcart pioneers might weep to see such suffering, but sympathy
and heroic assistance did not necessarily teach them how to accept
a woman's thanks, and those same men who risked themselves in
rescue might within a few months be meeting in secret to decide the
fate of an apostate or a particularly obnoxious Gentile. Hands that
had been tender with the frozen limbs of children could, and did,
cut throats.

In the years after 1856 the phrase "to save" a man came to have
the precise meaning of our modern euphemism "to liquidate." There
were almost surely not so many holy murders as the frantic Gentiles charged, and perhaps not so many as disgruntled avengers
confessed, but there were enough. This was the witch-hunt time
of Mormonism, its Inquisition, and neither fanaticism's excesses nor
the hierarchy's precise degree of responsibility has ever been fully
admitted and clarified. Instead, too many Mormon writers have
specialized in evasion, denial, or defensive citing of the provoca-
tions. Zion was persecuted, besieged, at war. The people the Gentiles called avengers either didn't exist, or were harmless, or were
policemen. Charges made by Gentiles could never be believed because they were part of a considered pattern of persecution. Add
to these obscurities the frequent absence of incontrovertible evidence (for even the confessions of Bill Hickman and John D.

Lee are the confessions of disgruntled men, and such exposés as those of T. B. H. Stenhouse and Ann Eliza Young were written by apostates) and the difficulties of arriving at an objective judgment are almost insuperable, especially when the archives of the Church remain sternly closed to such research as this. And so, though many of the suspected and confessed activities of the Sons of Dan took place on the trail, and hence have a claim to our attention, one is inclined to pass up those incidents until historical scholarship and a more enlightened Church policy with regard to its own history will let fact be separated from fiction and fury.

Whether or not Almon Babbitt, while bringing the pay of the territorial officials back from Washington in the fall of 1856, was ambushed and killed near Fort Kearney by Indians or, as the Gentiles said, "by Indians who spoke good English"—that is, by Porter Rockwell—is a troubling but insoluble question. Whether the many men who were "saved" by Rockwell, Hickman, Hanks, and others were really rubbed out on Brigham Young's orders, or for purposes of robbery, or while "resisting arrest" like young Lot Huntington —these are matters for several careful books of the kind that Juanita Brooks has written about the Mountain Meadows Massacre, and they will not be written by tomorrow. One thing is certain: it was a time of much killing, when the streets of Zion were hardly safer, at least for certain kinds of people, than the streets of the wildest mining camp. And a fair share of the killing was done by men of God. The massacre of the Fancher party at Mountain Meadows in 1857 may have been, though it probably was not, planned with the knowledge of Brigham Young. But whether it was or was not, the men who shed that blood were not what Brigham's apostate wife Ann Eliza called them, "fiends rather than men." They were a more dangerous order of beings than fiends: they were Christians just up off their knees.

Like that of any group, the solidarity of Mormonism was increased by hostility and threats from without. "Blessed are they who are persecuted for righteousness' sake," said many a Mormon brooding darkly on his wrongs or fancied wrongs. And blessed, many would have added, are they that strike their persecutors, or any reasonable facsimile thereof.

Neither the Utah War nor the Reformation is our present business, for to enter either of those thickets is to get lost. We note them only to pass them by after observing what they did to the trail and to the Gathering.

Intent upon re-establishing the credit of the handcart scheme, Brigham sent a batch of seventy missionaries eastward with carts on April 23, 1857. He sent them without a single team or wagon, and he told them to get there fast and to make it look easy. They did just that. Forty-eight days after they left Salt Lake City, they walked into Florence "feeling like young lions," their handcarts painted with mottoes and texts: "Zion's Express," "Merry Mormons," "Blessings Follow Sacrifice." For the whole distance they had averaged nearly twenty-two miles a day; from Fort Laramie to the Missouri, twenty-seven.

Those seventy vigorous men, and the immediate publicity given their walk, probably had the psychological effect that Brigham hoped for, and to some extent counteracted the disaster of the fall before. Certainly there was no apparent unwillingess of converts, this year or later, to go by the Lord's plan. Zion's sheep still trusted their shepherds. But the previous year's effort had not only exhausted the P.E. Fund, but left it in debt (one wonders if Brigham may not have been as furious with Franklin Richards for economic mismanagement as for risking the emigrants' lives), and so Orson Pratt, who had succeeded Richards as head of the English mission, had orders to ship none except those who could pay their way at least as far as the eastern states. Those who intended going straight through to the valley should deposit not only their ship fare, but $12.50 for railroad fare to Iowa City, plus fifteen dollars for a handcart. During the spring of 1857, Pratt sent off from Liverpool 2,181 people, of whom about 480 later walked across the plains in two handcart companies. During the year there were also six wagon-trains totaling something over 800 persons.

Whatever may have been their apprehensions, the first handcart company of 149 * made the trip without undue incident, leaving Iowa City on May 22 and arriving in Salt Lake City on September 11, well ahead of the bad weather but in the midst of the excitement about the invasion. The second company, composed of 330 Scandinavians, which left Iowa City on June 12 after only three days of acclimatization, suffered in the early stages from considerable sickness and in the later stages from near-starvation. The presence of hostile troops on the trail made it difficult for relief wagons to go too far eastward, but one of the charming oddities of Mr. Buchanan's expedition against the Mormons was that a detachment moving toward Utah traveled near this train of Danish plodders for a time beyond Fort Laramie, was thoroughly friendly to them, and on one occasion presented them with a crippled ox for beef.

This Danish company ran into a supply train on South Pass—whether Army, Mormon, or other is unclear—and was able to barter for flour enough to get through to the valley on September 12, only a day after the first company. From Fort Laramie on, it moved in the dust and noise of Russell, Majors, and Waddell's great army supply wagons and in frequent sight of troops, and in Echo Canyon it would have had to pass between the stone-wall fortifications that the young men of the Nauvoo Legion were building. Though it was met east of the city and escorted in, with the usual gifts of fresh fruits and vegetables, its greeting was surely more perfunctory than that of any train up to that time, for Brother Brigham had ordered his people to gather in their harvest and hoard it for an evil day, and had promised that if the United States Army entered Salt Lake City it would find the city and its houses and its fields in ashes. In October, over in Liverpool, Orson Pratt announced in an editorial in the *Millennial Star* that "in view of the difficulties which are now threatening the Saints, we deem it

* Hafen's figure. Wilford Woodruff, noting their arrival, set them at 154.

wisdom to stop all emigration to the States and Utah for the present."

Those difficulties, despite the fact that the Mormon guerrillas had stalled the army near Fort Bridger by burning its supply trains and running off its stock, were severe and looking to be more severe in the future. Once spring opened the trail, the angry Albert Sydney Johnston and his humiliated army were not going to be held back for very long. And his mere approach, the mere announcement of his coming, had already caused Brigham to make serious reductions in his ambitious program of empire—reductions most of which were never restored. The "Kingdom" had once been projected from the crest of the Rockies to the crest of the Sierra Nevada, and a number of anchor points had been settled: Fort Limhi on the Salmon River in Idaho, Genoa in the Carson Valley in Nevada, San Bernardino in California, Las Vegas on the Spanish Trail in the Nevada desert, and Fort Supply, once Fort Bridger, on the Overland Trail. If the original plans had matured, the Gathering would shortly have had a second route—or rather a third, since it was already possible to go by ship to San Francisco and cross the desert backward on the California Trail—by sea to San Diego and inland by San Bernardino and Las Vegas and the Southern Utah settlements.

The war stopped that, and stopped it for good. San Bernardino, founded by Amasa Lyman and Charles Coulson Rich, was abandoned, and its settlers recalled to Zion. The same thing happened to Genoa in the Carson Valley, and to the other Genoa far to the east on the Loup Fork, which had been hopefully colonized as a major supply station on the Mormon Trail, and to all the more ephemeral posts set up to serve the Y.X. Express. Deer Creek, Pacific Creek, Big Sandy, Fort Bridger and its close neighbor Fort Supply, were evacuated ahead of the expeditionary force, and both Bridger and Supply were burned to the ground to prevent their being put to use by the enemy.

And now their intimate knowledge of the trail and the country, the kind of frontier skill that had been developed by the migration, the Gathering, and the frequent relief and rescue trains, became the Saints' strongest weapon. They were able to operate freely, in any weather, far to the east of the valley. When two infantry regiments under Col. E. B. Alexander camped at Devil's Gate on the eve of the autumnal equinox, there was a camp of the Nauvoo Legion only a mile or so away—and those Nauvoo Legion Mormons had camped there on the Sweetwater many times, a lot of them with the rescue wagons the fall before. They knew where the best feed was, where a man or a body of men could see without being seen, where ambushes might be laid. They laid no ambushes, because Brigham's orders were to watch the army, not to fight it; to take every opportunity to delay it by stalling its supply trains and stampeding its stock, but not to start shooting.

Very shortly, but farther west on the trail, the Mormon captain Lot Smith met an unguarded supply train, confiscated all its freight, and turned it back toward Fort Laramie. That same evening, with only twenty-four men, Smith stopped two other trains totaling seventy-four wagons and burned them down to the irons. The animals he took, the drivers he started back on the trail. They might have died, but fortunately made it through. Even if they hadn't, Lot Smith would probably have remained the mythic hero, the cross between Robin Hood and Judas Maccabeus, that his people immediately made him into. With only a small band of riders, he stopped the United States Army in its own milling footprints. Caught at the edge of winter without supplies, unable to get any adequate information on Mormon fortifications or strength, Colonel Alexander tried to take his command through to Fort Hall, but ran into a terrible blizzard that drove him back to the ruins of Fort Bridger. That was where he was when Col. Albert Sydney Johnston came out to take over the command.

Johnston built a makeshift camp that he called Camp Scott, a little above old Fort Bridger on Black's Fork, and there sat down to wait out the winter until he could show this rabble what the United States Army could do. They were nearly as hard up for food as Dan Jones and his men had been at Devil's Gate the winter before; and they were so short of animals that squads of men were put in harness to haul wood down from the mountains on sleds. For company, Johnston had the newly appointed federal judges and territorial governor, with whom in his irritable frustration he did not always agree. His mood was not sweetened when the Mormons, still maintaining a skirmish line of riders within a few miles of the camp, sent over the ironic gift of a wagonload of salt.

Between Camp Scott and the valley, concentrated mainly at the barricades in Echo, Weber, and Little Emigration Canyons, were about eight hundred members of the Nauvoo Legion. But as the winter of stalemate wore toward spring, it became plainer and plainer to Brigham Young that this "war" must not come to shooting. Either out of awareness of the relative weakness of the Saints against the firepower of an organized and trained army with the whole United States behind it, or out of the perception that there might be more to gain by other methods, Brigham prepared to evacuate Salt Lake City if the troops came in, and announced his intention of burning it and scorching the earth. The Mormon people, he said, would move south ahead of the army threat, concentrating for the time being in the Utah Valley fifty miles south. Driven from their homes again and again by Gentile irregulars, mobs, and militia, they would now be driven by the uniformed army of their country. Uncomplaining, disciplined, obedient, blameless, they would submit once more to persecution until somewhere, deep in some desert or other, they would find a home where they could be let alone.

One can almost hear the speeches and the publicity releases. The sympathy and support that another driving would enlist in the States were surely a more reliable resource than a few thousand rifles and shotguns in the passes of the Wasatch. But gaining the kind of support and sympathy that could lead to an ultimate solution favorable to the Saints was a fairly desperate business. Brigham had to put his entire resources on the line, he had to be ready to move his whole people and burn his whole city and set fire to every field if the game developed that way. It is fair to assume that he was ready to do just that.

But now to the rescue, romantically disguised under the name of Osborne, and armed with letters from President Buchanan authorizing him to mediate if he could, came Thomas Kane, still the best and most influential friend the Saints had. He arrived in Salt Lake City on February 25, 1858, having come all the way around the Horn and across the desert from California. Until March 8 he stayed in the valley, conferring with Brigham and trying to reassure him that the intentions of the federal government were not so belligerent as Brigham had believed, and to establish the basis for a meeting with Governor-elect Alfred Cumming, still eating shoelaces without salt at Camp Scott. On March 8, Kane started for the mountains under the protection of Porter Rockwell and some others (Rockwell's descendants still treasure a fourteen-inch dagger given him by Kane). A dozen miles from Camp Scott, the escort stopped, and Kane rode in alone.

He had some difficulty with Johnston, who as an army man was hot to put down this rebellion by force—and who would lose his life a few years hence as a general in the army of another rebellion more to his liking—but little with Governor Cumming, who after his winter in the snow was perfectly willing to negotiate. There is every evidence of a Mormon plan to impress Cumming not only with Mormon strength but with Mormon orderliness, industry, harmlessness, and general civilized decency. The Nauvoo Legion went out of its way to show itself disciplined and well-trained, and it appears that every member of it, as Governor Cumming was escorted down Echo and Weber Canyons, lighted at least three fires on the hills and stood up at intervals behind twenty different rocks, to persuade him that the Mormon force was most alert, well-trained, warlike, and numerous. At Farmington, a little north of Salt Lake, the band serenaded him with carefully patriotic airs—a concert perhaps promoted by Kane, who had already expressed himself eloquently on the cultivated decency of Mormons and on the tone of their wind instruments. It may also have been a prepared display that Cumming saw as he rode into the city. He saw files of covered wagons, with stock and children and household goods, moving down State Street toward the point of the mountain, evacu-

ating families whose faces gave the lie to the horror stories and
scarehead rumors published about the Mormons in the eastern press.
If Cumming did not already know it, he would have been told that
some of these sad but uncomplaining people had previously given
up homes at Kanesville, and before that at Winter Quarters; and before that had been driven out of Nauvoo, and before that had fled
from Far West, and before that perhaps from Independence or
Kirtland. He would have been told that many whom he saw abandoning their homes in sorrow had come seven thousand hard miles,
the last fourteen hundred on foot, to find hope and safety in this
city from which the threat of the army was now driving them. He
would have been told that 25,000 of the 45,000 people in the territory were already on the road, and their houses prepared for the
torch.

No one refused Cumming his title of Governor, as he had expected them to. He satisfied himself that the Mormons had not, as
rumored, criminally destroyed the records of the federal courts.
By the time two commissioners arrived from Washington in June,
Cumming was nearly as pro-Mormon as Kane.

The result of Kane's intervention and Cumming's essential good
will and Brigham's prudent decision not to contest the army's entrance by force was a compromise. Brigham gave up any pretention
to the title of Territorial Governor and accepted Washington's
ostensible control of Utah's affairs, though he still retained much
of his power through his control of the Church that dominated
every Mormon's temporal as well as spiritual life. It would be a
long time before federal authority would be fully accepted. (From
1862 to 1870, in fact, the theocratic power of the Church was
supplemented by the ghost government of the ghost State of Deseret,
with Brigham as ghost Governor. This fully organized shadow,
whose legislature met after the regular territorial legislature, and
passed its own laws affirming or denying those passed by the regular
legislators, contained many of the same people who served the Territory, but their shadow enactments had more force for the faithful
than what was technically the law of the land.) In exchange for

Brigham's agreement to accept its occupation of the territory, the army agreed not to fix itself upon Salt Lake City, where its presence might create clashes, but to build a camp in Cedar Valley, twenty-five miles southwest. It said it would molest no resident of Utah in his daily business, which meant that it would not attempt to interfere in the practise of polygamy. So though Brigham had what he did not in the least want—an army on his doorstep, and an increased interference by Gentiles in Mormon affairs—he had it on something like his own terms.

On June 26, 1858, 3,000 men, with all their renewed accompaniment of wagons and stock, marched through Salt Lake City on their way to what would become Camp Floyd. The city, as dead as the sacked Nauvoo that Thomas Kane had visited years before, spooked them, or at least spooked the New York *Herald* correspondent who accompanied them:

> The streets were deserted, the city was deserted. Though surrounded by houses we were nevertheless in a place of desert loneliness. The quietness of the grave prevailed where it seemed that thronging thousands and rushing commerce ought to pour their tides along. The windows had been taken out of the major parts of the houses; the doors were locked; everything had been made ready for burning . . .

Until Johnston made it clear that the army would live up to the agreement reached with the peace commissioners, Salt Lake City's streets remained empty. Then finally Brigham called his people home. They came more than willingly, for some of the men had been out in the mountains all through the winter and spring, planting had been delayed or the chance for it lost, families had been camping or had crowded in with relatives and were eager to get back to the comfort of home. And for some, the dramatic demonstration of Mormon solidarity in beginning Brigham's policy of evacuation and scorched earth had been costly in more than time or crops or comfort. Among the casualties of the move was Irene Hascall Pomeroy, who during the retreat southward had burned her arm so badly that it had to be amputated. It never healed properly, and within three years she died of it, and so finally achieved her ambition to be immolated for her faith. There were undoubtedly others as eager to be tried as she, people who may have felt cheated that they were not actually called upon to pile hay against their homes and set them afire, and labor out through the desert in search of a new Canaan. Returning to a place that persecuting Gentiles had threatened must have seemed to some as difficult as the breaking of an old habit.

Still, they had had a satisfying time of discomfort. Blessed are they who are persecuted for righteousness' sake. They came back and planted the crops that could still be planted, and began to make money out of the soldiers by selling fruit, vegetables, and livestock to the camp. Within three years, on the outbreak of the Civil War, these regulars would be pulled out of Utah, and the Saints would buy Camp Floyd and all its gear for ten cents on the dollar.

Because of the closing-off of emigration from Liverpool during the uncertainties of the winter and spring, the Gathering of 1858 was barely a trickle. Kate B. Carter's census of the emigration shows only three small wagontrains, two from Iowa City and one from Florence, that carried altogether only 150 people, many of them undoubtedly returning missionaries slipping back home. But by the fall Conference in 1858 the situation in the valley was so far stabilized that the "trumpet-blast" tone was renewed in the instructions sent to the British mission. "Urge on the emigration so far as you have the power. Wherein the Saints are not able to come all the way through, let them come to the States, and then make their way through as soon as they can. We would like to strengthen at Genoa and Florence, and to make a large settlement on Deer Creek, and the Black Hills, and would not object [to] seeing about 10,000 Saints find their way to Utah the ensuing year."

The reference to Genoa, Deer Creek, and other stations is interesting, for it indicates that even though the mail contract for the Y.X. Express had been canceled and its stations broken up, Brigham had not abandoned his intention of controlling the road through the establishment and maintenance of colonized supply posts. In this, as in so many of his operations, the ecclesiastical and the economic were mingled. Control of the trail was useful, if not vital, to the Gathering; it was also useful to the freighting business, in which there were large profits and which increased with every increase in the population and commerce of Zion. In 1858, because of the "war," the Russell, Majors, and Waddell freighting operation alone had involved 3,500 wagons, 40,000 oxen, 1,000 mules, and 4,000 men.

On April 11, 1859, the *William Tapscott* sailed from Liverpool carrying 725 emigrants. Half of the ten wards into which the ship was divided were Scandinavian, a fact which indicates the growing importance of the Scandinavian mission in comparison with the shrinking pool of English converts. Iowa City was no longer the staging point, for by now the Hannibal and St. Joseph Railroad had been completed and allowed rail transportation clear to the Missouri. From St. Joseph the converts took a stern wheeler to Florence, rebuilt on the ashes of Winter Quarters in what since 1854 had been Nebraska Territory. For the next half dozen years the Mormon Trail would begin at the same point from which the pioneers had started.

One handcart company of 233 people * and four wagontrains totaling 1,206 (Carter's figures) got off from Florence in June, and all made the valley between the end of August and mid-September. They found the Loup Fork colony of Genoa abandoned except for three sharpers with cows who asked to join the company and then charged profiteer prices for their milk. These squatter entrepreneurs were symptomatic. There had always been some, even in the pre-pioneer days before 1847. During the late 1850's and early 1860's, with the development of regular stage and mail service, there was a growing number who tended stations, sold meals or beds or livestock, scavenged the trail, or turned alcohol into whiskey with the aid of water, cayenne pepper, and tobacco.

Two station attendants on the Big Sandy, seeing the Sixth Handcart Company drag by, came to the door of their shack with the

* Hafen; Mrs. Carter says 225.

contemporary equivalent of wolf whistles and in very short order talked two Scandinavian girls who were sick of walking into staying there and "marrying" them. The other Saints felt to deplore such weakness, and yet could hardly blame the girls. It was a very very long walk to Zion, and food was very short. Before they got in, two of that company dropped behind, unnoticed, and were later found half eaten by wolves.

A little exhausting, a little gruesome. Nevertheless, for handcart companies, a fairly routine trip. But it was not the vintage year that the Church had hoped for. Instead of 10,000, Kate B. Carter's census shows only 1,431 reaching the valley in 1859.

1860 saw two Mormon charter ships, the *Underwriter* which sailed March 30 with 594 emigrants, and the *William Tapscott* which sailed May 11 with 730. Again nearly half of the *Tapscott's* passengers were non-English, mainly Scandinavian and Swiss. They were unlucky, and would not have done as an advertisement of the well-run emigrating service, for smallpox broke out aboard and killed ten of them. But by the time the through passengers had organized at Florence they were past their trouble. Two handcart companies, the ninth and tenth of their kind, got off on June 1 and July 6. The ninth, with 233 people, suffered only one death while crossing the plains; the tenth, with 124, had none at all.

It is possible for historians scrutinizing the records to guess at some plausible reasons why. For one thing, these were not paupers on an economy run with minimal equipment. These handcarts were well-made of seasoned lumber; they were even painted. Where the Willie and Martin companies had had only twelve wagons altogether to carry the supplies and haul the lame and sick for nearly 1,100 people, the ninth company had six wagons for only 233, and the tenth, seven for 124. Even with that additional carrying capacity, both had to have relief supplies en route, the ninth company at Green River and the tenth at Three Crossings on the Sweetwater. And finally, they were past trying to set records or to prove something improbable: where the first three handcart companies of 1856, with their minimal supplies and few wagons, had all made the trip in less than seventy days, the ninth company took eighty-eight and the tenth eighty. Whatever the arguments about the delay that oxen could cause, they did mean more nearly sufficient food, and that in turn meant more leisure, lessened strain, less hardship, fewer deaths.

So the conclusion must be—and Mormon practise indicates that it was the conclusion of the hierarchy too—that handcarts were a perfectly feasible means of bringing the harvest to the valleys of Ephraim, *if:* if they started on time, if their carts were well-made, if they did not try to hurry, if they had relief supplies somewhere west of Fort Laramie, if they had enough wagons to carry food and to relieve the sick or feeble, and if the priesthood didn't get over-zealous about testing their charges. But just about the time when these conditions began to be acknowledged and met, the pattern of the emigration was abruptly changed. After 1860 there were no more handcarts, and very few of the old-fashioned kind of wagon-trains.

Everything on the trail was changing. The tenth handcart company, during its eighty days in transit, several times met or was passed by the overland stage carrying mail and passengers behind four good and frequently changed horses, and periodically the Pony Express riders scoured by their carts at a furious gallop. Both Pony Express and Overland Stage looked lovely and fast and comfortable from down in the roadside dust, but as the swift changes of the 1860's developed, neither was to last much longer than the handcarts. The Pony Express, that most brilliant and romantic of mail services, came and went like the clatter of advancing and then receding hoofs: it was dead the moment Edward Creighton carried his Overland Telegraph through to the West Coast from Omaha. The Overland Stage would die of an overdose of railroad in 1869. But until then, it would share the trail with the final form of Mormon transport, the so-called Church Trains.

The Church Train was primarily an economic development, part of the continuing Mormon movement toward self-sufficiency. By the end of the 1850's Utah was rich in livestock and plentifully equipped with wagons. There was no point therefore in buying new stock and new wagons at Florence, pouring good Mormon dollars into the hands of the Gentiles, if it could be demonstrated that trains could leave the valley early in the year, pick up freight and passengers on the Missouri, and return to Utah that same season. In 1860 Joseph W. Young, Brigham's brother, set out to demonstrate that the round trip was possible. He left Salt Lake City on April 30 with thirty-six wagons, most of them drawn by ox teams, and loaded with Utah-grown and Utah-ground flour and other supplies. On the way east he dropped off both supplies and spare teams at several depots. Reaching the Missouri in excellent condition, he picked up freight and some converts and started back after only a few days' delay. On October 3, well within the margin of safety from the weather, he was back in the valley, prepared to deliver a sermon in October Conference on the text of "ox-teamology."

His demonstration was decisive. With good teams, and with supplies and replacement stock available at a few stations, the Church could not only handle all its own freighting in its own wagons drawn by its own teams, but could create a market for its flour and other produce and livestock. Drivers could be, and promptly were, "called" for this six-month duty as men were called to missions, and were recompensed not in money but in labor-tithing credit. As a demonstration of Mormon cooperativeness and efficiency it was dazzling, and it at once put both the handcarts and the old style wagontrain out of business. The two handcart companies of 1860 were the last, and the seven wagontrains of the same year that brought 1,630 people to Zion (Mrs. Carter's figures), were nearly the last. What had once been a somewhat uncertain adventure had become the operation of a truck line; what had once been a trail was a road.

A search for dependable statistics on emigration during the period of the Church Trains is attended by the usual exasperations. Gustive Larson says that 1861 saw 1,959 converts reach the valley, all but 652 by Church Trains. But Mrs. Carter lists twelve wagontrains during that year, several of which left Florence in late May and early June—too early altogether to have come from the valley. Presumably the two systems overlapped during this year, and some emigrants would have gone in their own outfits, arranged by payment to the Church agents in Liverpool or New York. In 1865 and 1867, when Church Trains for some reason did not operate at all, Mrs. Carter's figures show emigration of only 800 and 500 people. But for the other years between 1860 and 1868 her totals are substantial: 5,036 in 1862; 3,625 in 1863; 2,474 in 1864; 3,126 in 1866; and 3,958 in 1868. In this last year of the trail, five hundred teams made the round trip from Salt Lake City, and $27,000 in special funds were raised for the "gathering of the Lord's poor." Larson's totals for the whole period 1861–1868 show 1,913 wagons sent east and back, with 2,389 men and 17,543 oxen. In all that period he finds only 726 emigrants who went with their own teams—a figure that cannot be tested against Mrs. Carter's because she does not distinguish between Church Trains and other trains. The total emigration for these years, as listed by the two compilations, shows considerable discrepancy, Mrs. Carter's list adding up to 23,010 and Mr. Larson's to 20,426.

By any system of computation, it was a steady and heavy flow of traffic, both in passengers and freight, and it was conducted entirely by professionals. No longer did captains have to instruct women, boys, or Welshmen in the mysteries of geeing and hawing oxen. No longer did they have to race against weather and failing supplies and growing exhaustion through the Black Hills and up the Sweetwater. Only when Indians ran off large numbers of animals, as they did in 1868, was it necessary to send any relief from the valley. No more buffalo stampedes panicked the camps and scattered the camp's tame herds—buffalo were getting rare in the Platte valley. There were no more days lost hunting quicksand fords, no more axle-breaking drops and climbs out of steep-banked creeks, no more loss of wagons to wind or current fording the North Platte: there were ferries and bridges on the major streams, and the approaches to the fords had been improved through twenty years. When the train was large and the leaders and drivers all experienced, there was little danger of being attacked by the Sioux or "picked by the Crows," as small or inexperienced companies sometimes were, and as Pony Express riders and the Overland Stage were often in danger of being. Converts headed for Zion in a Church Train were as safe as anyone on the trail—much safer than stage passengers since they did not have to eat the food that dirty and indifferent station keepers served up.

A trail is only a set of tracks, a road is a human institution. And it is a fact at first a little disconcerting to realize that what made the Mormon Trail into a human institution was actually as much the work of Gentiles as of the Mormons themselves. The Mormons popularized the route, and it turned out to be a better route in many ways than the Oregon-California Trail from Independence or St. Joseph. But the principle of the Gathering, the impulse to concentrate their strength in the "Kingdom," discouraged the permanent settlement of Saints along the way, and Brigham's plans to settle certain stations to serve his Y.X. Express were disrupted by the conflict with the federal government and the cancellation of his mail contract. The other stations which were established, essentially supply and stock depots for the Church Trains, turned out to be as ephemeral as the Mormon Ferry at Last Crossing—when the immediate need for them ceased, their people were likely to be pulled back to Salt Lake City. The Gentiles, who had from the beginning contributed trading posts, ferries, bridges, army posts, banditry, and other humanizing elements to the trail, in the end inherited it.

When the pioneers set out from Winter Quarters in April, 1847, there were only two permanent white habitations along the entire 1,035 miles. These were Fort Laramie and Fort Bridger, both adjuncts of the declining fur trade, and both Gentile. There were certain more peripatetic indications that the trail itself was potentially profitable—Miles Goodyear's trip up the Bear River to sell horses to the emigration, for instance. To these very tentative human intrusions upon the wilderness the Mormons added some of their own: the efficient ferry on the Elkhorn, the later ferries on the North Platte and the Green. Moreover, they did more for the trail itself than any before them, threw boulders out of the track, grubbed willows, dug the approaches of fords, and in consequence the Mormon Trail improved much faster than its rival across the Platte. At Windlass Hill above Ash Hollow, Oregon and California emigrants went on for years lowering their wagons on ropes—why should any of them do the road work necessary to make the descent easier when none of them ever expected to go that way again? If that hill had been on the Mormon Trail the descent would have been graded and improved by every company that used it, for the Mormon Trail was not a road of passage for random opportunists but a permanent way prepared for the Gathering of Zion.

Nevertheless, the very systematization of the Gathering meant that only when the Church saw need for it, as it saw need for the North Platte ferry in 1847, or for stations at Deer Creek and Genoa in 1857, was there likely to be any permanent or semi-permanent Mormon outpost on the trail. Most of the things that gradually developed at strategic points were the work of squatter entrepreneurs. Even Fort Laramie and Fort Bridger were in that category, and so were the bridge that John Richard built across the North Platte at Deer Creek in 1851 and the later bridge that replaced it, and the little whiskey posts that came and went along the trail (Antoine Roubidoux' near Chimney Rock, Bordeaux' on the Rawhide, the Chambeau and Semineaux post at Devil's Gate where Dan Jones wintered, others that lasted a season or two or were intermittently occupied). These were enterprises run almost always by French-Canadians, *métis*, the left-overs of the fur trade who were adapting themselves to the newer business opportunities of the overland migration. Often they combined with, or were taken over by, stations that served the several mail and stage companies. These stations, though inherited in the end by the Gentiles, were partially Mormon in their origin, for Mormons participated in an important way in the early mail service.

The first government mail service between Independence, Missouri, and Salt Lake City was supplied by Samuel Woodson, who in 1850 took the contract for four years. But well before that there had been a private Mormon service whose carriers were Porter Rockwell, Almon Babbitt, and others, and when Woodson after a little more than a year had to have help, Feramorz Little took over the route from Salt Lake City to Fort Laramie for the last two years and eleven months of Woodson's contract. From August 1, 1851 to April, 1853, Little and his helpers Eph Hanks and C. F. Decker rode that lonely and dangerous five hundred miles of mountains with no station and no change of animals except at Fort Bridger and, toward the end of their contract, at Devil's Gate.

The plan was to meet the carrier from Independence at Fort Laramie, as near as possible to the fifteenth of each month, to exchange mail sacks, and to ride back at once. It was a route, like any mail route, but it meant a thousand-mile round-trip every thirty days. Often they picked up travelers who for safety's sake wanted to ride with them, sometimes they were held up as much as three weeks by snow, once or twice they barely got through alive, several times they had encounters with the Crows, who were accustomed to "pick" small parties anywhere between Fort Laramie and Devil's Gate. On one occasion, in September, 1851, carrying the eastbound mail and escorting Dr. G. M. Bernhisel, who was headed for Washington as Territorial Delegate to Congress, Decker and Alfred Higgins were warned by Vasquez at Fort Bridger to look out for the Crows, who were up on Boxelder Creek, ten miles east of Deer Creek. When they reached Deer Creek they came upon an oddity: a photographer named Jones, who with five companions and a good outfit was engaged in photographing the route across the continent. Those pictures, if they had come through to us, would be absolutely priceless, but Jones was not the man likely to bring them through. When Decker and Higgins suggested that they travel and camp together, Jones replied that if they were afraid of Indians they had better hurry right along. He was staying to take pictures. Ten miles east, on Boxelder Creek, the mail carriers were stopped by a Crow war party demanding plunder. While some of the Crows were getting away with Decker's supplies, one tried to steal a revolver. Decker got it by the butt just as the Indian got it by the barrel. The Indian let go. Several Indians grappled with Higgins and he knocked a couple of them down. Just as a bloody fight threatened to develop, a squaw on a hill signaled and the Crows rode off, leaving the mail carriers to rescue their mail and part of their gear and make tracks for Fort Laramie. Behind them they saw the photographer's outfit starting to pitch camp. A day or two later, returning toward Salt Lake City, they met the shivering scarecrow Jones, well picked, dressed only in a breech clout, a castoff pair of Crow moccasins, and a piece of oil cloth. He had managed to hide and preserve a $1,200 poke of gold dust, but his outfit, including camera and pictures, was gone, and so was history's chance to know how the trail to that point looked in 1851.

Even by 1853, when Frederick Piercy came out with his sketching pad, it would have changed somewhat, and change was progressively faster with every year. By the winter of 1856–57, when Little and Hanks were again briefly carrying the mail in the interval between the abrogation of the McGraw contract and the signing of the contract with the Y.X. Express, the route between Salt Lake City and Fort Laramie could count on the use of trader cabins on the Big Sandy, at Pacific Springs, at Devil's Gate, at Independence Rock, and at the Platte bridge, and the great surge of hauling that accompanied the Utah War made those places into permanent stage stations. In 1860, when Richard Burton made his celebrated trip to Zion to study, among other things, the sex habits of the Mormons, he found Ward's Station two hours out of Fort Laramie on the Black Hills road; Horseshoe Station, run by Jack Slade, on Horseshoe Creek; a station "in the building" on the La Bonte; Wheeler's Station on Box Elder Creek; a Sioux agency and station on Deer Creek; a station on Little Muddy Creek; and the station of Louis Guenot, the bridge owner, near the Last Crossing. Beyond Last Crossing his stage stopped at Red Buttes Station, Willow Springs Station, Planté's station above Devil's Gate, the ranch of Luis Silva below the Three Crossings of the Sweetwater, the Three Crossings station itself, the Foot of the Ridge Station, a ranch run by two Canadians at Willow Creek, Pacific Springs Station, Big Sandy Station, McCarthy's station on the Green, Michael Martin's store farther down the Green, Ham's Fork Station, Holmes' station at "Millersville" on Smith's Fork, and finally Fort Bridger. Reported in Burton's garrulous and omniscient style, it seems a populous road.

Most of the stations west of Pacific Springs were run by Mormons; one, that on the Big Sandy, was run by Burton's driver, who happened to be one of the two men who had wolf-whistled Danish girls out of the Eighth Handcart Company in 1859. All of the stations, Gentile and Mormon, did more to add to than assuage the traveler's discomfort. Burton's world-traveled eye saw little to admire in any form of the American pioneer. French Canadian, American, Mormon—all struck him as lazy or sullen or uncouth, and all were shudderingly dirty. The *"ne plus ultra* of western discomfort" turned out to be the station on Ham's Fork, run by a dirty Scotch Mormon with two slattern Irish sisters for wives.

> Describing one I describe both sisters; her nose was "pugged," apparently by gnawing hard potatoes before that member had acquired firmness and consistency; her face was powdered with freckles; her hair, and indeed her general costume looked, to quote Mr. Dow's sermon, as though she had been rammed through a bush-fence into a world of wretchedness and woe. Her dress was unwashed and in tatters, and her feet were bare ... Moreover I could not but notice, that though the house contained two wives it boasted only of one cubile, and had only one cubiculum ... My first impulse was to attribute the evil, uncharitably enough, to Mormonism ... A more extended acquaintance with the regions west of the Wasach taught me that the dirt and discomfort were the growth of the land. To give the poor devils their due, Dawvid was civil and intelligent, though a noted dawdler ... Moreover his wives were not deficient in charity; several Indians came to the door and none went away without a "bit" and a "sup."

Burton's astringent travelogue is as good a way as any to take leave of the Mormon Trail. It reminds us that piety and ancestor worship are not the best foundation for the study of history—that the pioneer Mormons were no more seven feet tall and of a heroic gentleness and a saintly purity than their Gentile enemies were. They were frontier Americans with the frontier American virtues inextricably mixed with the frontier American coarseness and violence; or they were often immigrant paupers crusted with poverty's demoralization and dirt. They believed a different faith than their contemporaries, and their extraordinarily well-organized social system gave them great constructive and recuperative strength. But they were not demi-gods, and their often-slovenly humanity teaches us that much is lost when civilized people go out upon a frontier. The original Mormons were, as Thomas Kane testified, more civilized, better behaved, and cleaner than their neighbors. That advantage tended to dwindle under conditions of hardship and deprivation, and the influx of the underprivileged of Europe.

And partly what Burton saw along the trail reflected the change that had come in the trail itself. By 1860 much of the romance had gone out of an overland crossing, along with much of the uncertainty and danger. The human race had begun already to pollute its new environment; frontier naturalness and health and freedom had begun already to give way to the second stage of settlement, which is generally merely backward, dirty, and deprived. The Saints who stuck with the Gathering, and lived in tight Saintly communities in one of the valleys of Zion, had a much better chance to retain or to develop the qualities that Richard Burton would have thought civilized than those who "went Gentile" out along the trail.

The Saints might have said, with some justice, that the Gentiles were welcome to the trail—that having served its purpose as the route of the Gathering it was no longer necessary to the Mormons. They will probably, in angry repudiation of what Richard Burton said of their grandfathers and great grandfathers, insist upon the right of those ancestors to respect—for their faith, their endurance, their discipline. And they will be at least as right as Burton. A man who seldom washes may be, in his own way, a hero. A slattern barefoot girl who cannot spell may become as prolific and healthy a mother of a race as someone with cleaner linen or better grammar.

The new start that the Zion in the Valleys of the Mountains offered to Mormon converts was a real new start, however peculiar, and many of the essentially New England virtues of Mormonism have reasserted themselves in the society that the Gathering created.

I am just as glad, speaking personally, that I do not have to eat the meals served by the potato-nosed sister-wives of Dawvid Lewis at Ham's Fork. But from this distance, and with the whole history of the Mormon Migration before my eyes, I am glad to take off my hat and salute even these with a degree of respect. For what they and others like them did was not done easily or without sacrifice and suffering. They lived and acted, and sometimes died, for what they believed, and their intractable humanity ennobled them about as often as the excesses of their faith led them into tribal suspicion or their misfortunes into demoralization.

The story of the Mormon Trail is a story of people, no better and no worse than other people, probably, but certainly as sternly tested as any, and with a right to their pride in the way they have borne the testing.

12

┬┬┬┬┬┬┬┬┬┬┬┬

Pilgrimage Road

T HIS IS THE PLACE," says the tall granite shaft of Mahonri
Young's monument to the pioneers at the mouth of Emigration
Canyon. Whether Brigham actually said them, or Wilford Woodruff, or whether they crystallized out of history as myth crystallizes
out of the acts of living men, these are the right words. They say
what should here be said, what every good Saint has accepted as
revealed truth for 117 years.

This *is* the place, the Holy City, New Jerusalem, Zion in the
Valleys of the Mountains; and also a provincial capital, thriving
center of what the Chamber of Commerce likes to call the Intermountain Empire; and also, with a special passion of love and loyalty, home. This is not a city of people born where they do not
like to live. Though it exports its able young people to places of
wider opportunity, it keeps their affection, and often draws them
back. Though Brigham Young's dream of a Kingdom controlled
by the Saints was half frustrated by the larger Manifest Destiny of
which the Mormons themselves were a part, and has become the
Intermountain Empire dominated by certain industrial corporations
in which the Church generally has a solid share, Brigham did suc-
ceed in colonizing a heartland which in spite of Gentile intrusions
and the blurring years retains the stamp of its origin.

The Kingdom is a more cohesive society even yet than most Americans know. The Mormon zeal for genealogy, the temple rituals in which the living are baptized for the dead, the family reunions that may involve five hundred intricately related people, the persistence of undercover Fundamentalist polygamy, may be subjects of occasional joking, defensiveness, or embarrassment, but the Mormon family and the beliefs that sanctify it are nevertheless sources of a profound sense of community, an almost smug satisfaction. These people belong to one another, to a place, to a faith. They stand facing the rest of the world like a herd of rather amiable musk oxen, horns out, in a protective ring, watchful but not belligerent—full of confidence but ready to be reasonable, and wanting to be liked.

What was once a nearly universal paranoia has mellowed into a tolerant spirit of peaceful co-existence, though with certain emotional reservations and with an abiding sense that the Saints are a chosen people. On the other side, what was once a bitter Gentile antagonism has waned with the political and religious rivalry that used to exacerbate it, and with the official renunciation of polygamy in 1890. Within Salt Lake City itself, there is still a clash of economic interests and some suspicion between Mormon and Gentile, but elsewhere the Gentile world has pretty generally come around to admiration for the commonsense, thrift, industry, and efficiency which group solidarity and the rigors of desert settlement have built into the Mormon nature. Most material and most practical of all religions, Mormonism has come into its age of confidence and prosperity. The more the outside world bites its knuckles in existential despair, the more the Mormon is convinced of the value of his special sustaining faith as the basis for a healthy society.

This is the place. History, common effort, a quite remarkable social stability, and a notable cultural adaptation have made it so. The closest thing to it in modern history is Israel, and Mormons are not blind to the parallels. But this is Israel after more than a century, finally at peace with its ancient enemies. By now the strange and forbidding weathers and lights of the desert have been etched into the remembering senses of five generations; its farmers have their own crops and methods and calendars and institutions (what child but a Mormon child knows about Beet Vacation?); its valleys have their own local dialects, so that Cache can be distinguished from Sanpete by the flattening of a vowel; its people, who established themselves here as the "old settlers," and so put the Gentiles in the position of intruders, have retained the curious blend of provincialism and cosmopolitanism that has marked Mormonism ever since its half-literate farm boys—its Brigham Youngs and Heber Kimballs and Wilford Woodruffs—began missionarying around Europe in the late 1830's. This is the place Mormons go away from and return to. Though it changes, its keeps its integrity. May my right hand lose its cunning if I forget thee, Zion.

Mahonri Young's monument is shaped like the arms and upper shaft of a cross. At the foot of the central shaft are the bronze figures of Orson Pratt and Erastus Snow, one riding, one walking. Hats in hand, they cheer the panorama of the great valley as they cheered it on July 21, 1847, from the sudden top of Donner Hill. They make visual one of the great moments of Mormon and indeed of western history—such a moment as after months of effort and uncertainty William Clark caught with a scrawl in a notebook at the mouth of the Columbia on November 7, 1805: "Ocian in view! O! the joy." The commemoration here has a biblical, not a personal, flavor, and yet even to an unbeliever it seems to warm the stone it is carved in; an antique fervor glows from the words:

> "Hosannah! Hosannah! Hosannah! To God and the Lamb! Amen! Amen! Amen!" "And it shall come to pass in the last days that the mountain of the Lord's house shall be established in the tops of the mountains and shall be exalted above the hills; and all nations shall flow unto it. The wilderness shall blossom and the solitary place shall be glad for them, and the desert shall rejoice and blossom as the rose."

On both sides of Pratt and Snow, in bronze bas-relief, go the low-necked oxen and the hooped wagons that are as ineradicable a part of Mormon symbolism as the words of Isaiah are part of its vocabulary. On the back side of the horizontal structure, as if looking to the past rather than to the future, are individual figures of Indians and trappers and blackrobes, part of what to a Mormon view are the pre-history of the region; and the termini of the base are crowned by groups representing, on the south, Fathers Escalante and Dominguez, and on the north, the mountain men. On the back side of the vertical member the Donner party labors, doomed, going nowhere. But at the top of the shaft, more than life-size, dominating all this sculptured and preparatory history as they dominate the sweep of the valley, stand Brigham Young, Heber Kimball, and Wilford Woodruff, whose entry into the land made it officially Canaan.

As an expression of the Mormons' respect for their own history, and also of their interpretation of history, it is absolutely right. The pioneers who thought the Donner tragedy God's retribution upon a pack of quarrelsome Gentiles would approve the Donners' reversed and secondary status here, though it was they in fact who broke the trail. All would acknowledge as natural and right the elevation of Brother Brigham and the two apostles over the whole structure. William Clayton, if he could return for a look, would be especially gratified, for nowhere on the monument is an emphasized representation of Dr. Willard Richards, though as one of Brigham's counselors he might well have stood on the pillar in the place of Woodruff.

Temple Square, in the heart of downtown Salt Lake City, may be the true end of the Mormon Trail, and surely the museum there contains many trail relics, including the battered handcart of Archer Walters. But this monument is the symbolic end, and it is the proper place from which to make a pilgrimage backward toward the shrines that mark the origin and progress of the Church. It is a pilgrimage growing more and more popular among the pious and among Church and business groups anxious to advertise an anniversary with bearded and booted caravans. There are guide books to help the traveler locate routes and settlements and buildings that time has nearly effaced, and historical markers and monuments at the places of great trial or suffering. For in the tidal flow of history the direction of human dedication periodically reverses itself: those who with a whole heart set out to create the future find that instead they have created a past. These days, the Mormon Trail is most appropriately traversed backward, eastward, from the place where the Church finally achieved itself to the places where it began, from the realized fact to the forming idea.

Most common of the historical retracings of pioneer tracks—what might be called the short or economy pilgrimage, suitable for Sunday excursions or for Boy Scout weekends—is that from the This Is the Place monument to Henefer, on the Weber River. This stretch of thirty-six miles, the most difficult on the whole trail, took the Donner party sixteen days, Orson Pratt's road gang six. The highway opened on the old route as part of the Centennial piety will let a modern pilgrim drive it in an hour if he doesn't care about seeing anything. Even if he wants to see it all, he can do it in a morning.

If it is summer, the low mouth of Emigration Canyon will be brown on the hillsides, green along the creek. There will be flowers—blue pentstemon, creamy sego lilies, pink phlox—and in the canyon bottom soft maple and box elder, and on the slopes scrubby oak brush. Two miles up, the road crosses the creek to avoid going over Donner Hill; six and and a half miles up, at the marker indicating the last camp of Brigham's party before they entered the valley, it crosses again and begins the switchbacks up over the Little Mountain summit. Cutting across these swinging curves, the steep ruts of the old trail can be seen in a couple of places, plunging toward Emigration Creek. It does not look like a comfortable wagonroad.

From the Little Mountain summit, "like Moses from Pisgay's top," the pilgrim can look back and see a patch of trees and roofs and towers. On the other side he looks down into Mountain Dell, with the Mountain Dell Reservoir spreading up toward it from the west. Up Mountain Dell Creek a little way, just below a Girl Scout camp, Eph Hanks had a Pony Express station in 1860. Instead of following the old trail up the gulch, the modern road climbs the north slope, but from the summit the view is the same as that which Orson

Pratt and John Brown saw in 1847: the crowding peaks of the Wasatch, the falling ravine closed by its dark gun-sight mountain, with the floating crest of the Oquirrhs far beyond, and a glimpse of flat valley on each side. High as they are, the southward facing slopes up here are barren of everything but sage; the northward facing ones carry colonies of aspen, a species as groupy as the Mormons themselves.

The automobile road goes down the east side of Big Mountain north of the original grade, and thereby misses the ruins of the cobblerock "fortifications" that the Mormons threw up as their third line of defense when preparing for Johnston's army in 1857–58. But a ranch road leading back up Little Emigration Canyon from the MacFarlane Ranch, once the site of the Bauchmann Pony Express Station, leads to Mormon Flat, from which the fortifications can be reached by a short climb. They look very like a ruined stone wall, or a crude stone corral. The land here is posted against hunters, fishermen, and tote goats, but not against pilgrims—nor for that matter against the United States Army.

From MacFarlane's the automobile road leads down East Canyon to where the East Canyon Reservoir drowns eight miles of the old trail. Above the excruciating bottoms where the pioneers cut willows, bare cabins on a bare slope offer minimum mountain accommodation, a line of green rental rowboats is drawn up on the gravel beach, and a lonely *put-put* is trolling in a cove.

Here the old road climbed around on the western sidehill, but the new one goes straight up through Dixie Hollow, where the Donners and many later wagontrains camped and where in 1860 was the Dixie Hollow Pony Express Station. Above here, on Hogsback Summit, the ruts of the old trail, badly washed, are visible in the chalky white rock west of the road. From there it is six miles down Henefer Creek (Main Canyon) to the Weber and the town of Henefer with its flurry of historical markers commemorating the Donners, the Mormon pioneers, and the Pony Express, whose fourth station east of Salt Lake was at this spot.

This far, retrospective piety could take any Mormon family on a summer day's excursion. If a pilgrim chooses to go farther backward, he finds the characteristically Mormon aspect of this end of the trail—even the Pony Express stations were Mormon—progressively diluted and mixed with the history of the Oregon and California emigrations, and the jumps between places of specifically Mormon interest longer. Echo Canyon will not stop him unless he pauses to hunt up the Utah War fortifications or walk up to Redding's Cave. Fort Bridger, now a Wyoming state park, retains little from its period of Mormon occupancy, except a stretch of old stone wall. More truly a Mormon trail monument is the caravanserai, advertised for hundreds of miles in both directions, called Little America, out on the plains eastward. Its founder conceived the notion of putting an inn on that bleak plateau when as a young cowpuncher he nearly froze to death there one night. It is almost a parody of the Compleat Traveler's Rest, and its advertising corrupts a thousand miles of U.S. 30; but it is a thoroughly Mormon institution, comfortable and well-run and carefully friendly—a long step ahead of the crawling cabins that used to "accommodate" stage passengers. Like the Swiss, the Mormons make good hotel keepers; they know how to exploit their own special virtues and make them pay.

U.S. 30 crosses the Green River a good way below the old trail crossing, which was three miles below the mouth of the Big Sandy. In fact, the usual transcontinental motorist here diverges from the Mormon Trail, and if he stays on U.S. 30, does not pick it up again until North Platte, Nebraska. The pilgrim wanting to drive roads as close as possible to the old route must swing north, probably at Rock Springs, Wyoming, to strike the wagon route at Farson, on the Little Sandy.

Here is a spot for a Mormon to pause at, for it was here that the pioneers camped to confer with Jim Bridger. And taking Wyoming 28 up the long smooth slope toward South Pass, he is sure to stop at the historical marker where the California-Mormon Trail forked off from the Oregon Trail (Sublette's Cutoff) leading to Fort Hall. The time-worn, sagebrush-grown parallel grooves of the old trail are very plain here. It is a good place to stop for an hour and feel history, but the history is only peripherally Mormon: this forking road was here when they came, and all through their migration they took the left-hand fork.

Wyoming 28 follows the old route over South Pass only approximately, but for the ordinary pilgrim approximation is close enough. That high flat saddle is still as it always was, pushing up against the sky, with the Oregon Buttes southward and the Wind Rivers whitening the north, and that too is a good place to sit on a rock and feel history. Short of South Pass City the road curves off north to Lander, and then comes back southeastward again until it picks up the Sweetwater at the corner of the Rattlesnake Range, near Split Rock and Ice Spring. At Martin's Cove, just above Devil's Gate, the pilgrim may stop and try to imagine how that cliff-backed river-bottom might have looked to a shivering, exhausted, starving hand-cart emigrant in November, 1856. Though he shares the rest of the trail with the Gentiles, Martin's Cove, now in summer a green meadow threaded by the meanders of the river, seems peculiarly his.

Where Dan Jones and his companions lived through their raw-hide winter in the trader's cabins at Devil's Gate, there is a ranch: it cannot look too much different now from the way it looked then. Independence Rock is a state park enclosed in a woven-wire fence to protect its historic inscriptions from the inscriptional impulse of moderns. The Red Buttes show the edges of their tilted strata as they always did, Casper Mountain bends the North Platte eastward still, and near the state park preserving the ruins of Fort Casper the pilgrim will be able to locate some of the old abutment structures of the Mormon Ferry and the Upper Crossing bridge. But the river is not now what it was when it twirled Mormon wagons like straws and drowned the strong buffalo horse of Lewis Meyers, for it has been tamed by the Seminoe and Alcova dams, upstream.

Our highway now is a combination of U.S. 26, U.S. 20, and Interstate 25, and it is neither the old south bank nor the old north bank road. It stays south of the river, along the edge of the Laramie Range, until Douglas, when it crosses to the north side; crosses back south at Orin, where U.S. 20 breaks off; and recrosses again at Guernsey. Our pilgrim may drive off on a dirt road south of the river here, in order to hunt out the great grooved ruts where the trail climbed out of the bottoms—the best preserved and most impressive ruts anywhere on the route—or to search for the names of his ancestors among the inscriptions on Register Cliff.

What remains at Fort Laramie is not old Fort John, which the Mormon pioneers knew, but the skeleton of the military post that replaced Fort John in 1849. It is a charming place, a National Historical Park, but its parade ground, shaded by big trees and smooth with lawn, is a far cry from the gravelly treeless flat where the Sioux used to camp, and there is little of a specifically Mormon nature preserved there. The site of the Grattan Massacre eight miles east may be construed into a Mormon site, since it was the lame cow of a Danish Mormon convert that precipitated that swift bloodshed; and Rebecca Winters' grave, five miles out of Scott's Bluff on the Chicago, Burlington and Quincy right-of-way, is indisputably one. The Burlington's surveyors, closely following the old Mormon Trail route all the way from Northport, Nebraska, to Casper, discovered that lonely grave overgrown with grass and weeds, still hooped by an old wagon tire on which had been chiseled the inscription, "Rebecca Winters, Age 50." Mormon genealogical research has determined that she died on the trail during the Great Migration of 1852. The railroad obligingly diverted its tracks around the grave, and Mormon historical piety has marked it with a stone monument. Rebecca Winters, Age 50, is one of the very few of the thousands hastily buried along both sides of the Platte whose marker lasted more than a season or two.

At Fremont, Nebraska, the rendezvous point for the pioneer company and many a later one, there is a Mormon Pioneer Trail marker in a pleasant little park. But more important than all the trail markers put together, the shrine that marks the beginning of the last phase of the Migration, is the Winter Quarters Cemetery in Florence, Nebraska. As Mahonri Young's monument commemorates the life and safety into which they emerged, this quiet graveyard commemorates the suffering and death from which they fled.

Here too history is made memorable in sculpture, the one art for which the Mormons have shown a real aptitude. The monument by Avard Fairbanks, some of whose ancestors are buried in Florence, was dedicated in 1936. It is a bronze group of a man and woman clinging together, the man's right hand holding a shovel, the eyes of both lowered to the grave in which a child has just been laid. The man is booted, bearded, mighty-thighed, as becomes a pioneer; the woman hides her grieving face in the cloak that blows about her as if in a bleak wind. Across the rear of the base, in bronze bas-relief, goes that inescapable laboring train of covered wagons, and on the front, leaning against the mound of the new grave, a plaque lists the six hundred names of the known Winter Quarters dead. Anyone who is curious and has a few minutes can run through the list and discover that nearly a quarter of them were children under six.

This is the end of anything that can be called a consecutive pilgrimage. From here on it is widely separated sites, some of them all but lost, some swallowed up by Gentile settlement. Mt. Pisgah, these days, takes a little finding. But a pilgrim who makes his way to Talmadge, Iowa, and drives north on Iowa 169 will come after 2.3 miles to a cemetery on the left hand. Turning just beyond the cemetery, he will follow a country road around to the left until he comes to the crest of a ridge above West Wolf Creek, and there a marker will stop him and a stile invite him over a fence into a little meadow of perhaps two acres, in which are some elms and a white marble pillar. Nothing else—not a house, not a foundation stone.

The marker, perhaps reflecting the persistence of Gentile antagonism, does not give the Mormons anything. It says only, "1846, Mt. Pisgah, site of the first white settlement in Union County." But the marble pillar, erected by the Church and not by the local historical society, is more specific, if not always orthographically impeccable. It reads:

> This monument erected A.D. 1888 in memory of those mem-
> bers of the Church of Jesus Christ of latter day saints who
> died in 1846, 1847, and 1848, Dureing their exodus to seek a
> home beyond the Rocky Mountains. Interred here is William
> Huntington, the first Presiding Elder of the temporary settle-
> ment called Pisgah. Lenora Charlotte Snow, daughter of Elder
> Lorenzo & Charlotte Squires Snow. Isaac Phineas Richards
> son of Elder Franklin D. & Jane Snyder Richards.

So after long immersion in the history of the exodus we are back
at known graves. There are fifty-nine other names on the north,
west, and south faces of the pillar, but many listings reflect the terrible poverty and debilitation of the Saints during the late summer
and fall of 1846, the weeks when there were neither coffins nor
energies to bury the dead properly; many of the dead are remembered simply as "two other children," "Mr. Cook," "wife of Mr.
Brown." But they sleep very quietly in their westward-sloping
meadow, for no Gentile town filled in the cabins of Mt. Pisgah
when they were abandoned by the Saints, and the whole district
has gone back to farms.

Garden Grove, however, remains. It lies forty-five miles southeast of what was once Mt. Pisgah, a shady little farm village with
a village green and a bandstand, and near the bandstand one of those
markers that through the affectionate labors of devoted local historians so often manage to perpetuate error in bronze. The plaque
mounted on a chunk of pinkish-gray granite reads,

> Dedicated 1956   In memory of the Mormons who founded
> Garden Grove, Iowa, in 1847

They missed it a year, but at least they gave the Saints proper
credit. And whoever designed the plaque thought it appropriate to
include, in bas-relief, a couple of covered wagons.

There remains Nauvoo, in which the Church within the past few
years has begun creating an impressive shrine. The once-greatest
city in Illinois has shrunk to a quiet town known chiefly for a suc-
culent brand of blue cheese. The fields and orchards that Thomas

Kane found so fruitful and well-kept have been to a considerable extent replaced by vineyards growing Concord grapes for the manufacture of wine for sacramental use in synagogues. The mighty temple, now only a half-excavated foundation, is blocked off from its former view of the river by the mother house of the Benedictine Sisters. More awkward than any of these diminishments and ironies is the competition that the Church meets from within, or nearly within, the fold—from the Reorganized Church of Jesus Christ of Latter-day Saints, which was founded by Joseph's two sons and which has its headquarters in St. Joseph, Missouri. Though the Utah Church owns the temple site, Brigham Young's home, and some other houses, and though it has acquired a tract of land on the bluffs northward where it contemplates restoring the temple in something like its original imposing terms, the Reorganized Church has title to Joseph Smith's homestead, to the Mansion House, and to Nauvoo House, from which base it conducts a vigorous program of guided tours and propaganda. Its sign on Nauvoo House says that "it served as the last home of Emma, Joseph Smith's *only* wife."

Nevertheless this is not a competition which the Utah church, with its vastly greater resources, is likely to lose. Nauvoo is already less a town than a museum. In 1962 the National Park Service declared it a National Historic Site and authorized an able Mormon historian, David Miller, to write its history. Nauvoo Restoration Incorporated, "a non-profit corporation for the restoration of historic Nauvoo," works steadily with substantial Church support to acquire properties and put them back into their pre-1846 condition. Nauvoo the Beautiful, the Lord's chosen city, is not entirely turned over to the Gentiles.

Restored Nauvoo may not be a Bruges, an Avignon, even a Williamsburg. It will be such a nineteenth-century American town as New Englanders built many times in the Western Reserve of Ohio. But it will be more than a quaint anachronism, and more than a testimonial to Yankee influences on the frontier. For the temple, if indeed it is rebuilt, will give it back that touch of proto-Egyptian splendor that Joseph had added to the sober virtues of his followers.

And the long, sorrowful, hardly credible story of Mormonism's early years will make every old house on every old street of old Nauvoo into a shrine.

A surprising number of the solid houses they built survive in good condition, and like the graves on Mt. Pisgah's still hillside, these are the homes of people we know: Brigham Young, Heber Kimball, Wilford Woodruff, Orson Spencer, Willard Richards, John Taylor, Orson Hyde, Erastus Snow, Orson Pratt; and Sidney Rigdon, disappointed Prophet and Revelator, and John Smith the uncle of Joseph, and Loren Farr, who got into a fistfight with Joseph Tanner on the pioneer trip west and who later founded the city of Ogden. Leadership in the Mormon Church from the very beginning was likely to be associated with economic solvency, either as cause or result. Anyone who harbors the misconception that Mormonism was in its beginning a log-cabin movement should walk up and down Water Street or Kimball Street in Nauvoo. Though some early Mormons were born poor, and many achieved poverty, and many more had poverty thrust upon them, indigence was not their natural state, and they recovered from it with great promptness when left alone. Nauvoo, which was born out of disaster and had only six years to grow in before it was abandoned, strikes a visitor now as astonishingly substantial, even opulent.

It is the proper place to end this book. For though pilgrims may, and do, go farther eastward still, to Kirtland where the Reorganized Church owns the first temple and the spreading suburbs of Cleveland are inundating the land-boom Mormon farms of the 1830's; to the Hill Cumorah, near Palmyra, New York, where a landscaped hill and a monument to the Angel Moroni commemorate the finding of the Golden Plates; to Whitingham, Vermont, and the monument that marks Brigham's birthplace; finally to Sharon, Vermont and the granite obelisk, characteristically advertised as the tallest one-piece granite pillar in the world, that soars up from the spot where Joseph Smith was born—though pilgrims and tourists visit these well-kept premises and according to their nature scoff or feel reverence, the place for us to stop is here. Up to Nauvoo, Joseph was improvising and constantly re-creating; from here, after his death, the finished faith went forth.

It is a good place to stop. The state park that occupies much of the hill slope above the river is green and shady, and the seventeen-year locusts shrill in the trees as they shrilled for the ears of Ursulia Hascall, preparing her good-housekeeping wagon in the summer of 1846. The swampy shore is as rotten with the smell of dead Mormon flies, the full river air is as fresh. Strolling these shaded and mellow streets, past the substantial houses that he and his hierarchy were able to build in so short a time, and thinking ahead through the things that will happen to this people in the next five generations without swerving them more than a point or two from the line that Joseph laid down, even an unbeliever is brought to the perception that the man who started all this was no mere charlatan, Peepstone Joe. This was a mighty imagination, a man with an extraordinary capacity to move men. The Mormon Migration to the Salt Lake Valley was really Joseph Smith's operation, though Brother Brigham directed it. To stand in Nauvoo, as if in 1846, and look ahead to all of it is to be impressed, like Ursulia Hascall exclaiming at the multitudes of locks of Joseph's hair his followers had snipped from his bloody head, at how much of that whole history stems from Joseph.

At the western end of the Mormon Trail stands a city—a Kingdom, if you will. At the other end, ambiguous, unreliable, incautious, vain, charming, stands that most potent of living creatures, a man with a vision. Ultimately he is the object of every pilgrimage; for if we understand him we can understand it all.

A Word on Bibliography

The literature on the Mormons is enormous, repetitious, contradictory, and embattled, so much so that the late Bernard DeVoto refused to rest a judgment on any Gentile historian and rested it on Mormon historians only when they quoted official documents unavailable to him elsewhere. One is inclined to agree in general with that evaluation, and to follow whenever possible that procedure. For the posing of contrary biased opinions does not necessarily result in truth, nor does the citing of a charge with its counter-charge, or a pious delusion with the facts that debunk it. The more one wades into this morass the deeper he is mired, and the farther from firm ground. There *is* no firm ground here; there is only Mormon opinion, Gentile opinion, and the necessarily tentative opinion of historians trying to take account of all the facts and allow for all the delusion, hatred, passion, paranoia, lying, bad faith, concealment, and distortion of evidence that were contributed by both the Mormons and their enemies.

Trying to rely exclusively on original documents rather than on historical opinion does not avoid the difficulty, for those who wrote the original journals and letters, those who reported events as eyewitnesses, were very often blinded by pentecostal enthusiasm, tribal loyalty, or imperfect information. One dare not, often, accept their judgment of events; but for the events themselves they are the best documents we have, and whenever possible I have based this book on them.

Since the stance from which I have written will surely strike some as being just as biased as anything in the library of Mormonism and

anti-Mormonism, I may as well define it. I write as a non-Mormon but
not a Mormon-hater. Except as it affected the actions of the people
I write of, I do not deal with the Mormon faith: I do not believe it,
but I do not quarrel with it either. For the Church organization, historically and in modern times, I have a high respect. Of the hierarchy,
historically and in modern times, I am somewhat suspicious, in the way
I am suspicious of any very large and very powerful commercial and
industrial corporation. For the everyday virtues of the Mormons as
a people I have a warm admiration, and hundreds of individual Mormons have been my good friends for forty years. If I have a home
town, a place where a part of my heart is, it is Salt Lake City, and the
part of western history that seems most personal and real to me is
Mormon history. Nevertheless, I write as an outsider, and I make no
attempt to whitewash the Mormon tribal crimes, which were as griev-
ous as their wrongs.

Of all the historians who have dealt with the Mormon story, or any
phase of it, four seem to me worthy of complete trust: Mr. DeVoto
himself, at least in *The Year of Decision, 1846;* Fawn M. Brodie; Dale
L. Morgan; and Juanita Brooks. Ray B. West, Jr., though a little
inclined to blur the harsher aspects of Mormon history, has written
one excellent general book. And through the years from 1846 to 1869
there was a succession of intelligent, sometimes partial, sometimes
skeptical, but generally tolerant observers whose insights and judg-
ments are still worth our attention. These were Thomas Kane, Captain
Howard Stansbury, Captain J. W. Gunnison, Frederick Piercy, Jules
Remy, and Richard Burton. The illustrative anthology, *Among the
Mormons*, edited by William Mulder and A. Russell Mortenson, is
well-selected and without cant.

For the rest, the books below are listed either because they are the
best sources for the ground they cover, or because they are so representative and revealing in their bias that no student can afford not to
know them. *Caveat lector*. The works particularly useful to this book
are listed by chapters.

Of the journals and reminiscences, of which I read scores and heard
of many more that I was unable to obtain, I have listed only those
that I quoted, paraphrased, or otherwise directly used in the preparation of this book. They run all the way from 1846 to 1868, the last year
of the Church Trains, and there is necessarily a great deal of repetition
and monotony in what they record. In the beginning I intended, as a
by-product to this study, to compile a check list of all the known
Mormon Trail diaries, letters, and reminiscences, and with the help of
Juanita Brooks, Dale L. Morgan, and Chad Flake of Brigham Young

University I made a start toward it. But new records turn up regularly, even yet; and some are not made available for study by the Church library. It seems best to put off a Mormon Trail bibliography until the collection of documents is more nearly complete, and to leave it then to someone who is in the confidence of the Church Historian.

General Works: A Sampling

Bancroft, H. H., *History of Utah*. San Francisco, 1891.

Brodie, Fawn M., *No Man Knows My History*. New York, 1945.

Burton, Richard, *The City of the Saints*. New York, 1862. There is a new edition, with an informed introduction and careful notes, edited by Fawn M. Brodie, New York, 1963.

DeVoto, Bernard, *The Year of Decision, 1846*. Boston, 1943.

Gunnison, J. W., *The Mormons*. (No place of publication listed), 1856.

Jensen, Andrew, *Latter-Day Saints Biographical Encyclopedia*. Salt Lake City, 1901 (4 vols.).

Larson, Gustive O., *Prelude to the Kingdom*. Francestown, N.H., 1947.

Linn, W. A., *The Story of the Mormons*. New York, 1923.

Little, James A., *From Kirtland to Salt Lake City*. Salt Lake City, 1890.

Morgan, Dale L., *The Great Salt Lake*. Indianapolis–New York, 1947.

Mulder, William, and Mortenson, A. Russell, *Among the Mormons*. New York, 1958.

Nibley, Preston, *Exodus to Greatness*. Salt Lake City, 1947.

Piercy, Frederick H., *Route from Liverpool to Great Salt Lake Valley*. Liverpool, 1855.

Remy, Jules, *A Journey to Great Salt Lake City*. London, 1861.

Roberts, Brigham H., *History of the Church*. Salt Lake City, 1901–1906.

Stansbury, Howard, *An Expedition to the Valley of the Great Salt Lake*. Philadelphia, 1855.

Stegner, Wallace, *Mormon Country*. New York, 1942.

Stenhouse, T. B. H., *The Rocky Mountain Saints*. New York, 1873.

Tullidge, Edward, *The Women of Mormondom*. New York, 1877.

Werner, M. R., *Brigham Young*. New York, 1925.

West, Ray B., Jr., *Kingdom of the Saints*. New York, 1957.

Young, Ann Eliza, *Wife No. 19*. (No place of publication listed), 1876.

I: By The Rivers of Babylon

Chapter 1: For this, as for subsequent chapters, I have drawn details out of the whole range of general works and from some more special ones. To keep the documentation from becoming over-elaborate, let us say that this chapter is built primarily out of Fawn M. Brodie, *No Man Knows My History;* DeVoto, *The Year of Decision,* 1846; Thomas Ford, *A History of Illinois,* Chicago, 1854; Kane, *The Mormons;* Little, *From Kirtland to Salt Lake City;* Roberts, *History of the Church;* Tullidge, *The Women of Mormondom;* and the selected writings of Eliza Snow, published as *Eliza Snow, an Immortal,* Salt Lake City, 1957.

CHAPTER 2:   Most of the sources cited for Chapter 1, plus "Letters of a Proselyte: The Hascall-Pomeroy Correspondence," *Utah Historical Quarterly,* Vol. XXV (1957); and the journals of Oliver Boardman Huntington (typescript, Utah Historical Society), William Huntington (typescript, Brigham Young University), and Hosea Stout (typescript, Brigham Young University).

CHAPTER 3:   Primarily original journals, especially these: Hosea Stout; James Smithies (typescript through the courtesy of Mrs. Deon Lee, Castro Valley, California); Willard Richards (partial typescript in my possession); *William Clayton's Journal,* Salt Lake City, 1921; "Diary of Lorenzo Dow Young," *Utah Historical Quarterly,* Vol. XIV (1946); also Jensen, *Latter-Day Saints Biographical Encyclopedia,* and John Henry Evans, *Charles Coulson Rich: Pioneer Builder of the West,* New York, 1936; Rev. R. E. Harvey, "The Mormon Trek across Iowa Territory," *Annals of Iowa,* Vol. XXVIII (July, 1946); and Jacob van der Zee, "The Mormon Trails in Iowa," *Iowa Journal of History and Politics,* Vol. XII (1914), pp. 3–16.

CHAPTER 4:   The journals of Hosea Stout, Lorenzo Young, William Huntington, and William Clayton; *Eliza Snow, an Immortal;* Little, *From Kirtland to Salt Lake City;* the journal of Norton Jacob (typescript, Brigham Young University); the Hascall-Pomeroy Correspondence; Matthias Cowley, *Wilford Woodruff, History of His Life and Labors,* Salt Lake City, 1909.

CHAPTER 5:   Kane, *The Mormons;* DeVoto, *The Year of Decision,* 1846; Cowley, *Wilford Woodruff;* Little, *From Kirtland to Salt Lake City; The Autobiography of Parley Parker Pratt,* New York, 1874; O. O. Winther, *The Private Papers and Diary of Thomas Leiper Kane, a Friend of the Mormons,* San Francisco, 1937; Charles Charvat, *Logan Fontenelle, An Indian Chief in Broadcloth and Fine Linen,* Omaha, 1961; Tullidge, *The Women of Mormondom; Eliza Snow, an Immortal;*

the journals of Stout, Clayton, Norton Jacob, and Lorenzo Young; "Narrative of Franklin Dewey Richards" (MS, Bancroft Library); "Reminiscences of Mrs. Franklin D. Richards" (MS, Bancroft Library).

CHAPTER 6: DeVoto, *The Year of Decision, 1846*; Kane, *The Mormons;* Little, *From Kirtland to Salt Lake City;* journals of Stout, Clayton, Lee.

CHAPTER 7: Kane, *The Mormons;* Winther, *The Private Papers and Diary of Thomas Leiper Kane; Eliza Snow, an Immortal;* Evans, *Charles Coulson Rich;* Tullidge, *The Women of Mormondom;* DeVoto, *The Year of Decision;* the Hascall-Pomeroy Correspondence; the journals of Stout, Lee, Jacob, and Lorenzo Young.

II: THE MOUNTAIN OF THE LORD'S HOUSE

CHAPTER 1: Any general study of Mormonism deals with the pioneer trek to some extent. Little, *From Kirtland to Salt Lake City*, Nibley, *Exodus to Greatness*, and Tullidge, *The Women of Mormondom*, follow it fairly closely through the large use of journals. Andrew Jensen, *Day by Day with the Utah Pioneers, 1847*, is a mosaic of journal accounts, including passages from some journals not available to the public in other form. Morgan, *The Great Salt Lake*, contains meticulously accurate information on the pioneer trip, as do his more specific studies cited later. I have used all of these as a means of cross-referencing the individual journals and reminiscences, of which I have seen the following: William Clayton, Lorenzo Dow Young (together with the brief reminiscences of Clarissa Decker Young and Harriet Decker Young), Norton Jacob, James Smithies, and Appleton Harmon, all cited previously; also Levi Jackman (typescript, Utah Historical Society); Amasa Lyman (kept by Albert Carrington—typescript Brigham Young University); Orson Pratt (published as "Interesting Items concerning the Journeying of the Latter-Day Saints from the City of Nauvoo, until Their Location in the Valley of the Great Salt Lake," *Millennial Star* Vols. XI and XII (1849–1850); Howard Egan, published in *Pioneering the West*, Richmond, Utah, 1917; Erastus Snow, *Utah Humanities Review*, Vol. II (April, 1948); and William A. Empey, edited by Dale L. Morgan in "The Mormon Ferry on the North Platte. The Journal of William A. Empey, May 7–Aug. 4, 1847," *Annals of Wyoming* Vol.

XXI, Nos. 2–3 (July–October, 1949). The journal of Thomas Bullock is quoted a number of times in Jensen's *Day by Day with the Utah Pioneers,* as are those of George A. Smith, Wilford Woodruff, Clayton, Orson Pratt, Erastus Snow, Egan and Jacob. Not utilized in this "official" mosaic account are Lyman, Jackman, Lorenzo Young, Harmon, Smithies, and Empey. For the route which the pioneers established as the Mormon Trail I have used the *Guide to the Route Map of the Mormon Pioneers from Nauvoo to Great Salt Lake, 1846–1847.* Salt Lake City, n.d.; Olga Sharp Steele, "The Geography of the Mormon Trail across Nebraska," unpublished thesis, University of Nebraska; J. Roderick Korns, "West from Fort Bridger," *Utah Historical Quarterly,* Vol. XIX (1951); and William Clayton, *The Latter-Day Saints Emigrants' Guide,* St. Louis, 1848.

CHAPTER 2: The journals of the members of the pioneer company; Jensen, *Day by Day with the Utah Pioneers;* Edward Bonney, *The Banditti of the Prairies,* Chicago, 1850.

CHAPTER 3: The journals; Morgan, *The Great Salt Lake;* Morgan, "The Mormon Ferry on the North Platte."

CHAPTER 4: The journals; Morgan, *The Great Salt Lake.*

CHAPTER 5: The journals of Clayton, Jacob, and Appleton Harmon; Morgan, "The Mormon Ferry on the North Platte"; The Hascall-Pomeroy Correspondence; *Eliza Snow: An Immortal;* Little, *From Kirtland to Salt Lake City.*

CHAPTER 6: Kate B. Carter, "Church Emigration Overland," in *Heart Throbs of the West,* Vol. XII, Salt Lake City, 1951; Evans, *Charles Coulson Rich;* Gustive O. Larson, *Prelude to the Kingdom,* Francestown, N.H., 1947; Little, *From Kirtland to Salt Lake City;* Winther, *The Private Papers and Diary of Thomas Leiper Kane;* the journals of Hosea Stout and Oliver Boardman Huntington; the journal of John Pulsipher (typescript, Brigham Young University); Ann Eliza Young, *Wife No. 19;* Journal of the Council Point Emigration Company, 1852 (MS, Utah Historical Society).

CHAPTER 7: Frederick Hawkins Piercy, *Route from Liverpool to Great Salt Lake Valley;* Larson, *Prelude to the Kingdom.*

CHAPTER 8: LeRoy and Ann Hafen, *Handcarts to Zion*, Glendale, Calif., 1960; "Mr. Chislett's Narrative," in T. B. H. Stenhouse, *Rocky Mountain Saints*, pp. 312–332; Twiss Bermingham's journal, in Eliza M. Wakefield, *The Handcart Trail*, Carlsbad, N.M., 1949; Archer Walters' diary, in *Improvement Era*, Vols. XXXIX and XL (1936 and 1937); journal of Patience Loader (typescript, Brigham Young University); Kate B. Carter, compiler, *Heart Throbs of the West* and *Treasures of Pioneer History;* account of Josiah Rogerson in the *Salt Lake Tribune*, Jan. 14, 1914; John Bond, *Handcarts West in '56* (typescript, Utah Historical Society); Larson, *Prelude to the Kingdom*.

CHAPTER 9: Hafen, *Handcarts to Zion*, especially the diaries of rescuers and the speeches of Brigham Young and Heber Kimball included as Appendixes D, E, F, G, H, and I; journals of Patience Loader and John Bond; accounts of Josiah Rogerson and Chislett; the many brief accounts in *Heart Throbs* and *Treasures of Pioneer History;* Daniel W. Jones, *Forty Years among the Indians*, Salt Lake City, 1960; S. A. Hanks and E. K. Hanks, *Scouting for the Mormons on the Great Frontier*, Salt Lake City, 1946.

CHAPTER 10: Jones, *Forty Years among the Indians;* Bill Hickman, *Brigham's Destroying Angel*, Salt Lake City, 1904; Feramorz Little, "Mail Service across the Plains," (MS, Bancroft Library).

CHAPTER 11: Larson, *Prelude to the Kingdom;* Hafen, *Handcarts to Zion;* Winther, *The Private Papers and Diary of Thomas Leiper Kane;* Bancroft, Werner, West, and other general histories; Richard Burton, *The City of the Saints;* Carter, "Church Emigration Overland"; Little, "Mail Service across the Plains."

CHAPTER 12: William B. Smart, *Exploring the Pioneer Trail* (pamphlet), Salt Lake City, 1958; Alma P. Burton, *Mormon Trail from Vermont to Utah* (pamphlet), Salt Lake City, 1960; Howard R. Driggs, *Mormon Trail* (pamphlet), New York, 1947; Irene D. Paden, *The Wake of the Prairie Schooner*, New York, 1943; Steele, *Geography of the Mormon Trail across Nebraska;* Korns, *West from Fort Bridger*.

Index

Stenhouse, T. B. H., 277
Stoddard, Brother, 233
Stout, Anna, 60
Stout, Col. Hosea, 39, 41, 46–47, 49, 51, 53, 59–61, 65, 67, 69, 71, 74, 77, 92, 103–104, 106, 108, 118, 182, 187, 190, 199, 270
Stout, Hosea, Jr., 60, 77
Stout, Hyrum, 60, 104
Stout, Louisa, 59–60
Stout, Lucretia, 104
Stout, Marinda, 104
Stout, William Hosea, 104
Strang, James Jesse, 33
Strangites, 51, 112
Sublette, William, 141, 153
Sublette's Cutoff, 154, 160, 305
Sugar Creek, 43, 47, 49–50, 53, 56–57, 59, 74, 86, 182, 241
Suggs, Simon, 23
Sulphur Creek, 161–162
Sutter's Fort, Calif., 82, 192
Sweetwater Mountains, 150–151
Sweetwater River, 149, 151, 181, 185, 188, 203, 210, 235, 244–245, 251, 253–254, 260, 271, 281, 288, 291, 306
Sybille, Adams and Company, 142

Talmadge, 54
Tanner, Thomas, 133
Taylor, Allen, 205
Taylor, John, 22, 30, 51, 82, 116, 118, 159, 174–175, 211, 216, 227, 238, 311
Taylor, Stephen, 246, 250
Tennessee, 17
Tenth Handcart Company, 288–289
Teton Mountains, 157
Texas, 32, 45
Therlkill, George, 142–143
"This is the Place" monument, 113, 168, 299, 301–303
Thornton (ship), 227, 231, 238
Three Witnesses, Sons and Daughters of, 4
Toquatah, Chief, 267
Twain, Mark, 23
Twelve Apostles, 19, 38, 40, 42–43, 54, 60, 64, 66–68, 73, 77, 81, 86, 90, 92, 104, 114, 116, 118–119, 124, 126, 139, 143, 161, 170, 173, 181, 184, 186, 188, 190–191, 203, 208–209
    Quorum of, 33, 45, 47, 69, 117, 138, 204, 258

Uintas Mountains, 157
Underwriter (ship), 288
Union Pacific Railroad, 7
U. S. S. *Brooklyn*, 7
Utah, 1, 2, 7, 49, 71, 98, 223
    Sons and Daughters of, 4
Utah Indians, 122
Utah Mountains (*see* Uintas Mountains)
Utah Lake, 172
Utah Valley, 166, 173, 261, 282
Utah War, 220, 275, 278, 281–282

Valley Tan, 6
Valleys of the Mountains, 1
Van Buren, Martin, 76
Vancouver Island, 40
Vermont, 33
Vicksburg, 215
Virginia, 17

Wake of the Prairie Schooner, The (Paden), 7
Wales, 24
Walker, Henry, 233
Walker, Henson, 185
Walker, Joe, 153
Walters, Archer, 229–230, 232–235, 237, 302
Walters, Harriet, 233, 236
Walters, Henry, 234
Wardell, George, 93
Warsaw militia, 30
Wasatch River, 10, 49, 114, 167, 182, 235, 282, 304
Wayne County, Neb., 54
Weatherby, Jacob, 174–175
Webb, Ann Eliza, 199, 227
Webb, Chauncey, 227, 243
Weber Canyon, 10, 163–166, 182, 203, 282–283
Weber River, 303
Weber Valley, 7
Welling, Job, 232
Wells, Daniel, 92
Welsh, Madison, 185, 188

About The Author

The West has been Wallace Stegner's preoccupation and passion throughout his life. Born in Iowa in 1909, he was immediately carried westward, so that he can almost say, like Joaquin Miller, that he was born in a covered wagon headed west. He spent his childhood in North Dakota and Washington, his boyhood in Saskatchewan and Montana, his youth in Utah; and except for a seven-year exile while teaching at the University of Wisconsin and at Harvard, he has lived his mature years in California, where until 1969 he directed the writing program at Stanford University.

His books have reflected his western origins. Many of his short stories and novels, including *The Big Rock Candy Mountain, The Preacher and the Slave, A Shooting Star,* and more recently *All the Little Live Things, Angle of Repose,* and *Recapitulation,* have dealt with the past or present West, and he has several times turned his attention to aspects of western history: *Mormon Country* was a loving survey of the Utah of his youth; *Wolf Willow* an even more loving evocation of the prairies of his Saskatchewan boyhood; *Beyond the Hundredth Meridian,* his biography of the explorer and scientist John Wesley Powell, was said by the late Bernard DeVoto to have "added a basic book to the small shelf of books that give history basic knowledge of western experience."

The Gathering of Zion draws upon a lifetime of experience, reading, and writing about the West. This history comes living to the page because Mr. Stegner has a novelist's way with people, and because he knows in his very skin and eyeballs the lights and colors and forms of the country through which the Mormons made their painful way to Zion.